The Treaty of Portsmouth and Its Legacies

The Treaty of Portsmouth and Its Legacies

Edited by

Steven Ericson and Allen Hockley

Dartmouth College Press
Hanover, New Hampshire

PUBLISHED BY UNIVERSITY PRESS OF NEW ENGLAND

HANOVER AND LONDON

Dartmouth College Press
Published by University Press of New England,
One Court Street, Lebanon, NH 03766
www.upne.com
© 2008 by Trustees of Dartmouth College
Printed in the United States of America

5 4 3 2 1

For generous financial support of this publication, we are grateful to the Japan–United States Friendship Commission and to the John Sloan Dickey Center for International Understanding at Dartmouth College.

Frontispiece: "Bless you, my children!" *Harper's Weekly,* vol. 49, no. 2543 (September 16, 1905), p. 1352.

Library of Congress Cataloging-in-Publication Data

The Treaty of Portsmouth and its legacies / edited by Steven Ericson and Allen Hockley.
    p. cm.
Includes bibliographical references and index.
ISBN 978–1–58465–722–4 (cloth : alk. paper)
1. Russo-Japanese War, 1904–1905—Diplomatic history.   2. Japan. Treaties, etc. Russia, 1905
Sept. 5.   3. Russo-Japanese War, 1904–1905—Treaties.   I. Ericson, Steven J., 1953–
II. Hockley, Allen.
DS517.13.T74 2008
952.03'1—dc22   2008022109

green
press
INITIATIVE
University Press of New England is a member of the Green Press Initiative. The paper used in this book meets their minimum requirement for recycled paper.

Contents

9. Economic Engagement: Coping with the
Realities of the Globalized World / 142
Vladimir I. Ivanov

10. The Contemporary Implications of the
Russo-Japanese War: A Japanese Perspective / 157
Kazuhiko Togo

Acknowledgments

First and foremost, we wish to thank Ambassador Kenneth Yalowitz, the Norman E. McCullough Jr. Director of the John Sloan Dickey Center for International Understanding at Dartmouth College, for his unflagging support both of the Portsmouth Treaty centennial conference we hosted in Hanover and of this volume, which resulted from that collaborative, multinational project. We are indebted as well to Dartmouth Provost Barry Scherr, co-convener of the conference with Ambassador Yalowitz, for his many valuable contributions. Dartmouth Visiting Professor Ronald Edsforth deserves special mention for proposing the centennial commemoration and for coordinating the initial planning for it. We are also thankful to Margot de l'Etoile, Lisa Wallace, Robert Clough, Victoria Hicks, and Diane Casey of the Dickey Center; to former Dartmouth students and Presidential Scholar Research Assistants John Reidy '06, Aaron Sallen '06, and Lydia Yu '07; to Sally Eshleman, John Landrigan, and Amy Stockman of Dartmouth's Office of Foundation Relations; to Susan Bibeau and Thomas Garbelotti of Humanities Computing at Dartmouth; and to our editor at UPNE for their expert assistance.

For generous financial support, we are deeply grateful to the Japan-U.S. Friendship Commission; the Center for Global Partnership of the Japan Foundation; the Kennan Institute of the Woodrow Wilson International Center for Scholars; and the Dickey Center, the Office of the Provost, and the Dean of Faculty Office at Dartmouth College.

The Treaty of Portsmouth and Its Legacies

Introduction

Allen Hockley and Steven Ericson

The year 2005 marked exactly 60 years since the Russians took possession of the Kuril Islands immediately after Japan's surrender in World War II, 100 years since the Treaty of Portsmouth terminated the Russo-Japanese War of 1904–5, and 150 years since the Russo-Japanese Treaty of Amity inaugurated modern diplomatic relations between the two nations. Despite this long and eventful history of diplomatic engagement, Japan and Russia have yet to conclude a treaty formally ending World War II. The two nations have failed to do so primarily because they continue to dispute the issue of sovereignty over the four southernmost islands of the Kuril chain. In 2004, Prime Minister Koizumi Jun'ichirō and President Vladimir Putin announced their intention to accelerate talks on a bilateral peace treaty to make "concrete and substantive" progress before the 2005 anniversaries. To date a breakthrough remains elusive. The two countries have been near accord before, but despite positive steps by their leaders, the Russian and Japanese peoples have strongly opposed compromise. As a result, both parties have, for political reasons, sidestepped or dismissed previous proposals for diplomatic concession. Resolving this deadlock would set the stage for an economic and political partnership with powerful benefits for the entire Asia-Pacific region, while a continued impasse complicates regional security and economic well-being.

The Portsmouth Treaty remains the last peace agreement between the two countries. Seen from the perspective of more recent history, it provides an instructive record of successful Russo-Japanese diplomacy. With the United States as active mediator, the treaty established a framework that largely retained its validity through World War II. Although agreements made in 1945 rendered many of its specifics obsolete, it nonetheless continues to have regional ramifications. The treaty brought to a peaceful close the greatest international conflict prior to World War I, a conflict in which Japan and Russia engaged in battles of unprecedented scale over control of Manchuria and Korea. Viewing it as the first global conflict of the twentieth century, some historians have recently adopted the term World War Zero to refer to the conflict.[1] The Russo-Japanese War also ushered in a new era of war journalism that surpassed coverage of all prior conflicts in both detail and international scope.

The Treaty of Portsmouth likewise garnered international attention in both diplomatic circles and the world press. At the Japanese government's request, U.S. president Theodore Roosevelt served as intermediary in the 1905 peace negotiations, a service for which he received the Nobel Peace Prize in 1906—the first head of state to be accorded that honor. Both Russia and Japan made territorial and other concessions at Portsmouth, paving the way for peace and rapprochement between the two countries and offering the world a model of successful international diplomacy at the dawn of the twentieth century.

With Russia and Japan still seeking a peaceful conclusion to World War II and with cooperation on regional trade and security remaining a prerequisite for peace and stability in Northeast Asia and the Pacific, the centennial of the Treaty of Portsmouth provided an ideal opportunity to explore the background and making of that agreement as well as its long-term significance for international relations. "Portsmouth and Its Legacies: Commemorating the Centennial of the Russo-Japanese Peace Treaty of 1905," an international conference held at Dartmouth College on September 8–10, 2005, brought together Russian, Japanese, and American historians, policy analysts, and diplomats to revisit and reassess both the war and the treaty. M.I.T. historian John Dower opened the proceedings with a keynote address titled "Representations of a New Japan: Images from the Russo-Japanese War." Providing the focal point of the conference were four roundtable sessions on the Russo-Japanese War, the making of the Portsmouth Treaty, the cultural and political legacies of the settlement, and the implications of the treaty for current political and economic issues. The Dartmouth organizers commissioned eight essays—two per session—for the roundtable discussions and, to facilitate productive exchange, distributed them to all conference participants prior to the event. Authors presented brief synopses of their ideas to open each session. Discussants appointed to the task then offered their comments and critique to help guide the discussions that followed. The conference concluded with a two-part public panel focusing on opportunities for international cooperation on health issues in the Russian Far East and on the relevance of the Portsmouth Treaty for Asia-Pacific relations today.

This volume brings into print revised versions of the essays commissioned for the conference, reorganized according to three broad themes: diplomacy and the peace (part I), legacies (part II), and contemporary implications (part III). We have also included a later submission authored by Kazuhiko Tōgō, one of the conference participants. We conclude this volume with an appendix summarizing the discussion the original papers generated at the conference as well as an open discussion that focused on future research directions.

The first two papers, by David Schimmelpenninck van der Oye and Yasutoshi Teramoto, examine Russian and Japanese diplomacy before and after the conflict of 1904–5.[2] In his essay, Schimmelpenninck characterizes Russo-Japanese relations at this time as "an episode in the diplomacy of imperialism," the informal system that successfully kept the European powers from going to war over rival territorial claims in Africa and Asia between roughly 1880 and World War I. The principal flaw in that system was that it excluded rising non-European states. As a result, the basic cause of the Russo-Japanese War was the inability of an established member of the European imperialist club, Russia, to take seriously the colonial ambitions of an outsider, Japan. Complicating matters for Russia was the "highly erratic" nature of its East Asian policy, as the "pathologically indecisive" Nicholas II vacillated between moderate and hard-line approaches. Owing to such policy confusion and inconsistency, Russia was never able to respond appropriately to Japan's prewar proposals that the two nations negotiate their respective spheres of influence, as the European powers were effectively doing among themselves.

Teramoto shows in his paper that, in the months leading up to hostilities, Japanese officials led by Foreign Minister Komura Jutarō and Prime Minister Katsura Tarō became more and more resolved to settle the Manchuria-Korea question even at the risk of war, whereas their Russian counterparts, as Schimmelpenninck indicates, appeared to grow increasingly divided. Following the war, by contrast, while Japanese leaders "differed sharply" over aggressive versus conciliatory approaches to diplomacy, Russian officials became "relatively single-minded" in their foreign policy, seeking to avoid conflicts abroad while rebuilding at home. By the time of its 1907 convention with Tokyo, St. Petersburg had finally come around to recognize as legitimate Japan's imperialist interests in Northeast Asia. Meanwhile, Teramoto concludes that, although Japan thus continued the prewar framework of alliances and agreements with Russia and other European powers, it also began to develop a foreign policy toward the United States and the Asia-Pacific region independent of the Eurocentric system of international relations, a trend with profound implications for Japanese diplomacy leading up to the second Sino-Japanese and Pacific wars.

Working primarily from Russian sources, I. V. Lukoianov narrates a Russian perspective on the approach to the Portsmouth peace treaty and the negotiations that brought about its successful conclusion. He contends that maneuvers toward a settlement started as early as the summer of 1904 and continued throughout the war. Lukoianov sees in these processes a gradual development toward the positions Japan and Russia would eventually bring to the negotiations in Portsmouth. He exposes, in particular, the precariousness of Russia's position at the end of the war and during the approach to the peace negotiations. Factional disputes among Russian leaders after the defeat in the Battle of Tsushima provided a context in which Russia's negotiating position was gradually defined but still highly contested. The journey of Count Sergei Witte, Russia's representative at the peace negotiations, through Europe en route to Portsmouth, during which he met with representatives of Germany and France, provides Lukoianov with opportunities to explore the multifaceted negotiating strategy the Russian delegates were considering as they prepared for the conference. Witte's personal views and convictions, his diplomatic skills, and his ability to generate favorable public opinion, especially in the United States, constitute the narrative focus of Lukoianov's essay as he documents the successes and many near failures of the negotiations in Portsmouth. Lukoianov concludes that, although Witte's skills were critical to the process, the favorable result Russia achieved in Portsmouth was largely the product of Tsar Nicholas' unwillingness to concede on the most contested issues.

In their coauthored essay, "Roosevelt and the U.S. Role: Perception Makes Policy," Eugene P. Trani and Donald E. Davis explore the role of the influential journalist George Kennan (1845–1924) in shaping U.S. public opinion and policy toward Russia and Japan before, during, and after the Russo-Japanese War and the Portsmouth peace conference. Kennan had written extensively about Russia prior to the outbreak of hostilities in 1904 and was widely regarded at the time as the foremost U.S. expert on Russia. His 1891 book, *Siberia and the Exile System,* which characterized Russia as a land of misery, injustice, and tyranny, prefigured much of the war coverage he would supply for the distinguished and widely read *Outlook* magazine. The twenty-six articles (totaling 205 double-columned pages) Kennan authored for *Outlook* provide Trani and Davis with a wealth of primary sources from which to assess Kennan's views. Kennan's articles compared Russian and Japanese war preparations, officer corps, battlefield strategies, and treatment of POWs. He also provided detailed accounts of specific engagements. His postwar articles were more broadly conceptual, assessing, for example, the differences between Japan and Russia in terms of their moral culture; tolerance; respect for law, property, and personal freedom;

and virtues such as modesty, humanity, and fairness. Kennan's comments on the Portsmouth peace treaty, perhaps the most controversial in his *Outlook* series, suggested that Japan did not receive favorable terms and that the Hibiya riots protesting the settlement were thus justified. Noting that Kennan was a close confidant of President Roosevelt and had acquired through this friendship unprecedented access to members of Japan's military leadership and foreign ministry, Trani and Davis argue that Kennan was not only the most influential public authority on the two combatants but also determined to a great extent Roosevelt's attitudes and approach to the Portsmouth negotiations.

In their coauthored paper, "Lessons Lessened: The Near-Term Military Legacy of 1904–5 in Imperial Russia," Bruce W. Menning and John W. Steinberg address the effects of the war on Russia's military. They note that lack of unity and coherence plagued Russian military strategy both during and after the war, and postwar efforts to address the problem by creating an independent general staff and State Defense Council in 1905 ultimately foundered on tsarist politics and institutional infighting. Rather than providing overall direction and integration of imperial defense, these two new organs ended up simply adding to the fragmentation of decision making. Nicholas II remained the "final interpreter and arbiter" of military and foreign-policy matters. He eventually ignored the recommendations of the State Defense Council and the lessons of 1904–5 by pushing for construction of a Mahan-style blue-water navy at the expense of ground-force modernization, with serious consequences for Russian military preparedness at the outbreak of World War I in 1914.

In "The Absence of Portsmouth in an Early Twentieth-Century Japanese Imagination of Peace," Sho Konishi questions why historians of Japan have ignored the intimate cultural and intellectual relations between Japan and Russia in the early twentieth century. He argues that assessments of this period inordinately focus on the Russo-Japanese War and Portsmouth Treaty because they are skewed in favor of Western notions of modernity. Citing intellectuals associated with the early-twentieth-century Non-War Movement (Hisen Undō), Konishi explores an important but neglected alternative to conventional historical understanding of the war and treaty. Informed by the anarchist writings of Lev Tolstoi and Peter Kropotkin, advocates of the Non-War Movement argued that conflict was retrogressive, proposing instead that cooperation represented true progress and civilization. Central to their argument was the term *heimin*, a divisive term applied to commoners in a manner reflecting prevailing hierarchies of class structure. Non-War Movement intellectuals reconceptualized the word to connote a broad community in which race, ethnicity, and human possessions—including nation-states—

had no relevance. This form of modern subjectivity differed radically from Western notions of modernity in that *heimin* suggested the possibility of a transnational individuality. From this perspective, Non-War Movement intellectuals presented an alternative to imperialism and militarism, predominant characteristics of nation-states, thus forgoing any need to ascribe historical significance to the Russo-Japanese War and Portsmouth Treaty.

Shinji Yokote's essay, "Political Legacies of the Portsmouth Treaty," contradicts conventional characterizations of post-Portsmouth Russo-Japanese relations as hostile. He examines instead the spirit of cooperation the treaty engendered between Japan and Russia in the early twentieth century. Yokote notes that the wording of several articles in the treaty, especially those regarding the sovereignty of Korea and China over territory on which the combatants had fought, was ambiguous, perhaps deliberately so. This ambiguity enabled Japan and Russia to resist attempts by China—with the help of its allies, primarily the United States—to reassert control over its former assets in Manchuria. Yokote explores in considerable detail two examples to support this interpretation. With the backing of the United States, China resisted Russian attempts in 1908 to establish municipal administrations in cities along the Chinese Eastern Railway. The U.S. government even went so far as to propose neutralizing all foreign railways in Manchuria. Japan and Russia teamed up to veto this proposal by invoking the Portsmouth Treaty. The establishment of the Soviet Union threatened the continued validity of the treaty, especially with regard to Japanese and Soviet spheres of influence in Manchuria. Nonetheless, recognizing their mutual security and economic interests in the area, Japan and the Soviet Union successfully reinvoked the cooperative spirit of the treaty to assure peaceful relations and coauthority over Manchuria. From a broader perspective, Yokote argues, Russian-Japanese cooperation initiated by the Portsmouth Treaty created a new era in Northeast Asian regional politics that continued to exert influence on strategic and diplomatic thinking well into the twentieth century.

Focusing on contemporary implications of the Portsmouth settlement, the essays by David Wolff and Vladimir I. Ivanov shift attention from history to policy analysis. In "Riding Rough: Portsmouth, Regionalism, and the Birth of Anti-Americanism in Northeast Asia," Wolff argues that active U.S. participation in the Portsmouth peace marked the beginning of a century of anti-Americanism in Northeast Asia, as every country in the region—Japan, Russia, China, and Korea—found fault with Portsmouth and blamed the United States. Echoes of that anti-American feeling reverberate to this day, helping drive the expansion of divisive and destabilizing nationalist politics in the region. Wolff contends that anti-Americanism will likely continue to grow unless an Asia-Pacific community that includes the United States emerges as opposed to a more exclusive Northeast Asia that views America as an outsider.

In "Economic Engagement: Coping with the Realities of the Globalized World," Ivanov presents an optimistic portrait of the Russo-Japanese relationship, which, in his view, "is now qualitatively different" and "more positively focused" than it was at any point in the previous century. The relationship is undergoing significant transformation in large part under the influence of economic and other nonmilitary factors, such as investment decision-making and grassroots interaction, that are becoming increasingly nongovernmental in nature. Although bilateral economic links remain "relatively loose," Ivanov suggests, current trends and opportunities in trade, investment, and energy cooperation, especially the development of "megaprojects" like the Sakhalin oil and gas ventures, point to growing economic interdependence between Russia and Japan.

Utilizing current international relations theory, specifically the concepts of realism, liberalism, and constructivism, Kazuhiko Togo, in his essay, "The Contemporary Implications of the Russo-Japanese War: A Japanese Perspective," examines the effects of the war and Portsmouth Treaty on Japan, Russia, Korea, China, and the United States, the countries most directly affected. Togo provides a broad overview of each nation's historical experiences of the war and treaty, then traces their consequences for present-day international concerns. With a view to post–World War II international relations in Northeast Asia, he asks several pointed questions about the choices Japan made both in the conflict with Russia and in the peace settlement. Togo's essay thus encapsulates the overall theme of this volume—the Portsmouth Treaty and its legacies—while providing an overarching summary of the issues explored by the other contributors.

I

Diplomacy and the Peace

Chapter 1

Russia's Relations with Japan Before and After the War

An Episode in the Diplomacy of Imperialism

David Schimmelpenninck van der Oye

On the night of November 1, 1897, in a small village in China's Shandong Province, a group of peasants murdered two German Catholic missionaries in their sleep.[1] The crime appears to have been unpremeditated and was committed in the course of an attempted robbery.[2] Such incidents were part of the hazards of life abroad in an uncertain world, and the deaths might well have merited nothing more than an entry in the Roman Church's martyrology. Germany's bumptious Kaiser Wilhelm II, however, had been itching to join the European contest for concessions in the enormous but moribund Chinese empire. During the previous decade the Hohenzollerns had been almost shut out of the "Scramble for Africa," the race among Western powers great and small to carve up that continent in a patchwork of colonies. Wilhelm was eager for Germany not to be left behind this time around with only a few dregs of the Qing dynasty's carcass.[3] The misdeeds of a gang of bandits in Shandong presented the ideal pretext for action.

When news of the incident reached Berlin five days later, the kaiser immediately ordered his navy to occupy the port of Qingdao on Shandong's Jiaozhou (Kiaochow) Bay. A year earlier the ambitious Admiral Alfred von Tirpitz had identified the "unset pearl of Qingdao," with its sheltered harbor and populous hinterland, as the ideal candidate for a Teutonic Hong Kong.[4] Within a fortnight of the murders, on November 14, Admiral Otto von Diederichs of Imperial Germany's Pacific Squadron sailed into Jiaozhou Bay. The admiral secured Qingdao's garrison with a modest force of some seven hundred men and proclaimed himself the area's governor.[5]

St. Petersburg, which had ambitions of its own in northern China, had initially strongly objected to the move. Upon hearing that German vessels were on their way to Shandong, Russia's foreign minister, Count Mikhail Murav'ev, immediately informed his counterpart at the Wilhelmstrasse that he "deplored" this step. At the same time, should Berlin send ships to Jiaozhou Bay, the Russian navy would do likewise to reassert the tsarist claim to the port.[6] The brewing East Asian crisis took an ominous turn when Wilhelm bombastically reiterated his determination to occupy Qingdao and hinted darkly at "the complications that would arise from the simultaneous presence into the bay of both squadrons."[7]

In the event, the diplomatic squall ended almost as quickly as it had erupted. Rather than risk complications with his German cousin, in early December Tsar Nicholas II commanded his Pacific Squadron to seize Port Arthur, another harbor in the region.[8] Wilhelm quickly cabled his "congratulations" to Nicholas, adding in his characteristically florid prose: "Russia and Germany at the entrance of the Yellow Sea may be represented by St. George and St. Michael shielding the Holy Cross in the Far East."[9] As for the other European powers, France and Britain quickly followed suit by likewise extorting new Chinese naval stations from the Zongli Yamen, the Qing dynasty's foreign office.[10] Even Dutch and U.S. diplomats urged their home governments to seize naval bases, although their superiors wisely ignored such pleas.[11]

The Jiaozhou crisis was typical of the "diplomacy of imperialism," the mechanism for resolving colonial disputes that had evolved during the late nineteenth century.[12] Much like the "concert system," an unwritten code that determined relations among Europe's states on their own continent between the end of the Napoleonic Wars and the outbreak of the First World War, this system settled disputes that arose in Africa and Asia when rival claims clashed. Although the rules were never codified, they were fairly straightforward. Based on an implicit calculus involving a prior presence in the region, relative military strength, and at least the appearance of a sense of fair play, the diplomacy of imperialism was effective. Unlike the concert system, which had not always managed to head off war in Europe, this system successfully kept the powers from fighting each other over disagreements on other continents. Even when relations were at their most tense, whether at the oasis of Panjdeh in the Pamir Mountains in 1885, Fashoda on the upper Nile in 1898, or the Moroccan port of Agadir in 1911, "jaw-jaw" invariably prevailed over "war-war" through nearly a hundred years of colonial rivalries overseas before 1914.

The diplomacy of imperialism was not without its flaws. Chief among them was the inability of its practitioners to admit newly modernized non-

European states. Like an old-fashioned gentlemen's club, membership was open only to Europe's governments. Thus the tiny monarchy of Belgium was considered a legitimate colonial power, whereas the overseas ambitions of the United States and Japan were more questionable. It was this inability by an established member of the club—Russia—to take seriously the colonialist claims of an outsider—Japan—that led to the outbreak of war in East Asia on February 8, 1904.

Confusion at the Choristers' Bridge

The path to war between Russia and Japan began in 1895, with Japan's spectacular rout of China during a brief conflict over Korea.[13] The Sino-Japanese War had two major consequences. First, it laid bare to the world the utter inability of the Qing dynasty to defend its territorial integrity, thereby whetting the imperialist appetites of the European powers. Much as the Scramble for Africa had erupted in the 1880s, the Middle Kingdom's military humiliation set off the Scramble for Asia a decade later. At the same time, Russia's intervention to deny Japan a foothold on the Chinese mainland as the fruit of its victory aroused bitter resentment in the island empire. That intervention had come in the wake of the conclusion on April 17, 1895, of the Peace of Shimonoseki, which had marked the end of the Sino-Japanese War. Among Japan's demands had been possession of the Liaodong Peninsula near Beijing, with the strategically important naval base of Port Arthur at its tip. Although the Qing had agreed at Shimonoseki to cede rights to the peninsula, St. Petersburg mobilized Berlin and Paris in a triplicity that jointly demanded Tokyo's retrocession of Liaodong.

Significantly, Russia's démarche had come after heated debate among Nicholas II's counselors about how to respond to the dramatic turn of events in East Asia. Because of eastern Siberia's proximity to the theater of the Sino-Japanese War, the conflict aroused considerable interest on the banks of the Neva. Decision makers there were of two minds. One group advocated siding with Japan and joining in the former's grab of Chinese soil. Just as Russians had long tried to benefit from the decadence of the sick man of Europe, Ottoman Turkey, they should now see what they might get from the sick man of Asia. Chief among the Romanovs' desiderata was an ice-free outlet on the Pacific. With the Pacific port of Vladivostok hemmed in by frozen seas for four months a year, Russia lacked a suitable warm-water terminus for the Trans-Siberian Railroad then being built. Leading men in the tsarist admiralty suggested that the time was opportune for seizing a port in Korea, a view that Nicholas II enthusiastically shared. Without necessarily advocating such a step, the foreign minister, Prince Andrei Lobanov-Rostovskii, proposed making an arrangement with Tokyo for a new harbor in the region.[14]

Others in St. Petersburg backed a more cautious stance. The most powerful advocate of this approach was Finance Minister Sergei Witte, who saw good relations with China as essential for his ambitious plans to develop Russia's Far East. The finance minister never doubted that the Romanov dynasty would eventually dominate China. "The extension of Russia's railway through Manchuria . . . was far from being the final step in our advance to the Pacific Ocean," he wrote. "By historical necessity we [are] obligated to go further."[15] But the empire had to do so peacefully and through economic means. Railroads, banks, and trading houses should conquer the Middle Kingdom, not troops. Territorial annexations by war, Witte believed, were antiquated and counterproductive. Besides, he often reminded Nicholas, "for the sake of the general domestic situation in Russia it is exceedingly important to avoid anything which might lead to foreign complications."[16]

Despite some misgivings on the part of the tsar, Witte got his way, and Russia played the role of Beijing's savior in the wake of Shimonoseki. The finance minister quickly capitalized on China's goodwill by extending Russian influence through the means of informal empire or *pénétration pacifique*. He secured the Zongli Yamen's consent for his Trans-Siberian Railroad to take a shortcut through Manchuria, considerably shortening the line's eastern portion. More important, on June 3, 1896, the two empires concluded a secret treaty promising jointly to resist any future aggression by Japan.

Over the following years, St. Petersburg's East Asian diplomacy was highly erratic. A year after concluding a defensive alliance with China to protect it against any future Japanese predations, Nicholas abruptly changed course. Aping his cousin Willy's occupation of Qingdao, he seized the Liaodong Peninsula's southern part, including Port Arthur, for himself. Three years later, in the summer of 1900, Russia seemed to resume its original pro-Chinese direction and professed to help its neighbor as it suffered the ravages of the Boxer rising. But then Cossacks suddenly marched into the Qing dynasty's ancestral provinces of Manchuria. Although Nicholas' diplomats solemnly promised to evacuate, his military stayed put and even appeared to have designs on neighboring Korea.

This inconsistent line, veering wildly as it did between supporting Beijing and seeking to profit from its infirmity, reflected deep divisions in St. Petersburg's Far Eastern policy. The steadfast champion of a China-friendly orientation remained Sergei Witte, who was eventually supported by Count Vladimir Lamsdorf, foreign minister from 1900 through 1906. Arrayed against Witte was a changing coalition of hard-liners, including at various times the navy; Lamsdorf's opportunistic predecessor, Count Mikhail

Murav'ev (foreign minister from 1897 to 1900); the shady entrepreneur and retired captain of the guards Aleksandr Bezobrazov; and the tsar's eventual viceroy of the Far East, Admiral Evgenii Alekseev. Despite their differences, Witte and his various opponents generally agreed on one important point: whatever the means, Russia had to pursue an active role in Northeast Asia.

The Manchurian Question

Russia's occupation of Manchuria during the Boxer rising of 1900 and its subsequent reluctance to withdraw precipitously worsened relations with Japan. From the first, Nicholas II's ministers repeatedly assured the world that their country's troops had every intention of leaving the three provinces in the near future. Already on August 12, 1900, Count Lamsdorf asked his ambassadors to distribute a circular to foreign governments explaining that the occupation was a temporary measure, which would end as soon as life was back to normal. "Russia has no designs of territorial acquisitions in China," he pledged.[17] Yet Russian officials were also eager to win something in return for handing the region back to China. Although the tsarist army had sustained remarkably light casualties, the occupation had been expensive, and the railroad had suffered extensive damage at the hands of the Boxers. More important, tsarist officials wanted to be sure that popular unrest in China would never again pose a threat to Russian lives and property.

Opinions in St. Petersburg over the Manchurian question were sharply divided. Foreign Minister Lamsdorf and Finance Minister Witte argued that Manchuria should be handed back as soon as possible. Any reluctance to quit the region would only raise tensions there, they predicted. As Lamsdorf explained in a letter to Minister of War Aleksei Kuropatkin in the spring of 1902, "it would be advisable for us to evacuate Manchuria sooner, if possible, so as not to . . . provoke war with Japan."[18] Many Russians also advocated an evacuation for the simple reason that there were more pressing problems at home.[19]

While Count Lamsdorf was being cautious, Witte had other reasons for wishing a speedy evacuation. During the four years since the finance minister had won a concession to build a railway in the north, "Witte's kingdom" had flourished. Work on the Chinese Eastern Railway (CER) had proceeded at a frantic pace, with over 1,300 kilometers of the projected 2,500-kilometer line already on the ground by summer 1900.[20] The CER's headquarters in Harbin, initially set up in an old distillery at the intersection of the Sungari River and the future track in the spring of 1898, soon became the center of a thriving boomtown.[21] CER subsidiaries began to exploit the region's lumber and coal, and at the southern tip of the Liaodong Peninsula, near the new tsarist naval station of Port Arthur, Witte had equally ambitious plans to turn the harbor of Dalian (Talienwan), now officially renamed Dal'nii ("Far Away"), into a major commercial entrepôt.[22] To protect it all, the finance minister commanded an ever-expanding security force, derisively nicknamed "Matilda's Guards" after his wife, Matilda Ivanovna.[23] The army's presence in Manchuria during the Boxer rising had introduced a serious rival to Witte's own authority, and the sooner it left, the more quickly the Finance Ministry would regain its colonial monopoly.

There were influential advocates for keeping Manchuria. Military men, many of whom had begun their careers during the Central Asian wars, believed that Manchuria should be absorbed into the Russian empire, just as the khanates of Khiva, Kokand, and Bokhara had been in the late nineteenth century.[24] The most prominent hawk was Admiral Evgenii Alekseev. Based at Port Arthur, the naval officer had authority not only over the Pacific fleet but over the garrison on the Liaodong Peninsula as well. He also commanded Russian forces in the Far East during the Boxer Rebellion. Alekseev's mercurial temperament and ambition, combined with rumors that he was the illegitimate son of Alexander II, earned him the dislike of many contemporaries, especially Sergei Witte, who regarded him as a dangerous rival in Russia's Far East. Count Lamsdorf also distrusted the admiral and fretted about his "unfortunate propensity for adventures."[25]

Alekseev would emerge as the most forceful advocate for retaining Manchuria. He often argued that quitting the region would only make Russia more vulnerable to another rebellion as well as to an increasingly aggressive Japan.[26] Yet, if the admiral seemed to worry about defending his position on the Pacific, the international repercussions of a prolonged occupation did not bother him in the least. As he wrote the war minister: "Despite their protests against our intention to retain Manchuria, [the other powers] have long ago reconciled themselves to the matter."[27]

General Kuropatkin himself took an intermediate position on the Manchurian question. When the unrest first broke out, he strongly supported intervention and would come to oppose withdrawing the army prematurely. There were times when Kuropatkin was inclined to keep troops stationed in northern Manchuria, where the Chinese population was much smaller than in the southern province of Fengtien. Even then, however, he wavered between fully annexing the north and making it a semi-independent vassal, like the Central Asian emirate of Bokhara.[28] Weighing heavily on the war minister's considerations was Russia's vulnerable western border, where German ambitions posed a far greater danger to the security of the realm than any threats to the distant Pacific frontier.[29]

The pathologically indecisive Nicholas II characteristically wavered between the alternatives, although by temperament he favored the more adventurous course. Matters were not helped when he briefly befriended a retired guards officer, Aleksandr Bezobrazov, who concocted a baroque enterprise to occupy northern Korea's Yalu River basin in the guise of a lumbering enterprise.[30] The result was a confused and erratic policy that increasingly aroused the hostility of the other powers.

After over a year of difficult negotiations with a China emboldened by the support of St. Petersburg's rivals, Russia signed an agreement on April 8, 1902, in Beijing pledging a withdrawal from Manchuria in three stages over the next eighteen months.[31] St. Petersburg, however, proved unable to keep its word. Tsarist troops did carry out the first phase of their evacuation on October 8, 1902, pulling out of the southern half of Fengtien Province, including the ancient Qing capital of Mukden (now Shenyang). But the second step, promised for April 1903, was not taken, as Russian officials became increasingly divided over the merits of quitting the region.

Although now no longer the Japanese prime minister, Marquis Itō Hirobumi had tried to salvage his country's peace with Russia by undertaking a private mission to St. Petersburg in November 1901. While he had received the new government's approval for the trip, it was entirely at his own initiative. The elder statesman received a warm welcome, and Nicholas awarded him the Order of St. Alexander Nevsky, his dynasty's most prestigious decoration. In meetings with both Witte and Lamsdorf, Itō pleaded for a Korean-Manchurian deal. While the finance minister was sympathetic to such an arrangement, the foreign minister turned him down, and Itō returned to Tokyo empty-handed.[32] Though generally supportive of Witte, Lamsdorf was clearly heeding his sovereign's wishes. Earlier that month, Nicholas had told his cousin, Prince Henry of Prussia:

I don't want Korea for myself, but neither can I countenance that the Japanese set foot there. Were they to try this, it would be a *casus belli* for Russia. A Japanese presence in Korea would be like a new Bosporus for us in East Asia. Russia can never accept this.[33]

The Final Round

Despite a growing conviction in Tokyo about the futility of further negotiations and utter confusion at the Choristers' Bridge, in the summer of 1903 the two powers once again entered into talks to resolve their differences in East Asia. The initiative had come from Japan's prime minister, Katsura Tarō, after a series of discussions among cabinet members and elder statesmen earlier that year to determine his government's stance. As Yasutoshi Teramoto explains in his chapter, both Katsura and his foreign minister, Komura Jutarō, undertook the talks fully expecting war.

Russia's line had also toughened considerably as its diplomats resumed their negotiations with their Japanese counterparts. Finance Minister Sergei Witte, the principal advocate for peace in East Asia, was rapidly falling from imperial favor, while the hawkish Admiral Alekseev's star continued to rise. The tsar called the hard line he set in the spring of 1903 "the new course."[34] Its purpose, as he explained in a telegram on May 15 to his commander on the Pacific, was to ensure that there would be "no penetration of foreign influence into Manchuria . . . in any form whatsoever."[35] Russia would underscore its determination, he wrote Alekseev, by stepping up its military and commercial presence in East Asia. Nicholas promised:

We will upgrade our armed forces in the Far East as soon as possible, and without regard to budgetary prudence, to the level demanded by our political and economic tasks, thereby proving to the world our steadfast determination to defend our right to exclusive influence over Manchuria.[36]

Betraying his ambivalence and uncertainty, the tsar nevertheless added that his "new course" would be implemented "in connection with our final decision to comply with the agreement of April 8, 1902."[37]

Whereas Tokyo's resolve continued to grow more firm and distinct as the year progressed, each of the many conferences among tsarist officials to determine St. Petersburg's stance seemed to be less conclusive than the preceding one. Even Komura, the Japanese foreign minister, spoke of a "serious diversity of opinion in the counsels of Russia."[38] Tiring of the endless squabbling among his ministers, Nicholas did make two important decisions that summer. On August 12, he issued a decree appointing Admiral Alekseev as his viceroy of the Far East. As Nicholas explained to his new deputy, the position essentially made him the tsar's personal representative on the Pacific, with full authority for all policy in the region. All other officials, including diplomats, financial agents, and military officers, were answerable to him, not their own ministers in St. Petersburg.[39] And two weeks later, on August 28, Nicholas removed Alekseev's chief rival by dismissing Sergei Witte from his post as finance minister.[40]

Nicholas' decision to promote Alekseev had severe repercussions in Tokyo, which saw the appointment as highly provocative. Baron Roman Rosen, the Russian minister, reported that Japan had taken the naming of a viceroy for the Far East as an aggressive act.[41] The Japanese were particularly offended since the decree came a fortnight after their government had proposed new negotiations.[42]

Throughout 1903 foreign statesmen were confused, alarmed, and often angered by the frequent *voltes-face* in tsarist policy, further isolating Russia diplomatically. Along with Japan, England was the most troublesome power, and London did its best to disrupt Russian diplomacy in Asia. Meanwhile Germany was cynically playing off its European rivals by alternately assuring St. Petersburg of its support and promising strict neutrality to London and Tokyo.[43] The United States, whose secretary of state, John Hay, had taken the moral high ground by declaring China's doors open to all foreign commerce in 1899, expressed its indignation at Russia's continued attempts to close Manchuria to American business. At the same time, American public opinion, which had been aroused by news of recent anti-Semitic pogroms in the southwestern Russian town of Kishinev, was also hostile. Count Arthur Cassini, the tsar's ambassador in Washington, advised that "the United States will certainly not join in a war against us, but her moral and probably also financial support will go to Japan."[44] Even France opposed complications on the Pacific. Paris' partnership with St. Petersburg was meant to contain Germany, not Japan. Still smarting over Russia's lukewarm support of its African interests during the Fashoda crisis five years earlier, the Quay d'Orsay let it be known that it would do little more to assist its ally in the Far East.[45]

Despite the growing tensions in East Asia, a compromise might still have been possible even at this late stage. The tsar and his viceroy, however, still found it difficult to take Japan seriously. Nicholas certainly did not feel that the interminable talks merited interrupting his lengthy autumn holidays abroad or his hunts, while the convoluted four-way diplomacy among the traveling Russian court, St. Petersburg, Port Arthur, and Tokyo hardly simplified matters. Anyway, the tsar reasoned, "there will be no war because I do not wish it."[46] But the decision was not his alone to make.

As the negotiations dragged on inconclusively into winter, the Japanese cabinet finally concluded that there was no prospect of a peaceful solution. On February 6, 1904, Foreign Minister Komura summoned Baron Rosen to his official residence to announce that his government had lost its patience at the "futile negotiations." It had therefore decided to end them and break off diplomatic relations. He handed Rosen a telegram that concluded ominously:

... the Imperial Government reserves to themselves the right to take such independent action as they may deem best to consolidate and defend their menaced position, as well as to protect their established rights and legitimate interests.[47]

Upon returning to his legation, the Russian minister learned from the naval attaché that earlier the same day, at 6:00 A.M. local time, two Japanese squadrons "had weighed anchor for unknown destinations."[48] Shortly after midnight on February 8, 1904, torpedoes from one of them struck three Russian vessels at anchor off the tsarist Pacific garrison at Port Arthur. The two empires were at war.

From Adversary to Ally

Unlike its confused condition in the prewar years, in the immediate aftermath of the Far Eastern fiasco tsarist policy was relatively single-minded. Despite some revanchism in the military and the right-wing press, Nicholas' more senior statesmen clearly understood the urgent need to keep the peace abroad while the empire rebuilt at home.[49] Such sentiments were based on an objective assessment of the destruction that the Romanovs' Pacific adventure had left in its wake. As Bruce Menning has noted, although the Russian army had not been annihilated, it "came away from the Far East spent," while large parts of the Pacific and Baltic fleets were no more.[50] And the Black Sea mutiny on the battleship *Potemkin* suggested that the remaining assets were not necessarily reliable. Meanwhile, with the autocracy's finances in ruins, the treasury's top priority was to restore solvency. But the gravest challenge was political. For the first time in Russia's history, nearly all sectors of society—the peasantry, the urban masses, and the intelligentsia—had joined forces to rise against the regime. Nicholas II's decision to grant basic civil liberties and limited parliamentary rule had brought some calm back to the empire, but considerable tension and mistrust remained among his subjects. In the words of his prime minister, Petr Stolypin, "Our internal situation does not permit us to conduct an aggressive foreign policy."[51]

The only logical foreign policy was one of "*receuillement redux,*" a reprise of the diplomacy that Prince Alexander Gorchakov had conducted as chancellor in the wake of the equally disastrous Crimean War half a century earlier.[52] Like Stolypin, Aleksandr Izvol'skii, Russia's foreign minister from 1906 through 1908, was convinced of the need for prudence abroad. Upon assuming his new post, Izvol'skii recognized that his first task was to secure "our vulnerable frontier from the Far East right up to Europe."[53] Insisting that Russia needed at least ten years of peace fully to restore its strength, the foreign minister saw as his most immediate task the resolution of outstanding differences with his country's most dangerous rivals, including Britain, Germany, Austria-Hungary, and Japan.[54] Above all, the former envoy to Tokyo advocated disengagement from the Pacific. Izvol'skii's general approach, as he explained during a meeting with senior officers in 1907, was to "achieve a balance in the Far East through politics, so as not to waste any resources there and save our strength for the great challenges in Europe."[55]

In April 1906, the very month Izvol'skii was appointed foreign minister, Motono Ichirō, the Japanese minister to St. Petersburg, proposed renegotiating an agreement to restrict the movement of foreigners in Manchuria.[56] The pact was part of the unfinished business left from the peace of Portsmouth, which involved such details as new trade and fisheries conventions for the region as well as compensation for prisoners of war. In sharp contrast to its foot-dragging during the various talks before 1904, Russia responded with alacrity, and by July Izvol'skii and Motono were meeting to resolve these outstanding questions. It would take until the beginning of the following year to reach an understanding, but on the whole the conversations proceeded cordially and smoothly, going a long way toward establishing trust between the former adversaries.[57]

Although the Treaty of Portsmouth had obligated its signatories to settle some administrative details, by December 1906 Izvol'skii began to consider taking the dialogue a step further. The various commercial matters being considered seemed to suggest the need for a broader agreement that would delineate the two powers' spheres of interest in Manchuria. And the fact that Izvol'skii was in the midst of reaching a similar arrangement over Central Asia with Japan's ally, Great Britain, did not hurt matters. Accordingly, in January he asked a deputy at the Choristers' Bridge, Baron M. A. Taube, to draft a secret convention with Japan to that effect. A few weeks later the foreign minister presented the proposed convention to Motono, whose government responded favorably by the end of February.

On July 30, 1907, Aleksandr Izvol'skii and Motono Ichirō signed a convention "to consolidate the relations of peace and neighborliness which have happily been re-established between Japan and Russia."[58] The accord's two public articles pledged each power to respect the other's territorial integrity as well as that of China. More important were the three secret articles, the first of which solomonically divided Manchuria into two spheres of influence, with Japan gaining control over the Liaodong Peninsula and the surrounding area and Russia dominating the north, including the Chinese Eastern Railway. At the same time, Tokyo gained a free hand in Korea while Outer Mongolia fell under St. Petersburg's aegis. With this agreement, reinforced by two subsequent ones in 1910 and 1912, the former adversaries had at last resolved what nearly a decade of frustrated diplomacy had been unable to do. Thus, with the exception of Mongolia and the Liaodong Peninsula, the arrangement was not too different from the one Japan had been seeking right up to 1904—three years and nearly a quarter of a million lives earlier.

Conclusion

Scholars have often described the Russo-Japanese War as a classic imperialist conflict. Such assessments are only half right. Although rival expansionist urges led to a disagreement between St. Petersburg and Tokyo over Northeast Asia at the turn of the twentieth century, such competition was hardly unique during an age of rapid colonial conquest by the modern states. The four decades from 1880 through the outbreak of the First World War witnessed a number of confrontations in Africa and Asia among the great powers of Europe. None, however, erupted into open war; disagreements were invariably resolved by a diplomatic system that recognized the Western states as all having legitimate interests.

Russia's quarrel with Japan was unique because official St. Petersburg's highly traditional view of the world rendered it virtually impossible to accept the notion that Tokyo could play by the same rules. A few decades earlier, in justifying Russian conquest of independent khanates in Central Asia, the tsarist foreign ministry's jurist, Fedor Martens, had famously declared: "international law does not apply to savages." While views of Japan were less crude, many tsarist officials still found it difficult to consider the picturesque empire of geishas and origami as being in the same diplomatic league as its more familiar partners.

By no means did everyone involved in setting St. Petersburg's course for East Asia share this assessment. In fact, many at the Choristers' Bridge, including the foreign minister himself, Count Vladimir Lamsdorf, were well aware of the dangers inherent in ignoring Japan's repeated demands for a deal. The tragedy of tsarist diplomacy during the decade before 1904 was that it singularly lacked unity and focus. Riven as it was by bureaucratic and personal rivalries and led by a pathologically indecisive sovereign, the autocracy proved utterly incapable of setting a consistent path as it launched an ambitious course for the Pacific after Shimonoseki.

Making matters worse for Russia, the pattern of Meiji decision-making was the direct opposite of that of Nicholas II's regime. While confusion, chaos, and intrigue reigned on the banks of the Neva, Japan's cabinet and elder statesmen, despite the fluctuations of parliamentary politics, seemed to act with patience and single-minded determination in pursuing the nation's colonial interests before 1904. But, if Nicholas' dysfunctional Far Eastern diplomacy was an important contributing factor, the basic cause of the Russo-Japanese War was St. Petersburg's inability to take Tokyo seriously as a legitimate player in the imperialist game.

It would take the fall of Mukden and the sinking of the Baltic Fleet at

Tsushima to convince Russians to take Japan seriously. And, as the relatively smooth course of the negotiations after Portsmouth indicates, by 1907 the island empire's imperialist pretensions were seen as legitimate. Indeed, in the coming years, Russia and Japan would be the most aggressive and enthusiastic beneficiaries of China's agony. The economic development of northern Manchuria continued apace, and in 1912 Mongolia became a tsarist protectorate.[59] Thus, far from losing its imperialist appetite after 1905, St. Petersburg continued to pursue ambitions in Northeast Asia, albeit on a more restricted scale. Only now it did so with, rather than against, Japan.[60]

Chapter 2

Japanese Diplomacy Before and After the War

The Turning Point on the Road to the Pacific War

Yasutoshi Teramoto

*I*n the years immediately preceding the Russo-Japanese War, Tokyo increasingly saw the issue of control over the Korean Peninsula as a life-or-death matter from the standpoint of Japan's security. At the time Japanese leaders such as Prime Minister Katsura Tarō and Foreign Minister Komura Jutarō held that the Korea question was inseparable from that of Russian-occupied Manchuria and, distrustful of Russia's intentions, became more and more determined to resolve those questions even at the risk of war. After the conflict, Japan, while basically maintaining the prewar framework of alliances and understandings with European powers, began to develop a foreign policy toward the Asia Pacific region, and particularly toward the United States, that was largely independent of the Eurocentric system of international relations.

Japanese Diplomacy from the Tripartite Intervention to the Outbreak of the Russo-Japanese War

An Overview of Japanese Foreign Policy to 1900

During the Meiji era, Japan basically pursued an expansionist foreign policy toward the Korean Peninsula and China and worked toward a policy of cooperation with the major Western powers to obtain their consent for such a foreign policy. In this sense, Japanese foreign policy during the Meiji era had two facets: a policy toward Asia and a policy toward the Great Powers.

Beginning with the Kanghwa Island incident of 1875, Japan in its policy toward Korea under the Yi dynasty imitated the ways in which Western nations had opened Japan and sought to make inroads into the Korean Peninsula backed by military might. Before the Sino-Japanese War of 1894−95, Japan had struggled with China under the Manchu dynasty for suzerainty over the Korean Peninsula. The Japanese victory in the Sino-Japanese War broke the bonds of suzerainty between China and Korea.

After the tripartite intervention that followed the Sino-Japanese War,[1] Japan found itself struggling over the Korean Peninsula with Russia, which was pursuing a policy of southward advance in the Far East. Specifically, a pro-Russia faction seized the opportunity that the tripartite intervention provided to gain power within Korea. Incensed by this development, Japan instigated the assassination of Queen Min, in response to which King Kojong sought refuge in the Russian legation, and feelings toward Japan worsened in Korea. In 1896 Japan entered into two understandings with Russia, the Komura-Waeber Memorandum and the Yamagata-Lobanov Agreement, which allowed both countries to intervene in internal Korean affairs, but these agreements meant that Japan now had to negotiate on equal terms with Russia concerning the Korean Peninsula. Japan proposed an exchange of Manchuria for Korea (*Man-Kan kōkan*) on the occasion of the 1898 Nishi-Rosen Agreement, but Russia rejected this proposal. Under the 1898 agreement, Russia barely recognized Korean independence and Japanese economic supremacy on the peninsula, but the pact could hardly have been expected to establish Japanese political domination of Korea. In the event, Japan before the Russo-Japanese War continued to struggle with Russia for domination of Korea diplomatically, while at the same time strengthening its army and navy.

Japanese Foreign Policy from 1900 to the Start of the Russo-Japanese War

THE KATSURA-KOMURA LINE

The Boxer Rebellion of 1900 provided Russia with the opportunity to continue its occupation of Manchuria and forced Japan to reconsider its continental policy.[2] When forming his first cabinet in 1901, Prime Minister Katsura Tarō had already raised concluding an agreement with Britain and establishing Japan as the protector of Korea among the four planks of his political platform.[3] While showing a solid understanding of the pro-Russia views of Itō and others, Katsura judged that Russia would not end its occupation of Manchuria but would inevitably invade Korea. Therefore, a peace achieved through a pro-Russia policy would in the end only be temporary as far as Japan was concerned or would result in Japan's submission. On the other hand, Britain, exhausted by the Boer War, was pursuing a status quo policy in East Asia and did not wish to expand its territorial holdings; it was therefore interested in using Japan to oppose Russia's occupation of Manchuria. Thus, Katsura concluded that the best policy was for Japan to ally with Britain.[4] This view was shared by Katsura's mentor, the oligarch Yamagata Aritomo. Specifically, Yamagata had already argued in March 1890 for a national defense policy consisting not only of a "line of sovereignty" demarcating Japan proper but also of a "line of interest" covering the Korean Peninsula, with its close relationship with Japan,[5] and he also held that an alliance between Japan and Britain would best prevent the risk of a collision with Russia over its occupation of Manchuria.[6]

The most active promoter of Japanese diplomacy before the Russo-Japanese War was Foreign Minister Komura Jutarō. Komura was dubbed a "statesman diplomat"[7] owing to the characteristics of his diplomacy, whereby he sought to advance Japan's national interests from a broad viewpoint. The truth of this characterization is revealed by Komura's memorandum titled "Ten-Year Plan for National Political Diplomacy," which he submitted to Prime Minister Katsura upon assuming the post of foreign minister in 1901. In it, he argued that expanding Japan's national rights and interests and pursuing Japan's continental policy in the face of competition from the Great Powers in East Asia required not just exercising diplomacy but also wielding the domestic political tools of administration, finance, defense, education, and legislation as well as organizing and expanding transport and trade. He cited specific concerns such as the speedy completion of the Seoul-Pusan Railroad and the promotion of Sino-Japanese joint ventures and proposed the imperialist diplomatic line of establishing Japanese interests in both China and Korea.[8]

Komura also expressed his foreign policy toward China and Korea in his proposals for furthering Japanese business interests in those countries. The centerpiece of his foreign policy toward Korea was the administration of railroads such as the Seoul-Pusan and the Seoul-Hsinwiju rail lines. He argued for extending those railroads, which together ran the length of Korea, into Manchuria. Regarding China, he demanded the establishment of a Sino-Japanese bank and the investigation of potential business ventures in China. Thus, Komura focused his attention on railroads and finance, which played the most important role in the imperialist environment of those days.[9]

On July 22, 1900, after Russia had already succeeded in occupying Manchuria, Komura, then the Japanese minister to St. Petersburg, urged in a memorandum to Japan's foreign minister the doctrine of a Manchuria-Korea exchange, arguing that the most desirable outcome was to establish separate spheres of influence, with Japan and Russia each having a free hand in Korea and Manchuria, respectively, and each recognizing the other's freedom in terms of commerce within its sphere.[10] But Komura's years in St. Petersburg had hardened his views regarding Russia. His experiences in dealing with tsarist officials had convinced him that Japan would make its voice heard only through military strength.

When the Russian minister to Japan proposed Korea's neutralization on January 11, 1901, Komura, who was the Japanese minister to China at the time, replied that the Korea problem could not be solved unless the solution was linked to the Manchuria problem and that Japan could not accept Korean neutrality unless Russia agreed to Manchurian neutrality. If both territories could not be made neutral, Komura insisted that, in accordance with basic policy, there was no course but to follow the doctrine of a Manchuria-Korea exchange.[11] In this sense, the doctrine in question was a measure based on the notion that the Manchurian problem was inseparable from the Korean problem.

Komura developed his own theory regarding the policy of Japan toward Russia's occupation of Manchuria in "Memorandum Regarding an Anglo-Japanese Agreement," which he submitted to the Privy Council on December 7, 1901, following his appointment as foreign minister. China and Korea both had close relationships with Japan, and the fate of Korea, in particular, was a "life-or-death matter" to Japan. Therefore, Komura argued for a revised awareness that, were Russia allowed to possess Manchuria, Korea would be on the verge of losing its existence.[12] Komura indicated two alternative methods for resolving this situation: Japan should show a strong resolve not to rule out opening hostilities with Russia, or it should force Russia to compromise by allying with a third country. The first option he rejected because of the inadequacy of Japan's fighting capacity and the lack of a compelling casus belli at that time. This assessment left the second course as the better policy: Japan would force Russia to accede to its demands by putting pressure on St. Petersburg through an Anglo-Japanese alliance.[13]

Furthermore, Komura compared the advantages and disadvantages of concluding a Russo-Japanese understanding based on a Manchuria-Korea exchange versus opposing Russia by forming an Anglo-Japanese alliance. A Russo-Japanese understanding would fail to check future Russian expansion, not only in Manchuria but also in the rest of China, and therefore would only temporarily maintain peace throughout East Asia. It would bring some economic benefit to Japan in Manchuria but would cause Japan to lose the confidence of the Chinese people and make it difficult for the nation to oppose British naval power in the Far East. By contrast, an Anglo-Japanese alliance, he argued, would dissuade Britain from desiring to expand its territorial holdings in East Asia and therefore would maintain a relatively durable peace in the region. Such an alliance would commit the parties to the open-door policy of equal commercial opportunity and respect for China's territorial integrity, enabling Japan to gain China's confidence without risking censure by the major powers, and would facilitate the expansion of Japanese interests in China. Forming an alliance with Britain and forcing Russia to accept it would be the only way to resolve the Korea problem in a way that Japan desired. Britain had the potential to bestow on Japan great financial and commercial benefits, and an Anglo-Japanese alliance would make it far easier to oppose Russian naval power.[14] Finally, with British diplomatic backing, an Anglo-Japanese alliance could prevent a repeat of the tripartite intervention. Thus, Komura's approach had the advantage of accommodating broad concerns in areas such as diplomatic strategy, commerce, and finance without limiting Japan's options for responding to Russia's aggression in Manchuria.

According to Katsura and the foreign minister's confidential secretary, Honda Kumatarō, Komura was already planning to conclude an Anglo-Japanese alliance when he entered the cabinet. His purpose was to resolve the Manchuria-Korea problem even at the risk of war.[15] In the end, he believed, the best way to strengthen Japan's position was to join forces with Great Britain. In this sense, Komura followed a consistent policy toward Russia from the conclusion of the Anglo-Japanese Alliance to the outbreak of war with Russia.

Russia's occupation of Manchuria threatened the existence of Korea, which was closely linked to the security of Japan. Therefore, Japan could not consider separating the Korea problem from the Manchuria problem but decided to resolve the issue through military action once the limits of diplomatic negotiation with Russia became apparent. For Russia's part, placing the Korean Peninsula under Japanese control would cut off sea transport between Vladivostok and southern Manchuria, a situation that Russia would find unacceptable from the standpoint of its administration of Manchuria. Therefore, the Korean Peninsula was a life-or-death matter for Japan in terms of its security, and it was also essential to Russia for assuring its management of Manchuria. As a result, the problem of the Korean Peninsula was a matter on which neither country would budge, making war inevitable.[16] In that sense, Honda indicated that the guiding principles of Komura's diplomacy were the "inseparability of the Korea question from the Manchuria question" and the "inevitability of war with Russia" as the means for resolving those questions.[17]

SIMILARITIES AND DIFFERENCES BETWEEN THE
VIEWPOINTS OF KATSURA AND OF ITŌ HIROBUMI

The oligarch Itō Hirobumi, who immediately preceded Katsura as prime minister, did not initially oppose an alliance with Britain but considered its establishment impossible; he sought first to attempt a Russo-Japanese understanding and then to determine whether an Anglo-Japanese alliance or a Russo-Japanese agreement would be more advantageous to Japan. Katsura asserted that an alliance with Britain should come first and that a Russo-Japanese understanding should be permitted only insofar as it did not go against the spirit of the alliance with Britain.[18] In fact, Itō agreed on August 4, 1901, to prepare a draft proposal for negotiations leading to an alliance with Britain.[19] At the same time, Itō took the view that Japan could resolve the Manchurian-Korean problem only by dealing with Russia.[20]

Whereas Itō took the stance of negotiating with either Russia or Britain—whichever course was more beneficial for Japan's security and interests—Katsura felt that, even if Russia concluded an agreement with Japan, any compromise by St. Petersburg would be temporary. In terms of Russia's basic policy objectives, Katsura did not believe that Russia had any intention of yielding rights to Japan either in Manchuria or in Korea. According to Katsura, Itō's two-stage approach was also extremely risky, and the danger existed that Japan would lose in both negotiations. Katsura felt that Japan could never consummate an alliance with Britain unless it sought the alliance in good faith from the beginning.[21]

Itō believed that, without a Russo-Japanese understanding, an alliance with Britain, even if concluded under conditions favorable to Japan, would not substantially resolve the Korean problem and ultimately would only become a fuse that would spark a war with Russia, which Itō was anxious to avoid. In Katsura's view, however, it would be difficult to expect a satisfactory resolution for Japan in light of Russia's Far Eastern policy: any policy trend toward accommodation with St. Petersburg would be a diversion in the midst of Anglo-Japanese negotiations, and a wide gap in thinking between Russia and Japan was unavoidable.[22] In the end, after Itō and Katsura had reached their basic understanding on August 4, 1901, the Anglo-Japanese Alliance was concluded on January 30 of the following year.

According to Hara Takashi, Itō and the oligarch Inoue Kaoru were neither proponents of opening hostilities with Russia nor clear advocates of the antiwar argument.[23] Itō was cautious about opening hostilities in view of Japan's inadequate military preparation, especially in terms of its financial condition.[24] To the contrary, Komura had said that, if a country had enough money, arms, and independence under the kinds of international circumstances prevailing at the time, it would not need to go to war. Lacking those elements, Japan was obliged to do so.[25]

THE DECISION FOR WAR WITH RUSSIA

On March 15, 1903, oligarchs Itō, Inoue, Matsukata Masayoshi, Ōyama Iwao, and Saigō Tsugumichi met to consider policy toward Russia. The outcome of this meeting was extremely self-restrained: both Britain and Germany, pleading political realities, had no intention of blocking Russia's occupation of Manchuria; the oligarchs determined that it was dangerous for Japan to act alone, that the status quo in Korea should be maintained, and that an attempt should be made to strike an agreement with Russia if the opportunity arose.[26]

Russia agreed to evacuate its troops from Manchuria after the establishment of the Anglo-Japanese Alliance, but when it failed to meet the deadline for a second-phase withdrawal and, on the contrary, thrust new demands on China, the situation became critical at one stroke. Russia marched south from Manchuria to the Korean border area, occupied a wooded strip along the bank of the Yalu River, and leased land for a timber concession there.[27] Komura recognized that the Russians involved, though ostensibly merchants, were in reality military men, that their enterprise was not a private concern but a governmental one, and that their actions were in utter disregard of the stipulations of the concession and of Korean sovereignty.[28]

For Japan, however, it was a question not simply of competing for forest resources on the bank of the Yalu River but of being vigilant against a threat to the survival of Korea.[29] In reality, during 1902 and 1903, State Councilor Aleksandr Bezobrazov had the idea of utilizing the timber enterprise as a sort of "screen" or barrier against a possible attack on Russia by Japan and requested Admiral Evgenii Alekseev to send soldiers in civilian dress and a mounted rifle corps.[30] Even on November 27, 1903, Tsar Nicholas, while disregarding the objections of War Minister A. N. Kuropatkin, expressed confidence in Bezobrazov and agreed to send troops to the Yalu River Valley.[31]

On April 21, 1903, Itō, Katsura, and Komura met with Yamagata at his personal residence to refine policy toward Russia. There they firmly resolved not to compromise on the issue of exchanging Manchuria for Korea.[32] They determined that a Manchuria-Korea exchange would resolve the situation: Japan would have supremacy in Korea, in return for which it would recognize Russia's supremacy in Manchuria. This arrangement would result in a basic solution to the Korea problem. Japan, however, would not compromise on this policy, and fulfilling the demand for control over all of Korea required a determination not to avoid war. Placing Korea under Japanese control as far as the Yalu River meant occupying the military base that Russia administered on the flank of the Liaodong Peninsula. Subsequently, a Japanese army attack on Russia's flank beyond the Yalu River, by cutting off contact between Harbin and Port Arthur and threatening the Liaodong Peninsula, would signify failure for St. Petersburg's Far Eastern policy. The Japanese leaders, therefore, anticipated that Russia would find their demands to be unacceptable.[33] In that sense, according to Katsura, the April 21 meeting essentially meant the start of war with Russia.[34]

From the standpoint of the military, on May 12, Ōyama Iwao, chief of the General Staff Office, expressed to the emperor the urgent need to increase armaments to prevent a Russian invasion of Manchuria and Korea, which would then threaten Japan proper.[35] On June 8, at a top-level conference of the General Staff Office, a group of middle-echelon officers exerted pressure on Ōyama to support military action as a last resort if diplomatic negotiations aimed at preventing a Russian invasion of Manchuria and Korea proved unsuccessful. Ōyama did not respond to the officers' demand on the spot,[36] but on June 22 he submitted to the Katsura cabinet and the emperor a memorandum in which he advised that Tokyo begin negotiations with Russia before the military situation became disadvantageous for Japan.[37] According to Tani Hisao, a prominent professor at the Army College during the Taishō era (1912–26), the truth was that the military pushed Katsura and Komura to an early resolve on the inevitability of war with Russia.[38] In this sense, the military, particularly middle-echelon officers, intervened in the decision-making process leading to the Russo-Japanese War.[39]

On June 23, at an imperial conference on the Russian problem, Komura presented an "Opinion on Negotiations with Russia," building on the basic policy adopted at the April 21 meeting. In this opinion, he noted that the Korean Peninsula juts out from the continent like a "sharp dagger" and that Japan would find its security threatened, were Russia to occupy Korea. Meanwhile, Russia's continued occupation of Manchuria and establishment of various facilities on the Korean border would make Russia's footing in Manchuria absolute. Stating that this scenario would have the effect of threatening the survival not only of Korea, as a matter of course, but also of Japan, Komura urged that the main thrust of negotiations be to assure the safety of Korea and, with that goal in mind, to restrict Russia's activities in Manchuria. In terms of economic activity, Japan should quickly complete the Seoul-Pusan Railroad, acquiring the rights to lay a Seoul-Hsinwiju Railroad and connecting this line to the Manchurian network to form a railroad through the heart of Korea and Manchuria.[40] Komura expected that negotiating with Russia based on this policy would be problematic, however, and he counseled that Japan should enter negotiations with a resolve to surmount all difficulties and to achieve its demands to the fullest.[41] According to Katsura, he and Komura both started negotiations on the Korean problem determined from the beginning not to avoid war.[42]

Katsura held that the struggle with Russia over the Korean problem, not the Manchurian one, was a "life-or-death matter" for Japan, and he was resigned to going to war with Russia to resolve that problem. Nonetheless, he took the attitude that, in conducting negotiations, Japan should aim for a peaceful solution and avoid hostilities. By contrast, Komura, emphasizing Russia's continued occupation of Manchuria, was resolved to go to war with Russia from the moment he assumed the post of foreign minister.[43]

Yet, when Itō asked at the June 23 imperial conference whether resolving to "surmount all difficulties" meant war, Navy Minister Yamamoto Gonnohyōe explained that this phrase simply indicated that Japan would negotiate with a firm resolve, pursuing peaceful, friendly talks while enduring whatever conduct Russia might display. Itō agreed with this interpretation.[44] In a September meeting of the Privy Council, Yamagata proposed that Japan dispatch its army to Seoul and prepare for any eventualities in view of Russia's deforestation of the Yalu River and its incursion into Korea. Yamamoto, however, opposed such action because of the potential harm to Japan's international relations and the lack of preparation on the part of the Japanese army; Ōyama then responded that the government could not dispatch the army overseas without the consent of the navy, given the navy's command of the sea.[45] Japan was simply not in a position to open hostilities and would have to pursue diplomacy as much as possible.

Looking at the course of foreign-policy-making from the Privy Council meeting in March through the April 21 meeting and the June 23 imperial conference, one can say that Katsura and Komura hardened their Manchuria-Korea policy after participating in the April meeting. One can also state that during this period the leadership in Japanese diplomacy on Manchuria and Korea gradually shifted from the senior oligarchs to Katsura and Komura.

Though Japan entered negotiations with Russia on the basis of a Manchuria-Korea exchange,[46] Russia in its counterproposal demanded that Japan not use Korea for strategic purposes and that Korea north of 39° north latitude be set aside as a neutral zone. Japan rejected these demands. The middle-echelon military officers, however, viewed this response as insufficient. One of them, Seigo Iguchi, deplored the situation, writing in his diary that Katsura lacked any resolve to open hostilities and that Ōyama and Ya-mamoto likewise had no will to take decisive military action even in Octo-ber.[47] In fact, after Japan received Russia's first reply on October 3, Katsura could not decide whether to open hostilities and still had some desire to come to a diplomatic solution.

After Russia delivered its second reply on December 11, the Privy Coun-cil, including cabinet members, held a meeting on December 16. On the Manchuria problem, the participants decided to seek a solution by diplo-matic means. On the Korea problem, they resolved to insist on placing Korea outside Russia's sphere of special interest and Manchuria outside Japan's sphere and on establishing a neutral zone of fifty kilometers on each side of the Manchuria-Korea border; they agreed that, if Russia did not ac-cept Japan's proposal, war would be unavoidable.[48]

Russia's second reply convinced Katsura to go to war, and even the cau-tious Itō finally came around to this way of thinking.[49] Katsura stated in a letter to Yamagata on December 21 that the Manchuria problem would be negotiated by diplomatic means but the Korea problem required insistence on Japanese demands, which Tokyo had to fulfill even by resort to war. Therefore, he concluded that there was no prospect of a peaceful solution; war was inevitable.[50] Even Itō, in a letter he sent to Yamagata on December 20, now discussed the effort Japan was making to complete preparations for war.[51]

In its reply of January 6, 1904, Russia continued to demand a ban on the strategic use of Korea and the establishment of a neutral zone north of 39° north latitude, but it did not refer to the territorial integrity of Manchuria. This reply meant no substantial change in Russia's position as far as Japan was concerned.[52] Although on January 13, 1904, the Japanese government urged Russia to reconsider its demands, St. Petersburg had made no reply even by the end of January.[53]

In a meeting with Yamagata, Katsura, Yamamoto, and Komura on Janu-ary 30, Itō insisted that even if Russia compromised on its demands for es-tablishing a neutral zone and prohibiting the strategic use of Korea, in light of Russia's overall strategy, Japan would obtain but a few years of respite and would clearly be forced sooner or later to open hostilities. None of the oth-ers at this meeting contested this view.[54] Ōyama reported to the cabinet on February 1 that any more delay would play into the hands of Russia, which was awaiting the arrival of forces by sea and by the Trans-Siberian Railroad; he insisted on seizing the advantage of making a head start and on match-ing political and military strategies.[55]

On February 4, the cabinet formally decided that wasting time under these circumstances would plunge Japan into an irretrievably disadvantageous position both diplomatically and militarily and decided on a final communication breaking off Russo-Japanese negotiations.[56] The next day Komura directed the minister to Russia, Kurino Shin'ichirō, to communicate Japan's rupture of diplomatic relations and its commencement of independent actions to defend itself and vested Japanese interests.[57]

On February 7, Alexander von Benckendorff, the Russian minister to Britain, met with Foreign Minister Henry Charles Lansdowne and told him that in its next reply Russia was going to accept all of Japan's demands concerning Korea and declare support for the territorial integrity of Manchuria. Lansdowne reported this conversation to Hayashi Tadasu, Japan's minister to Britain. Hayashi dismissed this report on the grounds that considering such a reply would continue an unsatisfactory situation in view of Russia's previous delays and asserted that, even if the Russian central government was in earnest, its branch offices could not be trusted and, on the contrary, were likely to maneuver for advantage. He added that a positive Japanese response would have been possible a week earlier but was now pointless, the reason being that Japanese military authorities had been promoting a fighting spirit since the end of the previous year and this spirit could no longer be easily suppressed. When Hayashi asked Lansdowne why Russia had not made this proposal earlier, Lansdowne answered that Russia was playing "a game of bluff." Furthermore, when the British foreign minister asked Hayashi why Japan was suing for war, Hayashi explained that Tokyo had waited for a response from St. Petersburg for three weeks, which was far too long in the face of an urgent threat of war, and had pressed many times for a response.[58]

According to Sergei Witte, the Japanese proposal for a Manchuria-Korea exchange was, on the whole, acceptable, but Russia's domestic decision-making process regarding the Far Eastern region prevented acceptance; and Russia's protracted way of negotiating compelled Japan to resort to armed force.[59] If Russia had observed its treaty for withdrawing troops from Manchuria, avoided Bezobrazov's adventure in Korea, and agreed to Japan's proposal, the war would not have broken out.[60]

Ultimately, there was a grave perception gap between Russia's bluff toward Japan and Japan's distrust toward Russia. In fact, strong distrust toward Russian diplomacy greatly influenced judgments on the Japanese side, as Russia halted its troop withdrawal from Manchuria, marched south toward the Korean border, and postponed negotiations with Japan. Japanese leaders believed that any further postponement of negotiations would lead to an irretrievable breakdown in the balance of military power.

In the end, Japanese diplomacy leading up to the Russo-Japanese War followed the strategy that Mutsu Munemitsu, foreign minister at the time of

Japan's war with China a decade earlier, had pursued: maintain "a nonaggressive diplomatic attitude" while being "prepared to seize the initiative militarily should developments warrant such action."[61]

Japanese Foreign Policy after the Russo-Japanese War

The Three Lines of Postwar Japanese Diplomacy

Japan had already established a diplomatic line on Korea by the time of the Russo-Japanese War. The focal point of Japanese diplomacy after the war shifted from Korea to Manchuria. Although Japanese decision makers generally agreed on consolidating and expanding their empire's control over Manchuria, they differed sharply over how best to achieve those aims.[62] Japanese foreign policy had three lines of diplomacy concerning Manchuria after the Russo-Japanese War. The Japanese army took the hardest line on continuing the occupation and administration of Manchuria; the diplomacy of Komura in the first Katsura cabinet (1901–6) aimed to achieve new imperialist development in Manchuria after the war; and the diplomacy of Hayashi Tadasu in the first Saionji cabinet (1906–8) emphasized seeking the approval of the Great Powers with regard to Japanese interests in East Asia and the Pacific.[63]

The Japanese army sought to strengthen Japan's position by continuing the military administration it had begun of the occupied territory in southern Manchuria. The army called for forcibly subjugating all of Manchuria, seizing every opportunity to acquire concessions, and following the same administrative policy as in Japanese territory.[64]

After the war, however, both Britain and the United States strongly protested Japan's repeated violations of the numerous declarations it had made to open Manchuria in order to gain Anglo-American diplomatic and financial support before and during the war.[65] The U.S. secretary of state, Elihu Root, protested in the strongest terms that room for trade in Manchuria by foreign countries following the completion of the Japanese troop withdrawal was slim or nonexistent and that exclusionary promotion of Japanese interests there would bring about "acute disappointment"; he went on to urge "serious reflection by the Japanese government."[66] Even Japan's ally, Britain, issued a strong warning directly to Itō through its ambassador in Tokyo, Sir Claude MacDonald, that Japan's behavior in ignoring the countries that had shown sympathy to it and supplied it with arms during the Russo-Japanese War would be a "suicidal policy."[67]

Alarming reports were also arriving in succession from Japanese representatives in Manchuria. Uchida Yasuya, the minister to China, reported that top-level Chinese officials were angry, saying that "Japan is nothing but Russia."[68] Similarly, Consul Segawa Asanoshin stated that abusing the power resulting from victory would be "following in the footsteps of Russia" and would also have a profound effect on future policy toward China.[69] Secretary Hagiwara Shūichi reported that the Japanese military administration was humiliating the Chinese and that local authorities were holding grudges, which would be difficult to extinguish.[70] According to another report, any errors committed by the military administration would invite censure from abroad, tarnish the glory of victory, and have a negative impact on policy toward China and on relations with friendly nations such as Britain and the United States.[71]

Responding to the Anglo-American protests and Japanese reports from Manchuria, Prime Minister Saionji Kinmochi embarked on a one-month inspection tour of Manchuria on April 15, 1906, to ascertain the situation there firsthand.[72] On May 22, at a meeting on the Manchurian problem following the premier's return to Japan, Itō pointed out the risk of international isolation raised by the severe criticisms of Japan from Britain, the United States, and individuals such as Yüan Shih-k'ai; he argued that Manchuria was not a Japanese possession but was purely Chinese territory and rejected the doctrine of direct administration of Manchuria expounded by Chief of the General Staff Kodama Gentarō.[73] Saionji voiced support for Itō's views; as a result, Japan abolished the Manchurian Occupation Military Administration and reorganized the wartime Guandong Government-General into a peacetime government-general.

Meanwhile, Marshal Yamagata, who regarded the Portsmouth settlement as nothing more than an "armistice treaty," adopted a precautionary stance anticipating that Russia would try to take revenge.[74] On April 4, 1907, the Japanese military decided on its first postwar "Imperial Defense Policy," which shifted strategy from defense to offense on the premise that, since the war, Japan was becoming a continental power. The military designated Russia as the first hypothetical enemy nation, followed by the United States, Germany, and France. For the army, the target of military preparedness would be Russia's Far Eastern Force and, for the navy, the U.S. Navy.[75] Yet after the Russo-Japanese War, while Japan's relations with Russia improved, its relations with the United States deteriorated.

The second line of postwar diplomacy was that of Komura, who pursued an imperialistic foreign policy that sought to further Japan's acquisition of concessions.[76] Komura set as the goal of peace negotiations the acquisition of three major types of concessions in southern Manchuria: railroads, mines, and forests.[77] To secure the concessions in southern Manchuria that Russia had ceded under the Portsmouth Treaty, the cabinet decided that Japan could continue military occupation of the region if China were to suspend negotiations with Japan and refuse to acquiesce in the cession of absolutely essential items such as the Liaodong Peninsula leasehold and the South Manchuria Railroad.[78]

Komura's diplomatic attitude at the Beijing Conference in October 1905 was that Japan's victory at tremendous sacrifice had had the favorable result for China of restoring concessions from Russia and that Japan had earned the right to demand "reward" for this outcome.[79] Accordingly, the foreign minister maintained, China should embrace the notion of thanking Japan, which should feel no debt to China. Thus, Komura's diplomacy toward China had at its nucleus the acquisition of major concessions and the assurance of a Japanese sphere of influence in southern Manchuria. As a result of Komura's strenuous negotiations in Beijing, on December 22, 1905, Japan concluded a treaty with China by which it achieved these objectives in Manchuria.

The third line of postwar diplomacy was that of Hayashi Tadasu aimed at implementing a policy of international cooperation with the Great Powers.[80] As vice-minister of foreign affairs during the tripartite intervention after the Sino-Japanese War, Hayashi had received direct notices from the ambassadors of the three intervening countries, and this striking experience had a major formative influence on his later diplomatic thinking.[81] As a result, he stressed the need for Japan to pursue a policy of forming alliances with the Great Powers, and in 1895 he proposed that Japan become a partner of Britain, which was not expanding its territorial holdings in East Asia but rather was seeking to maintain the status quo.[82]

Hayashi could be called exceptional among the policy makers of his time in having reasonable and rational ideas. He tried to treat China with "fairness" and thought that concluding a treaty required a spirit of "mutual concession."[83] He held that Japan should avoid using military force to solve diplomatic problems and should adopt a moderate approach as much as possible.[84] Hayashi noted that history offered no examples of countries that prospered for a long period after expanding their territories through war and maintained that for Japan to take over areas with different histories and customs—that is, different peoples—would sap national strength and endanger relations with the Great Powers.[85] He also pointed out that misconduct by the military administration in Manchuria after the war had had a negative effect on Japan's foreign relations.[86]

When concrete negotiations with China on Japan's acquisition of various concessions in Manchuria did not advance under such a moderate policy, however, Itō, Yamagata, Katsura, and others severely criticized Hayashi's diplomacy as a failure.[87] In response to this criticism, Hayashi held that Japan had fought the Russo-Japanese War for its own national interests and had based its actions on "self-preservation" but, to China, Japan was nothing but the "wolf at the back gate," following Russia.[88]

Yet Hayashi struggled hard with the Chinese court's procrastinating attitude toward negotiations. He also insisted that the Sino-Japanese treaty on Manchuria prohibited China's planned construction of a Hsinmintung-Fakumen railroad as being "proximate and parallel" to the South Manchuria Railroad. When Japan made no progress on resolving Manchurian problems such as the Yentai Coal Mine, Hayashi tried to force his way by threatening military action.[89]

The foreign minister also rejected the draft of a proposed Japanese-American understanding as a vague agreement that did not address the problem of Japanese immigration and would produce unnecessary anxiety between Japan and the United States. Judging that no cause for war existed between the two countries, on February 18, 1908, he instead concluded a gentlemen's agreement covering only the immigration problem.[90]

The diplomatic stance of Hayashi Tadasu was basically a moderate and rational one emphasizing mutual concessions and fidelity in relations with China: in other words, a diplomacy of international understanding. Yet, faced with the rising movement in China to reclaim rights, Hayashi advocated harsher policies such as dispatching a garrison force or proposing the use of military power, exposing the limits of his rationalistic attitude. Even Hayashi, in the final analysis, adopted a diplomatic stance that would fulfill Japan's national interests.[91]

In the end, Itō played an important role in rebuffing the diplomatic line of the military in Manchuria. Through Komura's diplomacy, Japan was fairly successful in acquiring concessions in Manchuria by treaty. Thanks to Hayashi's diplomacy of international understanding, Japan succeeded in securing the international approval of the European powers through agreements with France and Russia, for example, and also succeeded in calming the problem of Japanese immigration to the United States through the gentlemen's agreement.

Nonetheless, Japanese diplomacy after the Russo-Japanese War, whether the diplomacy of Komura or that of Hayashi, cannot be called successful in resolving the fundamental problems between Japan and China. Komura's imperialist diplomacy sparked an increasing backlash of Chinese nationalism, while Hayashi's moderate and rational foreign policy faced severe criticism at home as a diplomatic failure. In other words, postwar Japan, pressed by domestic demands for a strong continental policy, the rise of Chinese nationalism, and Anglo-American warnings against its advance into the Manchurian market, was unable to establish a stable diplomatic line. Japan's conflicted foreign-policy structure, adjusting, expanding, and reproducing itself, was to continue as a dilemma until the outbreak of the second Sino-Japanese and Pacific wars.

Transformation of the International Political Framework after the Russo-Japanese War

The nature of international politics in East Asia centering on Japan's relations with the United States and China around the time of the Russo-Japanese War remains understudied. The popular view of the international political framework after the war is that the Asia-Pacific region by and large lacked autonomy: it was incorporated into a Eurocentric world, and Europe and Asia more or less became one entity.[92]

An alternative view is that international relations in postwar East Asia began to grow more and more independent of the international politics of Europe through specific regional conflicts and friction.[93] In studying the beginnings of Japanese-American confrontation over Manchuria, one can argue that relations between Japan and the United States after the Russo-Japanese War, although greatly affected by European power politics, had a different dynamic independent of the international politics of Europe, producing new frictions in East Asia and the Pacific. To be sure, for Japan during this period, the alliance with Britain was "the main axis of Japanese foreign policy," while the Franco-Japanese and Russo-Japanese understandings supplemented this alliance and provided an international guarantee of Japanese imperialist concessions. Japan was clearly maintaining close relations with the European powers. In the end, while Japan's relations with Britain deteriorated after the war, its ties with Russia evolved into a substantial alliance by the time of their third postwar agreement in 1916.

Still, one can say of international politics in the period following the Russo-Japanese War that, while a large focal point leading to the First World War was forming and intensifying in Europe centering on the Balkan Peninsula, another focal point independent of Europe centering on Japanese-American relations was germinating and steadily forming in East Asia and the Pacific with repeated crises in the relationship between Japan and the United States. In the course of managing these crises, Japan, although basically maintaining a framework of alliances and understandings with European nations, began to develop a foreign policy toward the United States based on an independent logic shaped by specific incidents in the Asia-Pacific region, creating, as it were, a "multilayered diplomacy." The Washington Conference system of multilateral treaties among powers with interests in the region established in 1921–22 furthered the autonomy of international relations in East Asia and the Pacific, but rising Chinese nationalism directed against the rights and interests Japan had acquired in southern Manchuria after the Russo-Japanese War and worsening Japanese-American relations over Manchuria and the Pacific generated the causes of the second Sino-Japanese and Pacific wars.

Chapter 3

The Portsmouth Peace

I. V. Lukoianov

TRANSLATED AND EDITED BY JOHN KOPPER

*N*o sooner had it gone to war with Russia than Japan began thinking about the upcoming peace. It assumed that the campaign would be brief, with one or two battles sufficing for the utter destruction of the Russian army. Thus as early as the summer of 1904 Tokyo began actively to work on the terms of a peace settlement. Komura Jutarō, the minister of foreign affairs, assumed that Japan should engage in direct talks with Russia to end the war, avoiding an international conference and third-party mediation (although Japan's position did not exclude help from others in organizing the negotiations). Komura also composed a hypothetical list of conditions on which Japan should insist. The list included these main points: the payment of an indemnity; freedom of action for Japan in Korea; removal of Russian troops from Manchuria; cession of the Liaodong Peninsula to Japan; cession of the South Manchuria Railway (henceforth SMR), from Harbin to Port Arthur as well as Sakhalin (which Japan had not yet occupied); granting of fishing rights to the Japanese in Russian coastal waters; freedom for the Japanese to navigate the Amur as far as Blagoveshchensk; and, finally, the opening of the ports of Nikolaevsk, Khabarovsk, and Blagoveshchensk to foreigners.[1] Japan's initial military successes turned the heads of its leaders, and this led them to place exorbitant demands on Russia, unacceptable not only for their content but for their overall premise and tone. Japan immediately raised the threat of something that had not hitherto been the object of its claims and had not been a reason for war with Russia: Sakhalin and de facto supremacy in the entire Russian Far East.

John Kopper is Professor of Russian and Comparative Literature at Dartmouth College.

Tokyo's position transformed a war over influence in Korea and Manchuria into a contest for Russia's Far Eastern possessions. St. Petersburg thereby became the victim of aggression, which guaranteed it international support, although until 1904 its claims in the Far East had left it almost completely isolated.

Moreover, a sharp decline in Russia's influence in the Far East—should Japan attain its ends—suited neither England nor the United States. Both nations allowed the war to proceed so that they could receive, at the hands of the Japanese, freedom of action in Manchuria.[2] On many occasions, both at the beginning and the end of the war, Theodore Roosevelt repeated: "It is in our interest that the war between Russia and Japan be prolonged, that both powers be as debilitated as possible, and that their boundary clashes not be eliminated by the conclusion of a peace."[3] Keeping pace with the success of Japanese arms, efforts to bring about peace increased dramatically in Washington and to some extent in London. For this reason, on June 6, 1904, the Japanese envoy in Washington, Takahira Kogorō, held a private discussion with President Theodore Roosevelt about a conference of world powers at the war's end.[4] There were many reasons why Tokyo looked to the United States for support in future peace negotiations. Because of its extremely poor relations with St. Petersburg, London could hardly be of assistance to Japan. Testing the waters, Roosevelt promised the Japanese that, depending naturally on the outcome of the war, Korea should belong exclusively to Japan's sphere of interests.[5]

In Russia, on the other hand, it would appear that in the early stages of the war only the former finance minister, Sergei Witte, spoke in favor of a swift conclusion. In many respects Witte had been responsible for the Russian Empire's Far Eastern policy in the decade leading up to the war. The first attempt to start peace negotiations occurred in the summer of 1904. It must be pointed out, however, that sources depict this differently. According to the memoirs of Witte himself, during July 1904, the Japanese ambassador to London, Hayashi Tadasu, proposed to Witte through intermediaries that they begin peace negotiations. The chair of the Committee of Ministers, then in Berlin, wrote about this proposal to Nicholas II, but did not receive an answer.[6] This event is represented differently in Japanese sources. Hayashi reported to Tokyo that Witte had actually approached him twice with a proposal to meet.[7] However, Komura, the minister of foreign affairs, vetoed Hayashi's trip to Brussels. In Tokyo's view, the conditions for concluding the war had not yet ripened. The version of the Japanese diplomat appears more plausible. Indeed, he had no serious reasons to seek contacts with highly placed Russian officials to discuss peace conditions advantageous to St. Petersburg. Witte, in contrast, clearly dreamed about donning the laurels of a peacemaker, hoping in this way to restore his own influence on the Russian political scene.

In neither the latter half of 1904 nor early 1905 did Nicholas II show any inclination to sue for peace. He recollected Aleksei Kuropatkin's prediction of an arduous and long but ultimately victorious war for Russia. Likewise the Bezobrazovites (partisans of Aleksandr Mikhailovich Bezobrazov, personal adviser to Nicholas II and a notorious war hawk) maintained a certain amount of influence over him. They were convinced of the ultimate triumph of Russian arms and were prepared to establish in the Far East the rule they wished for. In the spring of 1904, at the behest of Nicholas II, Aleksei Abaza compiled a program of action for Russia-as-victor. It provided for Russia's annexation of all of Manchuria and Korea. To soften the dissatisfaction of the foreign community, the tsar intended to introduce a tax-free zone into the entirety of their putative Far Eastern protectorate for a period of twenty-five years. This program was not an object of open discussion in the government. It was developed secretly, and besides Nicholas II and Abaza, only K. I. Vogak and Evgenii Alekseev were let in on its contents. The tsar had smiled as he said: "If [Vladimir] Lamsdorf knew about this, he would die from horror."[8] As late as June 1905 the Bezobrazovites did not doubt a Russian victory and continued to prepare for the annexation of Manchuria and Korea as well as the inclusion of Mongolia, Chinese Turkestan, and even Tibet in St. Petersburg's sphere of influence.[9] One need not take these pipe dreams too seriously, but they reflect the existence in some circles (predominantly military ones) of a conviction that the war could still be won.

The year 1905 opened with the fall of Port Arthur and the beginning of the first Russian Revolution. Despite their chronological proximity, it cannot be asserted that these events were interconnected. The revolution introduced some changes in the conduct of the war, but these occurred several months later.[10] After the surrender of the fortress, a sentiment to end the war appeared in Russia for the first time. But this proved to be brief and without consequence.[11]

The Japanese were much more active on the peace front, but it is difficult to say how serious the intentions of Tokyo were. Even in November 1904, before the surrender of Port Arthur, Hayashi suggested preparing peace terms at the initiative of Japan. The diplomat proceeded from the assumption that the capture of the Russian fortress would strengthen antiwar sentiments in Europe and the United States. In his opinion, if Japan were not to appear the principal culprit in continuing the war, it had to demonstrate a readiness for peace. If Russia agreed—and it would be even better if it did not—this would only strengthen the image of Japan as a peace-loving power.[12] On

January 14, 1905, Theodore Roosevelt and Takahira discussed possible peace terms. The American president stated that, given the results of the war, Japan should acquire not only Korea but also Port Arthur. He proposed carving out of Manchuria a neutral zone under the international control of the great powers (so that it would not fall into the hands of the Japanese). However, on this point the American leader encountered strong resistance from the Japanese, who feared that in a "neutral" Manchuria all the great powers would begin to arm themselves and inaugurate a dangerous rivalry with Japan.

At the same time, the president actively searched for a means of influencing St. Petersburg, sending out feelers in Paris and Berlin before and after the Battle of Mukden.[13] Russia, however, did not react. The failure of this attempt confirmed the correctness of the position of Komura, which he presented on January 12, 1905, to the English ambassador Sir Claude MacDonald: "As long as the Baltic Fleet is not defeated and does not return to Russia, and as long as the Japanese do not gain a decisive victory at Mukden, the Russian government will not want . . . to make any peace proposal."[14]

Nevertheless, in February and March of 1905 a new attempt was made to bring about direct Russo-Japanese contact, much like the effort made in the summer of 1904. Here the Russian and Japanese versions are again diametrically opposed. According to data in St. Petersburg, Hayashi let it be known through a third party in London that he was ready to renew a "private exchange of views."[15] St. Petersburg, however, rejected the proposal on the grounds that it would be strange to start negotiations immediately after a military failure like the surrender of Port Arthur.[16] On the one hand, the state of the Russian army had not yet reached a critical point, but the surrender had sharply worsened any possible negotiating position for Russia. According to Japanese records, the initiative again came from Witte. Hayashi responded that an official proposal from Russia was a prerequisite for beginning negotiations.[17] Here again the Japanese version appears more plausible. Indeed, in Russia at this time perceptible pro-peace sentiments had appeared in high government circles, and Witte probably intended to make use of them. An indirect confirmation of Witte's initiative can be found in his emotional letter to Nicholas II on February 28, 1905, which contains a proposal to end the war.[18] But the tsar did not react to Witte's communiqué. On this occasion as well Russian government officials had grounds for assuming that Tokyo's goal in negotiations was something other than a peace treaty. They thought the Japanese might be circulating rumors about a swift end to the war to abet the success of the bond issue they were negotiating in London.[19] In general, rumors reaching St. Petersburg about Japan's desire for peace were displaced by information coming from various sources about Japan's difficult economic situation. According to this latter theory, Japan's economic position was driving her toward the negotiating table. A reasonable response in this situation would be for Russia to wait it out. And Russia did so. Roosevelt summed it up when he declared: "No side wanted to take the first step."[20]

Nevertheless, on March 8 (21), 1905, the Russian ambassador to Paris, A. I. Nelidov, was ordered to exchange views with the French foreign minister, T. Delcassé, on the prospects for peace and the contents of a peace agreement.[21] There ensued a discussion in the French press, organized by Delcassé, about possible peace conditions. On March 23 (April 5), Delcassé himself spoke with Japan's minister to France, Motono Ichirō, about peace conditions that would prove inadmissible for Russia: payment of an indemnity, loss of her own territory, withdrawal from the Chinese Eastern Railway (henceforth CER), and restrictions on her navy.[22] The Japanese, with whom Delcassé was speaking off the record, understood that his words did not reflect a Russian initiative, but rather Paris's concern that the Russo-Japanese conflict would benefit Germany. Tokyo concluded that the French initiative was not directly connected with St. Petersburg's position.[23] An exchange of views also took place between Washington and St. Petersburg in which Russia let it be known what terms were inadmissible: territorial concessions and an indemnity. While unofficially demonstrating a readiness for peace, Nicholas II still wished that Japan would take the first step.[24] However, moods soon shifted in St. Petersburg in favor of continuing the war.

The turning point in Russia occurred after the defeat of the Russian navy at Tsushima on May 14–15 (27–28), 1905. Eager for a change in the military situation in the Far East, the Russian leadership had placed enormous—but ultimately unjustified—hopes on the campaign of Zinovy Rozhestvensky's squadron. After its destruction, Russian leaders for the first time seriously entertained the possibility that Russia could lose the war. The Russian Empire had essentially lost its entire Pacific fleet. However, in spite of a series of failures, Russia's land-based forces had not been destroyed. The dilemma was obvious: should Russia continue the war with Japan or, before it was too late, seek peace? All other problems, including Russia's revolutionary movement and the impending crisis in her finances, were eclipsed by the war predicament. Reacting to Tsushima, Finance Minister Vladimir Kokovtsov wrote a letter to Nicholas II, in which he posed a narrowly military question: was the army capable of resisting a Japanese attack, and was Vladivostok "truly secure"? If the answer was yes, in his opinion the war should be continued. But, if the answer from the military was no, then it was necessary to conclude a peace treaty immediately, or a Japanese army would soon be standing on Russian soil.[25]

Kokovtsov's emotional message was but a weak reflection of the panic that had flared up in St. Petersburg. Following the loss of the fleet, the government immediately recalled plans for convoking the "Zemskii Sobor," the traditional consultative assembly of the tsars, and submitting to its judgment the question of continued military action. This would be a way of shifting responsibility away from the tsar. In the days between May 18 and 23, apparently, several plans were made for convening a Zemskii Sobor. However, the confusion did not last long. Nicholas II took the responsibility for defeat on himself, and on May 24 (June 6), 1905, a military council was summoned to discuss continuation of the war.[26]

At the council Nicholas II agreed with Grand Duke Vladimir Alexandrovich's view: "Now we find ourselves in a situation which, if not desperate, is extremely trying. Our internal welfare is more important than victory. It is imperative to try to ascertain Japan's peace terms immediately." Despite the fact that no official resolution was taken at the end of the conference, the discussion is evidence that the leadership's intense concern, partly about internal affairs but also about further military failures, outweighed all other considerations. For this reason, the Russian government decided to pursue peace.

In some measure Nicholas II would be pushed toward peace by growing pressure from abroad. On May 23 (June 5), the tsar received a letter from Wilhelm II (its contents were reported to the American president). The kaiser had approached Roosevelt about initiating negotiations and was making an insistent appeal to end the war.[27] On May 24, the recently accredited U.S. envoy to St. Petersburg, G. Meyer, asked for an audience with the tsar. Nicholas II received Meyer the next day. The tsar reluctantly agreed to Roosevelt's peace initiative, fearing that otherwise the Japanese would seize Sakhalin.[28] Over the course of these days in Washington, Roosevelt personally tried to persuade the Russian diplomat A. P. Cassini that the war was hopelessly lost.[29] Nonetheless, St. Petersburg proved stubborn: even at the beginning of June, Vladimir Lamsdorf continued to assert that Russia did not want peace until Japan declared her own readiness.[30] This declaration was certainly a reaction to the peace conditions likely to be required by Japan—payment of indemnity, transfer of territory, and restrictions on the navy—and the sentiment was mainly intended for Japanese consumption.

Other important events prior to the beginning of the Portsmouth conference took place largely in negotiations between St. Petersburg and Washington. On May 26 (June 8), 1905, Roosevelt sent the tsar an official offer to mediate. On May 30, in a special diplomatic note, Russia agreed to a meeting between Russian representatives and the Japanese plenipotentiaries. There was a short discussion about the choice of a locale. Russia tried to insist on The Hague but rapidly yielded to an American venue (not Washington or New York, "because of the lethal summer heat," but any other "serene summer spot").[31]

Preparations then began in St. Petersburg for the upcoming peace conference. First the ambassador to Paris, A. I. Nelidov, refused an offer to head the Russian delegation, then the ambassador to Rome, N. V. Murav'ev, likewise refused, despite the fact that their names had already been communicated to Roosevelt and, accordingly, to the Japanese.[32] Both were in a weak position to represent Russia's Far Eastern policy. A team of specialists was therefore selected for the trip to America and prepared with detailed instructions. The delegation included the military attaché in Japan, Colonel M. K. Samoilov, naval attaché Aleksandr Rusin, and an attaché of the finance minister in China, Dmitry Pokotilov. The following were also enlisted to negotiate the peace: Fyodor Martens, the professor and well-known specialist in international law; Ivan Shipov, the director of the State Treasury and an old colleague of Witte; General Nikolai Yermolov, chief of the Division of Military Statistics on the General Staff; and, joining them in Washington, the envoy Roman Rosen, who had worked for a long time in Tokyo and was designated as deputy for the Russian delegation during the negotiations. Also in the delegation were embassy attachés from the financial sections in the United States and Japan, Grigorii Vilenkin and N. A. Raspopov. Georges Plançon, a diplomatic official on the staff of deputy Evgenii Alekseev, was named secretary of the delegation. Ivan Korostovets served as personal secretary to the Russian plenipotentiary.

After the refusal of the two ambassadors to lead the delegation, Nicholas II, in spite of his unwillingness, was forced to appoint Sergei Witte as Russian plenipotentiary. His nomination was met with universal approval. The former minister of finance had a reputation for being pro-peace, and he was considered by all as the most appropriate choice for the peace conference. In the language of diplomacy, his selection meant that Russia truly intended to end the war.

The Japanese in turn were planning to send Marquis Itō Hirobumi, a longtime supporter of an accord with Russia.[33] After learning about the proposed composition of the Russian delegation, however, the Japanese rejected this idea. They concluded that the position of Itō, one of the leading political figures of Japan, did not correspond to that of either A. I. Nelidov or N. V. Murav'ev. As a result, the minister of foreign affairs, Komura Jutarō, was named head of the Japanese delegation. Komura supported a hard line toward Russia.

The preparation of instructions for the Russian delegation was scarcely an easy task. First, views of various officials were solicited, including the

ministers of the army and navy, the minister of finance, and Evgenii Alekseev. The War Ministry was strongly opposed to the conclusion of a peace,
but if negotiations were a foregone conclusion, then it favored independence for Korea and the restoration of Manchuria to China and Liaodong to
Russia, with the subsequent transfer of the peninsula to Beijing.[34] These
were the terms of an undefeated nation and fully reflected the attitudes of
the generals. Naval officials were more modest and insisted only on the inadmissibility of any limitations on the Pacific fleet or the surrender to Japan
of ships interned in neutral ports during the war.[35] Vladimir Kokovtsov outlined the most thorough and useful answers for the peace negotiators and
formulated in clear terms his basic stance: "From a financial point of view,
the conclusion of a peace is extremely desirable, but for Russia at present it
should not be seen as necessary to conclude peace at whatever cost." Furthermore, the minister of finance was the first to emphasize that the accord
with Japan must be "sincere and as lasting as possible." This would require
a long-term oversight of interests. In essence, Kokovtsov's proposed peace
terms amounted to no cession of Russian territory, no indemnity beyond
compensation for the care of prisoners of war, the withdrawal of forces from
Manchuria and the return of Manchuria to China (together with Liaodong),
and the CER to remain in Russian hands (with the transfer of the greater
part of the SMR to Beijing a possibility).[36]

Kokovtsov's proposals formed the basis of the extensive and detailed instructions given to the Russian delegation.[37] In St. Petersburg officials had
correctly evaluated both the current situation ("certain neutral states are interested in the swift cessation of hostilities, fearing too dominant a Japanese
influence in the Far East and therefore ready to exert pressure on the Tokyo
cabinet") and the position of Japan with respect to the continuation of war
(it "also desires the end of war, having exhausted its military and financial
resources and cost itself innumerable casualties"). The instructions defined
a limit beyond which the delegation could not go. Four inadmissible conditions were the cession to Japan of any Russian territory, the payment of indemnity, restrictions on sea power in the Far East, and the loss of any part
of the CER.[38] The Russian Foreign Ministry understood exactly the wishes,
and the range of possibilities, open to Tokyo ("among the more reasonable
Japanese statesmen there apparently prevails some effort to use their present advantageous circumstances to end the war, which in the future can
only cause aggravation and uneasiness among those powers that had at first
sympathized with the Japanese"). Assuming that Japan would attempt to
insist on the cession of Sakhalin, Russia categorically rejected the possibility but was ready to grant the Japanese fishing rights in coastal waters instead.[39] The Russians intended to neutralize the remaining Japanese de-

mands through recourse to existing international agreements (the return of Manchuria to China; the affirmation of Korean independence; and the recognition of Beijing's sovereignty over Changchun, a key junction on the southern spur of the CER) and through private concessions.[40]

St. Petersburg correctly predicted the majority of Tokyo's conditions. These were discussed by the Japanese government on June 17 (30), and on June 22 (July 5) they were affirmed by the emperor. The demands were divided into three groups. The first were those that the peace delegation had to insist on categorically: freedom of action in Korea, withdrawal from Manchuria, and the transfer of Port Arthur and the SMR to Japan. The second were relatively important conditions: the payment of an indemnity, the transfer of Sakhalin, the acquisition of Russian vessels interned in neutral ports, and the granting of fishing rights in coastal waters. And, finally, the third group of conditions, which were viewed as supplementary: curtailment of Russian naval forces in the Far East and the demilitarization of Vladivostok.[41] One can easily see that the minimum Japanese demands and the maximum Russian concessions on the whole did not contradict one another. This gave the peace negotiations a realistic chance of success.

Russia also had an important source of information to help it prepare for the conference—an efficient system for secretly reading the diplomatic correspondence of a number of embassies in St. Petersburg as well as the correspondence of Japanese embassies in Paris and The Hague.[42] Nevertheless, the head of the Russian delegation departed for Portsmouth without feeling optimism about the outcome of negotiations. Witte considered too categorical the official instructions that were given to him, taking it for granted that he would not succeed in carrying them out completely and that it would be necessary to yield on Sakhalin and the question of an indemnity. On this point the Russian plenipotentiary preferred to pay any sum necessary to secure the return of the island occupied by Japanese troops ("I am utterly convinced that it will be impossible to conclude an accord the Japanese would agree to if it meant returning Sakhalin to us without some corresponding monetary payment").[43]

Before his departure, Witte met with Nicholas II. At the meeting he apparently insisted on his idea of an accord with Japan that included the allies and received additional instructions on this point.[44] The discussion probably did not touch on the possibility of any new concessions, but the additional instructions included the phrase that with the landing of Japanese troops on Sakhalin "some considerations, cited in the aforementioned instructions, have now lost their import." It is possible that, in order to cement an alliance, the tsar agreed orally to make more substantial concessions to Japan. Subsequent events force one to draw this conclusion.

Witte left St. Petersburg on July 6 (19), 1905. In Germany, the Russian plenipotentiary asserted one thing and while in France something completely different. In Berlin on July 7 (20), Witte met with E. Mendelson and revealed to him in secret the concessions Russia was prepared to make: Korea, Manchuria, half of Sakhalin, the SMR (the CER's main line would remain Russian), and an indemnity of up to 500 million rubles. In fact Witte was convinced that Russia would undoubtedly lose all of Sakhalin and the indemnity would be higher. It is highly improbable that all these conditions came from Witte himself. His frankness can be explained as the result of calculation. With a meeting of the two emperors slated to take place several days later, Witte hoped to put pressure on Nicholas II through Wilhelm. To make the German leader as convincing and determined as possible, Witte frightened Wilhelm with the prospect of growing revolution in Russia ("there will be rivers of blood") and other thoroughly unpleasant consequences of continuing the war (humiliation, the return of a defeated army, and so forth).[45]

In contrast, in the French capital the Russian plenipotentiary expressed the wish to obtain another loan for Russia and discussed the desirability of a continental, anti-English alliance. But he did not find a sympathetic audience. The French frostily noted that Russia would be able to obtain funds only after the end of the war. Moreover, the projected English-French rapprochement excluded a radical reorientation of France's policy.[46] Witte was more successful in sounding out the potential reaction of Europeans to the peace conditions. The plenipotentiary met with a number of individuals (the French premier M. Rouvier, the German ambassador G. Radolin, and others). To everyone Witte asserted the same thing: Russia would not pay an indemnity but was prepared to let go of Korea and southern Manchuria. Of course, this position immediately became known to the Japanese.[47]

Apart from all this, Witte was looking for insurance in case the negotiations failed. He intended to use the trip to the United States to prepare the groundwork for an American loan. Russia needed money in any case. The former minister of finance understood that he would not be able to draw, as in the past, on the resources of the Paris market and that support in Berlin could not be guaranteed. Witte worked out a plan to attract American public opinion to his side, particularly Jewish opinion, hoping to overcome the negative image that prevailed abroad of Russia as a despotic autocracy.[48] This would hardly have a direct effect on the forthcoming negotiations, but in the event of failure the head of the Russian delegation hoped to rectify the financial position of the empire.

Furthermore, through E. Dillon, the St. Petersburg correspondent of the *Daily Telegraph*, Witte again approached Hayashi. Hiding nothing, the Russian plenipotentiary asked that word be passed to the Japanese ambassador that his (Witte's) position was very difficult and that he would like Itō to be given authority, before the Portsmouth Conference began, to hold preliminary discussions about both a peace agreement and an alliance. Hayashi, however, disappointed Witte, replying that his hopes for Itō were groundless and that a Russo-Japanese alliance was impossible: how could two parties conclude an amicable agreement when they did not trust each other?[49] In spite of his refusal, the Japanese ambassador expressed optimism about the outcome of the upcoming negotiations, at the same time firmly stating that Japan was counting on an indemnity.[50] It is not surprising that, after receiving this reply, Witte left Europe in an exceptionally poor frame of mind, more convinced than ever of the imminent failure of the peace conference.

On July 10–11 (23–24), 1905, while Witte was in Europe, Nicholas II and Wilhelm II signed a treaty of alliance at Björkö, Sweden. It is difficult to say whether the upcoming Russo-Japanese negotiations and the meeting of the two emperors were connected. B. A. Romanov has suggested that the tsar embarked on an alliance with Germany because he was searching for any form of support whatsoever on the eve of Portsmouth.[51] The tsar's action would have required the correct calculation, with no room for error, that in order to detach St. Petersburg from Berlin, France—and, through France, England—would respond with a countermove, putting pressure on the Japanese to come to peace. Indeed France and England were noticeably worried. Judging by the activities of Russian diplomats who rushed to calm London and Paris, however, it is unlikely that Nicholas II had thought through his plan in advance. This would have required maintaining pressure and feeding the sense of alarm.[52] Another explanation is more likely: the tsar was dissatisfied by the conduct of Paris during the entire course of the Russo-Japanese War and did not sense any French support for Russia. This indignation was reflected first and foremost in the tsar's impulsive decision to sign an accord with Wilhelm II.[53]

Witte reported to St. Petersburg the results of his meetings in Berlin and Paris. He insisted on the inevitability of the payment of money (in France "all are of this opinion"). The naval minister, N. M. Chikhachev, moved closer to Witte's position (better to pay any amount of money than lose Sakhalin), but not the minister of finance, Vladimir Kokovtsov, who rejected any indemnity. Witte meanwhile continued to think that the instructions he had received allowed for loss of the island ("I could agree to the cession of Sakhalin"), whereas on the issue of payments Nicholas II had stated his position to him "much more categorically."[54] Witte clearly wanted to obtain permission to negotiate an indemnity.

On July 14 (27), the German steamship *Kaiser Wilhelm the Great* left the

French port of Cherbourg with the Russian delegation on board. During the crossing, Witte spent less time preparing for the forthcoming negotiations than grumbling incessantly about Russia's previous policy in the Far East and especially about the Bezobrazovites. No serious work was conducted by the delegation as a whole. The upcoming negotiations were discussed largely over dinner. Witte openly declared that "he was not in a position to decide anything or ascertain the exact state of affairs until the arrival in America of Captain Rusin, who was coming from the theater of war and would bring precise information about the army."[55] For himself, though, the Russian plenipotentiary formulated rules of conduct for the negotiations: "(1) do not show in any way that we desire peace; behave in such a way as to produce the impression that, if the Sovereign had agreed to the negotiations, it was only in view of the general wish of almost all nations to see the war ended; (2) maintain a bearing that befitted a representative of Russia, that is, the representative of a great empire, to whom a minor unpleasantness had happened; (3) keep in mind the enormous role of the American press and be particularly obliging and accessible to all its representatives; (4) draw over to our side the American population, which was 'highly democratic,' by behaving in a simple, unpretentious, and democratic way with them; and (5) in view of the significant influence of the Jews, in particular in New York and in the American press generally, do not treat them with hostility."[56]

While still en route to the United States, Witte began his campaign to win over American public opinion. During the crossing he often gave interviews to journalists, a large number of whom were accompanying the Russian delegation. They arrived in New York on July 20 (August 2). (Komura had arrived a week before.) Once having set foot on American soil, in every way the Russian representative emphasized his sympathy and respect for the American people and their president. Before his departure for America, Witte had persuaded Nicholas II to agree to the lifting of import duties on products of the American machine industry and to award the United States most-favored-nation status in its trade with Russia. In observance of diplomatic niceties, this was officially announced to Roosevelt only after the end of negotiations, but Americans knew in advance about Russia's decision. On July 21 (August 3) Witte visited the New York Stock Exchange and on August 1 (14) met with the most powerful American Jewish bankers.[57] The conversation with the financiers led to a certain softening of attitudes toward Russia's autocratic state, a development that indirectly contributed to the conclusion of a peace.

An unpleasant surprise awaited Witte on his arrival in the United States. On July 18, with Nicholas II's agreement, Lamsdorf had sent a telegram from St. Petersburg with additional instructions. The minister emphasized that no one had given the Russian plenipotentiary the right to concede Sakhalin.[58] This could mean only one thing: that the previous understandings Witte had with the tsar had been disavowed. With obvious irritation Witte replied to Lamsdorf that he would see that the orders were carried out.[59] After this, the official position of the Russian plenipotentiary would diverge sharply from the intentions he had expressed while still in Europe.

On July 22 (August 4), the Russian representatives had a private conversation with Roosevelt. Here the question was raised that had appeared insurmountable—the issue of an indemnity. Denying that he knew anything of the Japanese conditions, Roosevelt suggested that Russia should agree to the demand for payments.[60] Witte objected and declared that he represented an undefeated power.[61] The Russian delegates and the American president parted with a pessimistic presentiment about the outcome of the talks.

The first official meeting of the delegates took place on Roosevelt's yacht, with the president's participation. Then everyone left for Portsmouth. Because fog slowed travel by sea, the participants did not arrive until July 27 (August 8). Witte left the yacht on July 24 (August 6) in Newport, Rhode Island, and made the rest of his way to Portsmouth by rail. When he arrived in Boston, it was reported that the Russian plenipotentiary "shook hands with the entire train crew, and even kissed the engineer." In fact Witte did nothing more than tip the engineer and fireman and shook outstretched hands, but newspapers fanned this episode into a major story. However, the "legend of the kiss did more for the popularity of the Russian mission . . . than our diplomatic courtesies."[62] In point of fact, from this moment on, the Russian delegation, and especially Witte, began to be met not just with interest and sympathy but with cheers. Hitherto, the prevailing American opinion had been that Russia was a land of dreary absolutism and reaction.

Negotiations began on July 23 (August 5). Sessions were conducted almost every day, both official (with the writing up of protocols) and unofficial, when the sides privately attempted to settle the most controversial questions. As before, Witte was pessimistic. "He is worn down and despondent and, once this task is completed, ready to give it all up and walk away."[63] There was an obvious reason for the Russian representative's state of mind. He did not know how to carry out the instructions given him, especially after the failure of his idea to conclude an alliance with Japan. It is hardly an exaggeration to say that the main difficulties he anticipated came not from the Japanese but from St. Petersburg, for he feared the fickleness of Nicholas II and the influence of the "war party" on him. On July 28 (August 10), the Russian delegation received a written text of the Japanese conditions.[64] The demands made on Russia proved to be extensive and, on half the points, exceeded the limits acceptable to Russia.[65] In particular, there were the matters of the payment of an indemnity, the transfer of Sakhalin and interned vessels, and limitations on Russian naval forces in the Far East.

When they received the Japanese conditions, the Russian delegation immediately conferred. Witte decided to give an answer even before obtaining instructions from St. Petersburg, presumably to avoid giving the Japanese the impression that their conditions "produced a strong impression on us or caused confusion."[66] The conference was brief, lasting three hours. But it was exceptionally important for an understanding of the entire subsequent course of negotiations. Witte formulated his basic approach to the peace treaty. He proceeded from the assumption that the Japanese side, not trusting Russia, was reasoning approximately thus: "If Russia doesn't pay an indemnity and holds on to Sakhalin and Vladivostok, while still maintaining control of the remainder of its navy and building a new one, she will profit from the experience she gained in losing to us and will attack. . . . The only way to ensure peace is to weaken Russia in the long term."[67] But this wish was unrealistic to say the least. Even if Japan succeeded in insisting on the greater part of its requirements, the country would not so much ensure its future security as create extra incentives in St. Petersburg for revenge. In other words, however paradoxical it sounded, the more Russia was forced to concede, the more the future danger to Japan would increase. Both sides, however, were to a certain extent interested not only in concluding peace but in establishing a state of affairs in the Far East that neither side would have cause to reexamine later. A prerequisite for this outcome was the elimination of distrust, and therefore Witte took it upon himself to calm Japan, again proposing an alliance to help consolidate the results of the peace process. Thus he returned to an idea already rejected by Hayashi and the Tokyo leadership not long before the beginning of negotiations. Desirous of an alliance with Japan, the Russian plenipotentiary was prepared to make concessions to Tokyo that would be unacceptable to St. Petersburg ("if we could convey the idea that . . . we are prepared to bind ourselves to the preservation of Japan's gains, this would calm the Japanese and the whole world, which would see the sincerity of our intentions. If we say to the Japanese that we have obliged ourselves to protect the rights recognized as theirs, then we can facilitate the acceptance of our own conditions"). It was a question of giving back Sakhalin to Japan (that is, doing what the Russian representative had spoken about before his departure from St. Petersburg). Witte intended to use this concession to obtain acceptable results on other points. But the hard line of Nicholas II tied the hands of the Russian plenipotentiary and prevented his pursuit of this strategy.

The Russian reply of July 30 (August 12), made even before instructions were received from St. Petersburg on July 31 (August 13), in fact produced as strong an impression on the Japanese, who had not expected this gambit, as it did on the Americans. At a minimum Witte attained one goal: the swiftness of his answer was interpreted as a sign of Russia's willingness to make peace. Of course this did not dispel suspicion on the Japanese side, but it did somewhat shake it. Furthermore, the Japanese conditions were leaked in the press (obviously not without the assistance of the Russian delegation). However, when the Japanese raised this question at the conference (since they had previously agreed that the course of negotiations would be confidential), Witte proposed to make all the discussions open, that is, to communicate all details to the news staff. The Japanese side rejected this openness, thus allowing the Russian delegation to garner even more sympathy in the court of American public opinion.

In other respects matters did not proceed as well. In their reply to the Japanese, the Russians certified that they were ready to give up Korea and Changchun and that Manchuria would become Chinese, without any special privileges for the Russians. But to the questions of the cession of Sakhalin, payment of indemnity, neutralization of the CER, and limitations on the navy, the answer was a firm no.

Witte was consoled by the news that Nicholas II approved of his answer. The tsar considered the same points to be unacceptable.[68] However, the important thing for the Russian plenipotentiary was not so much agreement with St. Petersburg as fresh evidence that the war party had not increased its influence and that the intention of the tsar to conclude a peace was as strong as ever. Witte decided that he had to act, and he attempted once again to put pressure on his sovereign. That same day he sent Ivan Korostovets to publicly request a timetable of the next steamships bound for Europe.[69] He purposely did this with great flair, not so much for Japanese consumption as for St. Petersburg's—it was likely that in a day or two everyone would read in the newspapers that, because of its hard line, the Russian delegation had to prepare to leave. Witte next sent a panicked telegram to St. Petersburg: "In view of the huge differences in the terms of the two parties, an accord will not be achieved."[70] Prepared to break off negotiations, he wrote: "We must handle this matter in a way that brings . . . a large part of public opinion in Europe and America over to our cause, . . . and if a peace cannot be reached, we will be able to publish with a clear conscience all the negotiation documents and submit the entire case to the judgment of humanity."[71] This was a hint to Russia: let the Japanese weigh their position again and think about possible concessions. But Witte lacked reasons to hope that his démarche would lead to success.

In spite of the gloomy expectations of the Russian plenipotentiary, the

Japanese did not break off negotiations. A concrete discussion of the Japanese conditions began, article by article. The error of Witte's betting on an alliance with Tokyo was confirmed immediately. On July 30 (August 12), Komura "rather drily declared that Japan did not need Russia's support."[72] For several days both sides competed in making eloquent and artful arguments in support of their positions. Witte repeatedly panicked in the course of the discussions. On August 1 (14), he wrote from Portsmouth to Vladimir Kokovtsov about the need to prepare for the war's continuation, and he sent Lamsdorf a list of proposals that he had prepared in case negotiations failed.[73] Discussion ended on August 5 (18) with outstanding differences remaining on four points (Sakhalin, an indemnity, vessels in neutral ports, and limits on naval forces in the Far East).

Witte was ready to yield to the Japanese on almost all the disputed points. He took it for granted that the question of vessels had no serious practical significance and was important only from the standpoint of national pride. Witte's position on restrictions on armed forces in the Pacific was analogous, since, even with no restrictions, "in the next few decades Russia could not construct a fleet in the Far East capable of fighting the Japanese." On the other hand, Russia's retention of Sakhalin appeared to the Russian plenipotentiary an insoluble problem: the Japanese had already occupied the island, so "I do not foresee the opportunity, at least in the next few decades, to take back the island." The one thing that Witte categorically rejected was a war indemnity, which he thought, in a moral sense, "would grate on the Russian soul."[74] But morality is one thing, and peace negotiation quite another. In Witte's opinion, a breakdown of negotiations and "the continuation of war would be the greatest calamity for Russia."[75] Witte's perspective on concessions had changed diametrically. Before sailing from France he had caustically written about the "accounting" approach of Vladimir Kokovtsov, but now he completely accepted it. The impression persists, nevertheless, that the Russian plenipotentiary was privately inclined to yield even on the question of reparations. True, he recognized that the handover of all of Sakhalin to Japan, without any indemnity payment, would be the best possible outcome. But the Japanese categorically refused to make this linkage.[76] Strictly following his instructions, Witte decided for the present to leave all these problems for St. Petersburg to decide.

During the ensuant pause the Japanese, with the help of Roosevelt, organized a movement to put pressure on St. Petersburg, with the participation of Berlin and, to a certain extent, of Paris.[77] Simultaneously, on August 6 (19), during a meeting with Roman Rosen, Roosevelt promised to nudge the Japanese toward concessions. He assumed he would be able to persuade them to drop their demands for the return of interned vessels and the curtailment of Russian armed forces in the Pacific. The president hoped that in exchange Russia would cede Sakhalin to Japan, while he proposed submitting the question of an indemnity to the judgment of two mediators, that is, to solve the issue only in general terms. This sequence of steps, however, presupposed that Russia would be willing to deal with the question of compensation; and, after that, it would be easier to press Russia to make other concessions.[78]

It turned out, nonetheless, that the president's negotiations with Rosen had no effect. While in discussions with Russia's deputy, Komura proposed, after specifying that he did so in his own name and without Tokyo's knowledge, a new combination of terms. The Japanese side dropped its demands for the return of interned vessels and the limitation on Russian naval forces in the Pacific and also was willing to return to Russia the northern part of Sakhalin (to the 50th parallel) for 1.2 billion yen (about $600 million in today's dollars).[79] The proposal of the Japanese representative surprised everyone, including the American president. At this point Roosevelt lost all initiative at the negotiations, and his potential role as a mediator was practically reduced to zero. Witte immediately seized on the new Japanese proposal. Understanding that he would not be supported by Nicholas II, the Russian plenipotentiary attempted to maneuver around the tsar. Witte asked Kokovtsov, with whom he could be more open, to exert all his efforts to have the new Japanese initiative accepted in St. Petersburg "after consultation with our most prominent, high-ranking officials," above all D. M. Sol'skii and K. P. Pobedonostsev.[80] Witte hoped in this way to paralyze the influence of the war party on Nicholas II, making use of the experience in state affairs of the "prominent officials" and playing on their fears of revolution. Kokovtsov responded to the request, but most likely did not act with particular zeal in supporting Witte. The fact was that relations between the two were less than serene. Furthermore, the minister of finance himself had somewhat different—and quite unshakable—ideas about the peace terms, and he believed that no indemnity should be paid.[81]

The tsar, however, was immovable. On August 4 (17), he stated his resolution over Sakhalin in a telegram to the Russian plenipotentiary: "Not an inch of ground, not a ruble for military costs."[82] Neither Kokovtsov nor Lamsdorf succeeded with their idea to hold a meeting to consider the Japanese peace terms.[83] The only thing the tsar agreed to was to canvass the views of the military and naval ministers as well as Grand Duke Nikolai Nikolayevich, that is, the very representatives of the war party whose influence in St. Petersburg Witte so feared. The head of the Russian delegation tried to stand his ground, calling on Kokovtsov to report his request not only to D. M. Sol'skii but to D. F. Trepov, the influential governor-general of St. Petersburg, that a peace resolution be adopted by "a conference chaired by the Sovereign and with the participation of at least a significant number of prominent class representatives."[84] One can look on this proposal as a call to convene something like a Zemskii Sobor. But this time Witte's ploy did not win support: D. M. Sol'skii refused, and D. F. Trepov pretended not to understand what "class representatives" Witte was talking about.[85] On August 8 (21), Witte himself attempted to convince Nicholas II to soften his position for at least tactical reasons: "If we want the blame for a failed conference to fall exclusively on Japan, then we cannot reject the cession of Sakhalin or compensation for military expenditures."[86] All in vain. In the end, the Russian delegation received a directive from St. Petersburg on August 9 (22). The Japanese condition of "half of Sakhalin in exchange for money" was deemed unacceptable. The delegation was instructed to break off negotiations if the Japanese did not drop their demand.

From the moment it became clear that the main obstacles were twofold—the fate of Sakhalin and indemnity payment—the center of decision making shifted to St. Petersburg, and Nicholas II began negotiations with the American envoy G. Meyer, who represented the voice of Roosevelt.[87] The American president insisted that exchanging North Sakhalin for money was a "just and honorable" condition for Russia. In the event that the war continued, he warned Russia about the prospect of further calamities and, in particular, the loss of the entirety of eastern Siberia.[88] G. Meyer, who was instructed to relay instantly Roosevelt's opinions to the tsar, was received by Nicholas II on August 10 (23). In the course of a two-hour audience, the tsar firmly stated: "I prefer a temporary loss of territory to the humiliation of our country with an indemnity payment, as if we were a conquered nation." If Japan refused, the tsar was ready to continue the war. So that Meyer would understand that he would not yield to any pressure, Nicholas II showed him a telegram from Wilhelm II, in which he advised Russia (according to an agreement with Roosevelt) to conclude a peace, which, in the kaiser's opinion, St. Petersburg could not do without agreeing to an indemnity.[89] The Russian autocrat intended only to "generously pay all maintenance costs of Russian prisoners-of-war, but not a sum which could be interpreted as an indemnity."[90] However, the tsar consented to return the southern part of Sakhalin "on the grounds that it has only belonged to Russia for thirty years, and therefore can be regarded like Port Arthur, and not native Russian territory."[91] After receiving a less than reassuring reply from Meyer, Roosevelt once again, on August 13 (26), tried to push his proposal. The language reveals that Roosevelt was acting in concert with the Japanese: "Otherwise Japan, perhaps, will drop the idea of concluding a peace." Further: "If peace is concluded on the terms I proposed [!—I. L.], Russia will come out of this war without significant harm, and its national honor and interests will be salvaged."[92] Before this, on August 12 (25), Lamsdorf had reported to the tsar that the French government had come out in favor of an indemnity payment.[93] However, the obvious game that the Japanese were playing did not succeed. Meyer reported that Russia would not pay an indemnity and that "on this point the government is supported by the press and the entire nation, even the peasants."[94] Following this answer, Roosevelt gave in, having realized that for all practical purposes his role as mediator had come aground on the question of "Sakhalin versus indemnity" and was now a complete failure. He advised the Japanese nevertheless to conclude a peace accord.[95]

For the relatively honorable conditions of the Portsmouth peace, Russia was indebted, first of all, to Nicholas II, who demonstrated an uncommon firmness of spirit (a rare example in his reign). He did not yield to the persuasion or threats of Witte, Roosevelt, and Wilhelm II. On the night of August 15/16 (28/29), the Russian delegation received a directive from him: "Send Witte my order to end negotiations tomorrow no matter what. I intend to continue the war rather than wait for gracious concessions from the Japanese."[96] The autocrat reached his decisions not so much by making sober calculations as by relying on an inner voice. This time it proved to be right. A firm decision did not come easily to Nicholas II. He fully understood what he risked. After receiving on August 17 (30) a telegram from Witte about the successful conclusion of negotiations, the tsar wrote in his diary: "After this I spent the whole day in a fog!"[97]

The American president had informed the Japanese of his failure to pressure the tsar. On learning that Nicholas II had faith in his army in Manchuria and therefore had decided absolutely not to pay an indemnity or return Sakhalin, the Japanese delegates began to prepare themselves for a fruitless conclusion to the negotiations. They composed an announcement about the breakup of the conference and planned to leave Portsmouth on August 13 (26). Although he had the authority to make concessions, Komura could not bring himself to do this again without preliminary agreement from Tokyo. But most of all he feared the collapse of the peace conference. On August 13 (26) there was a private meeting between the delegations. Witte reported to the Japanese that they could receive only the southern part of Sakhalin, without any indemnity. The Japanese were noticeably upset. "They asked Sergey Yul'evich [Witte] to speak to them not as the Russian plenipotentiary, but as a government official, that is, as if he stood in their position. With complete sincerity he advised them to agree to the peace."[98]

The final word, however, remained Tokyo's. The Japanese government indeed had a great deal to ponder. On August 6, Makino Nobuaki, Japan's ambassador to Vienna, reported from Vienna that, according to his sources, in St. Petersburg the war party was again gathering strength and was insisting on stiffening the instructions given Witte.[99] Inoue Kaoru sent analogous reports from Berlin.[100] Japan knew the contents of the conversation between American ambassador Meyer and Nicholas II, in which the tsar categorically rejected the possibility of an indemnity and territorial concessions.[101] All this clearly contributed to the softening of Tokyo's position. At a session of the Japanese government held on the night of August 14/15 (27/28), it was decided that, in view of the prevailing military and financial situation of Japan, a peace treaty was necessary. Therefore, on August 15 (28), Prime Minister Katsura Tarō gave Komura permission to take questions about an indemnity and Sakhalin off the table, after first trying, nevertheless, to insist on the handover of the whole island.[102] At the time it was reaching its decision, Tokyo already knew from Roosevelt that Nicholas II had agreed to return southern Sakhalin.

The Russian delegation was prepared for a rupture, too. Therefore, when the words "complete agreement of the Japanese" resounded at the session of August 16 (29), it seemed "to everyone there to be absolutely unexpected. Everything had been readied for departure." "Around 11 o'clock Witte came out of the conference hall. He was flushed and smiling. Stopping in the middle of the room, he said excitedly: 'Well, gentlemen, it's peace. Congratulations! The Japanese yielded on everything.'"[103] As one Russian delegate observed in a letter to Kokovtsov: "Foreigners and Americans are overjoyed. They greet Russians with open arms. The Japanese look confused. They do not share in the general happiness. They are in mourning."[104] The delegations then discussed a number of technical questions, but the main thing was accomplished: peace was concluded.[105] The Russian delegation felt and behaved like a victor. This was Russia's first success in war that was won at the negotiating table. Witte took advantage of his accomplishment in Portsmouth both in America and on his return to Russia. He reached an important understanding with the Morgan Bank to float Russian bonds in America; and, in Paris, he paved the way for a major loan deal. Witte's success in Portsmouth became a springboard for his political career. In October 1905 he was named head of the united government that had just been created in Russia and became the first prime minister in the history of the empire.

The Portsmouth peace was well received by all the great powers. Only England, perhaps astonished at the tractability of the Japanese, maintained a demonstrative imperturbability.

In Japan the Portsmouth peace aroused universal disappointment. On his return, Komura was met by an enraged crowd. He was soon dismissed from his post as minister of foreign affairs. Even during the negotiations, Japanese public opinion had demanded the cession not only of Sakhalin but also of Vladivostok and the Russian littoral.[106] The Japanese press wrote that weak diplomacy had lost the nation its victory in the war.[107] With news of the signing of the peace accord on conditions far from expected, there were outbreaks of disorder in Tokyo. A crowd of people was angry that a coalition of nationalist organizations opposed to the peace had not been given permission to conduct a meeting in Hibiya Park, in the center of Tokyo. The crowd began throwing stones at the building of the Home Ministry, set fire to wooden structures next to the minister's residence, and destroyed about one hundred police stations, thirty tramcars, and three Christian churches. Order was rapidly restored only when the emperor introduced martial law in the capital and a division of the Emperor's Guards entered the city, securing government buildings. Demonstrations against the peace took place in other major Japanese cities. Seventeen people died in mass protests.[108]

In Russia Witte was equally reproached for having returned to Japan the southern part of Sakhalin. Malicious wags even added to the honorific of "count," which Nicholas II had awarded the head of the delegation in recognition of the successful treaty negotiation, dubbing Witte "Count Polusakhalinskiy" (Count Half of Sakhalin). In spite of the fact that the tsar himself had agreed to the cession of southern Sakhalin, the question lingered: would it not have been possible to get by without any territorial losses at all? Probably yes. But, under the conditions of the time, a completely uncompromising attitude on Russia's part appeared too dangerous, and in any case both sides were considerably interested in a speedy end to the war. If the negotiations had failed, the continuation of military action at a time when the fires of revolution were spreading would have been extremely risky and probably impossible to sustain. The cession of half of Sakhalin doubtless engendered among Russians a certain revanchism, especially heard among the officer corps and in drawing rooms and salons. Even Nicholas II himself assumed that, after some period of time had elapsed, the empire would make amends for its failures and recover what it had lost. However, this would happen under a different regime.

Chapter 4

Roosevelt and the U.S. Role

Perception Makes Policy

Eugene P. Trani and Donald E. Davis

Introduction

In 1998, I (Eugene Trani) was the guest of John Podesta, President William Clinton's White House chief of staff. As we passed through the Roosevelt Room, I was drawn to the main display, President Theodore Roosevelt's 1906 Nobel Peace Prize that was celebrated on May 5, 1910, at the National Theatre in Oslo, where the former president gave his Nobel Lecture on international peace. He suggested arbitration treaties, a court of arbitral justice, and a league of peace. It was then that I reminisced about my efforts as a young Ph.D. candidate to capture TR's triumph at Portsmouth in 1905. If I were to rewrite my 1969 monograph, *The Treaty of Portsmouth: An Adventure in American Diplomacy,* what might the intervening thirty-six years add to my study? There is, after all, at least one important new source for American scholars, the Archive for the Foreign Policy of the Russian Empire (AVPRI) in Moscow, which has already begun to be utilized. Also, there are about twenty-five additions to the literature, especially new collections of printed documents, a half-dozen or so fresh articles, and approximately a dozen books, amongst them some biographies.

My own interest in America's foreign policy has considerably broadened. In 2002, I coauthored, with Donald Davis, *The First Cold War: The Legacy of Woodrow Wilson in U.S.-Soviet Relations,* and we are now working on a study tentatively titled "Romancing the Bear and Dragon: The Story of America's Love-Hate Relationship with Russia and China in the 20th Century." In this forthcoming book, we look at the U.S. and Russian relationship from a wholly new perspective, one that begins with TR at Portsmouth.

In my 1969 Portsmouth book, I devoted a chapter to "Roosevelt and the Russians," basing much of it on George von Lengerke Meyer, and I followed that with an article on Meyer's activities as American ambassador to St. Petersburg during the 1905 revolution, titled "Russia in 1905: The View from the American Embassy." It then crossed my mind, and has preyed upon it ever since, that Americans have had, and continue to have, a very negative view of Russia and Russians, whether tsarist, commissarist, or federationist. I wondered where that attitude came from, how it has prevailed, and the various forms it has taken from the time of TR to President Ronald Reagan. In the case of TR, there was one American who particularly shaped his views on this subject, the elder George Kennan, who became America's first preeminent expert on Russia. (He was the distant cousin of the diplomat George Frost Kennan.)

A body of material exists showing Kennan's direct influence on TR. The president asked Kennan to make his views known to Japanese "men of influence" in Tokyo: "Japan must hold Port Arthur and she must hold Korea. These two points are already settled."[1] TR went on to say that "I have, from the beginning, favored Japan and have done all I could do, consistent with international law, to advance her interests. I thoroughly admire and believe in the Japanese. They have always told the truth and the Russians have not." Through journalist Richard Barry, TR asked Kennan to use this quote in order to convince Japan not to make outlandish demands.[2] Amongst others, Kennan had a two-hour interview with Japan's foreign minister, Komura Jutarō. Certainly, President Roosevelt and George Kennan were not alone in their positive assessments of Japan and negative views of Russia.[3]

Part 1

Winston B. Thorson's 1948 article, "American Public Opinion and the Portsmouth Peace Conference," proved that newspapers and journals remained favorable to Japan and negative to Russia throughout the conference, contrary to what Tyler Dennett, Howard K. Beale, and others believed.[4] Members of the Russian delegation, especially its chief plenipotentiary, Sergei Witte, had attempted to create a pro-Russian view. Thorson looked for evidence of their success: "when one turns to the most likely sources for confirmation, these sources are silent and that confirmation is lacking." He concluded: "there was no shift of American public opinion of the kind or degree claimed." Even media neutral or critical toward Japan "shifted to unqualified support of the Japanese position before the Conference was concluded."[5] Nor should any supposed pro-Russian bias be confused with President Theodore Roosevelt's legitimate concern over too big a Japanese victory and America's need for "Asiatic balance and the safety of the Philippines."[6] The secret Taft-Katsura agreement (1905) recognized Japan's dominant position in Korea in exchange for Japan's disavowing "aggressive designs" on the Philippines; that agreement raised little concern. Japan's restoration of Manchuria to China and its promises to sustain the Open Door won American press approval. Witte's warnings about Japan's Far Eastern domination gained little public support: "[the press] was clearly not taking up an anti-Japanese, let alone a pro-Russian attitude on the issues of war and peace."[7]

Public opinion backed TR's intervention in the peace process and compromise solution on the indemnity and Sakhalin items: Russia would pay Japan for the northern half of that island rather than calling the compensation an indemnity. Roosevelt's support of the Japanese is well known and often quoted: "[They] have impressed me most favorably. . . . [and] I am far stronger pro-Japanese than ever."[8] Even the Tokyo riots, as the terms of the treaty were made known, failed to shift U.S. opinion.[9]

American negative feeling toward Russia was nothing new. The most famous and earliest expression of such sentiment had come from Neil S. Brown during his ambassadorship to St. Petersburg, 1851–53. According to Brown, the most disagreeable features of Russia were its secrecy, surveillance, distrust, undue ceremony and delay, overbearing police, censorship, and espionage, including opening communications and spying. He wrote that nothing worth knowing was made public. Display was a passion with the Russian government. He concluded: "A strange superstition prevails among the Russians that they are destined to conquer the world."[10]

America's full-blown negativism toward Russia began in 1891 with the publication of George Kennan's *Siberia and the Exile System.* These two volumes initiated a widespread American public opinion swing from an inconsistent ebb and flow to what Frederick F. Travis, Kennan's biographer, calls a "universal hostility." Travis concludes that by 1902–3 "diverse elements of opinion [began] to coalesce."[11] Kennan had maintained that Russia was a land of misery, injustice, and tyranny. In his own account, he wrote, "I know more about the exile system than any man in the Russian Prison department . . . and if I could go before a court of justice with power to summon and protect witnesses I would prove a state of affairs that would disgrace the Russian Government in the eyes of the whole civilized world and make Alexander III blush with shame under his clothes."[12]

When Admiral Tōgō Heihachirō sank part of the Russian fleet and blockaded the rest at Port Arthur on February 8, 1904, U.S. opinion—even though considering this a sneak attack—supported Japan's war effort against what Kennan had termed Russia's "barbaric despotism." As Travis notes, "Only a few American voices supported Russia during the war; even though the Japanese had initiated hostilities, the tsarist empire was considered the aggressor, and the American press often expressed the idea, first pronounced by Kennan, that the war was a 'struggle of civilization against barbarism.'"[13] The president himself came closest to expressing this view, which he shared with Kennan, while at a White House luncheon, stating that he "would not hesitate to give Japan something more than moral support against Russia" if he were sure of public support.[14]

With threats of war looming in January 1904, Kennan had predicted a Japanese victory and a Russian revolution due to bureaucratic inefficiency and popular discontent. By March, he headed for Japan to cover the war for *Outlook,* the distinguished magazine he had worked for since 1898. After a series of Russian defeats, though more fighting was in store, President Roosevelt was already reiterating to the Japanese in February 1905 that he favored Japan's obtaining the fruits of her victory. He did this through an indirect channel, as earlier mentioned, in a letter to Richard Barry, a writer for *Collier's,* who gave TR's conditions to Kennan in Tokyo. Kennan, as a confidant of Roosevelt, was in close touch with Japanese leaders. It was Roosevelt's intention that Kennan relay his views. In March, Kennan did so verbatim to Prime Minister Katsura Tarō.[15]

"In Kennan's war coverage," Travis argues, "Japan represented the forces of modern civilization while Russia, because of its government, represented 'medieval' barbarism." Travis lists about thirty articles of between five and ten double-columned pages each that Kennan published in *Outlook* throughout 1904–5. Part of Kennan's effort was a crusade to stir up trouble amongst Russian prisoners of war (POWs) against the autocracy. Secretary of State Elihu Root, who assumed office shortly after John Hay's death in July 1905, was concerned that American consulates, especially the one in Yokohama, should not be involved in Kennan's propaganda efforts. Nevertheless, over a ton of such material was distributed to approximately seventy thousand Russian POWs.[16]

Most important, Kennan shaped American opinion; TR considered him one of the most influential journalists of the time. As a Washington, D.C., correspondent, he had a good relationship with the president, one that Roosevelt cultivated: "Kennan himself was an occasional luncheon guest and often corresponded on important issues with the president or members of his cabinet."[17] TR courted Kennan because he valued Kennan's support and considered *Outlook* a valuable instrument for advancing his foreign policy. During the war, TR wanted Kennan to keep him informed, especially about the infamous and anti-Semitic Kishinev trial, and he assured Kennan that he shared the writer's feelings about Russia. The printed page mattered to TR, and Kennan was the premier maker of American public opinion on Russia. Because of this, it is worthwhile to consider what Kennan had to write on Russia in *Outlook;* it helped set the course of public opinion and contributed to Roosevelt's Portsmouth policy.

Part 2

Kennan's twenty-six articles on the Russo-Japanese War—205 double-columned pages—constituted an important extension of his views, which he had circulated widely since the publication in 1891 of his pathbreaking *Siberian Exile System.*[18] All along, he had made his perception of Russia known with increasing clarity and directness. His attitude toward Japan was new and provided a valuable contrast to his views about Russia. Even by the time of his initial piece on the war in the June 11, 1904, issue of *Outlook,* "First Impressions of Japan," he had decisively influenced American public opinion to be hostile toward Russia. In addition, he also served as a messenger to the administration because, as his editor, Lyman Abbott, then noted, Kennan had obtained "access to the most authoritative sources of knowledge about the Eastern problem in its large relations. Letters of introduction from the highest diplomatic officials in the United States to members of the Japanese Ministry and private letters to Japanese men and women of high rank and influence open to Mr. Kennan opportunities quite exceptional."[19] Kennan was quick to point out Japanese patriotism, how peaceful things appeared there, and the "friendly feeling that the Japanese have for Englishmen and Americans."[20] He elaborated on these themes in his second article, "Japan at War" (June 18, 1904), by contrasting the two antagonists. Whereas in Russia only two and a half years previously, in every city from St. Petersburg to Irkutsk, there were "indications of potential, if not of actual, war . . . to be seen at almost every step," in Japan, "there was absolutely nothing to suggest war, or even preparation for war." Though in Russia there was a "show of military power," there was little efficiency compared with Japan. The Russian government professed "to be fighting the battle of European civilization against Asiatic barbarism." The Japanese press, on the other hand, pictured the Russian bear sinking in a torpedoed battleship or the sleeping Russian Gulliver with Lilliputian Japanese soldiers crawling all over his body.[21]

This contrasting of Russia and Japan continued. Kennan wrote of how the Japanese had "prearranged" the war through careful planning. The Japanese character excelled in "intelligent and painstaking forethought." He was impressed with Japan's modernity, accomplished in just fifty to sixty years and, especially, the education of many of her officers at Harvard and Yale. There was a "strong influence that America has exerted, and is still exerting."[22] At a Japanese naval school, he witnessed the splendid education, training, and long practice sessions of the cadets. Though Russian and Japanese naval equipment rated about equally, the Russians were "far inferior" in the use of theirs.[23]

The Japanese Red Cross was blended into the service in time of war.[24] As to the Russian POWs it cared for, when Kennan asked how they were treated, the POWs replied, "very well." Kennan judged that these POWs had more vigor than the Siberian exiles he had written about in 1891. The Russian POWs felt that the Japanese fought well and that Russian strength in Manchuria was "overestimated." Kennan concluded: "Japan treats her enemies better than Russia does her subjects."[25]

Kennan was allowed to visit Admiral Tōgō at his fleet's base just off Yentoa Bay, nestled in the Elliot Isles, fifty-five miles north of the blockaded Russian fleet at Port Arthur and thirty-five miles north of Dal'nii. Since the very narrow entrance to Port Arthur was partly blocked with sunken, stone-laden vessels and was guarded by torpedo boats, destroyers, and mines, the Russian fleet would be slow to escape, and Japanese wireless could notify Tōgō if it tried to get away. Before any Russian ships could break out, the main Japanese fleet would have arrived from the Elliot Isles. Yentoa Bay had become the center for supplying General Nogi Maresuke's Third Imperial Army besieging Port Arthur. The bay was guarded by a colossal ten-mile boom, stretching from Terminal Head to Sump Isle. From there, the navy could assist the First Imperial Army on the lower Yalu River as well as the Second Imperial Army in Manchuria. Kennan concluded that the Russians had "underestimated the strength and ability of their enemy" and that they were up against "one of the first military powers of the civilized world."[26] By contrast, the Russians had done "few things thoroughly and efficiently." Furthermore, Japanese proficiency, especially in the production of its own war matériel, meant that the cost of the war would be comparatively small for Japan.[27]

Kennan devoted a total of sixteen articles to the war itself—one evaluating General Aleksei N. Kuropatkin and his Manchurian army, twelve on the siege of Port Arthur by General Nogi's Third Imperial Army, and three on the war at sea between Admiral Tōgō and Admiral Zinovii P. Rozhdestvenskii. On the siege of Port Arthur, he gave a vivid eyewitness account, starting with his arrival there on October 23, 1904. The first thing that he noted was how well supplied Nogi's army of between 200,000 and 300,000 was, and he considered that its fighting spirit was high.[28] His trip from Dal'nii, some fifty miles north of Port Arthur, proceeded through rugged terrain, and he wondered why General Anatolii M. Stëssel had not made a stiff defense in these steep hills with at least 30,000 to 40,000 troops before retreating to the forts ringing the port: "if the Russians had defended these positions with half the courage and obstinacy that they afterward displayed . . . they might have inflicted immense losses . . . and might have made it impossible [for Nogi] to begin siege operations before the end of October or November [but instead] they allowed themselves to be greatly outnumbered at almost every point of attack, failed to entrench properly the naturally strong position that the country afforded . . ." As far as Kennan could ascertain, Stössel "very likely had never studied the topography of the peninsula in connection with a possible plan of invasion." This resulted in a much earlier investment of Port Arthur than if Nogi had lost 15,000 or 20,000 men before he even reached it.

In all of this—from not trying to prevent the boom construction and not harassing the landing at Yentoa Bay to neglecting a second line of defense on the Kinchow Isthmus and not entrenching between there and Port Arthur— Stössel had shown "lack of foresight, lack of energy, and lack of strategic skill."[29] This allowed Nogi quickly to gain a commanding view of the twelve-mile semicircle of Russian forts guarding Port Arthur. Yet, when Kennan first saw them, he was "surprised by the great natural strength of the Russian position[s] . . . [for he had] wholly underestimated both their power and their extent."[30] Even so, by the end of July, Nogi's troops had thoroughly invested those positions. After storming the outermost forts in August, though at a high cost, Nogi decided on a general assault of Port Arthur on August 16, ending on the 24th; it cost him 15,000 casualties, and it failed.[31]

Nogi had not realized the strength of these forts, each with its long glacis, deep moats, high parapets, strong counterscarps, and barbed wire entanglements. His gamble was that, if Port Arthur could have been seized in August, it would have freed his army for duty in Manchuria and Vladivostok as well as giving Tōgō other tasks than just the blockade.[32] It was now plain that siege operations of zigzag trenches and parallels were necessary. Nogi would have to bring into range his Krupp eleven-inch howitzers from Dal'nii. All these efforts began in early September. Most notably, the howitzers were able to lob a constant barrage of five-hundred-pound explosives into Port Arthur with deadly accuracy, directed as they were from high observation points, with all sixteen howitzers resting on concrete bases with steel mountings.[33] A steady bombardment allowed Nogi to move his units of sappers within three hundred yards of two outlying positions of the twenty-seven forts and entrenchments on either side of the old Chinese wall in front of the city.[34] A second assault from September 19 to 22, 1904, also failed, at the cost of another 12,000 to 15,000 troops. After that, it was a question of digging.[35] It was necessary to undermine the casemates and caponieres and to blow up the counterscarp walls.[36]

With the badly outnumbered Russian defenders also suffering heavy casualties and facing dimming prospects for holding out in the absence of reinforcements, Kennan complained: "If the Czar and the Grand Dukes of the 'war party' could only be forced themselves to take such ghastly chances, they might perhaps put a stop to a contest in which they have shown neither ability nor humanity."[37] By contrast, he discussed TR's gung-ho character with his Japanese friends: "I only wished that he were there to give the Japanese an 'appreciation' of his own character, because he would have been much more 'delighted' with the situation than I was."[38] Part of "the situation" was that General Nogi's Third Army was being reinforced by the Seventh Division—an additional 4,000 fresh troops.[39]

The work of filling in the moats before selected forts was accomplished by sinking shafts into the glacis, laying and exploding mines behind the counterscarps, and pushing the resulting debris back into the moats. Nothing was done by General Stëssel to prevent this. The Russians seemed unaware of what really was going on. If Stëssel could have held out to February or March, that would have prevented General Nogi from participating in the decisive Battle of Mukden. And, contrary to the Russian general's later comments, plenty of supplies and ammunition remained to do the job.[40] Stëssel's great mistake was allowing the Japanese to get close and stay within fifty feet of his positions in order to tunnel under and set their explosives. As Kennan explained, this blunder stemmed from the "failure of the Russians to discriminate between operations that were really threatening and dangerous and movements that had little if any importance."

With news of the approach of Russia's Baltic Fleet, the Japanese emperor ordered Nogi immediately to take Port Arthur, whatever the costs. The final assault was planned for November 26, 1904, with an additional 20,000 fresh troops.[41] It was preceded with the fierce assault of 203-Meter Hill in order to gain a clear view of the Russian fleet still trapped in Port Arthur's harbor. That effort cost 12,000 troops. Once the Japanese had captured this lookout, their eleven-inch howitzers took out four battleships, two cruisers, one gunboat, and a number of other vessels. Only the battleship *Sevastopol* escaped the harbor; it was sunk by torpedo boats.[42]

On January 2, 1905, Stëssel sent a truce flag to Nogi, and the articles of capitulation were signed at 9:45 P.M. Kennan described the considerable stores that were still held by Stëssel, in contradiction to the Russian general's later statements. The Russians, Kennan concluded, had been "badly led" and "outclassed." No matter what the "self-excusing and self-justifying" reports said, Kennan maintained that the "oversights and mistakes of the Russians, in the course of the siege, were many and great."[43]

In discussing General Kuropatkin's Manchurian army prior to the Battle of Mukden (February 23 to March 10, 1905), which the Russians subsequently lost, Kennan called attention to the army's "disorganization" and "demoralization." He concluded: "the picture of disorder, confusion, and incapacity . . . is enough to raise more than a doubt as to the ability of Russia ever to make any effective stand in Manchuria."[44] Though the Russians lost 89,000 troops and the Japanese 75,000, Kuropatkin's army escaped northward, and the Japanese were "too exhausted" to pursue. Japan had "reached the limit of its capabilities."[45] As to the destruction of Admiral Rozhdestvensky's Baltic Fleet, his thirty-two vessels were disabled and put out of action by accurate Japanese fire at a distance of three to four miles.[46] The opposing fleets were nearly equal in strength, yet after thirty hours the Russian fleet lost twenty vessels and was practically destroyed, while Tōgō lost only three torpedo boats. Kennan claimed that long-range marksmanship as well as accurate intelligence reports and the superior speed of the Japanese vessels accounted for this astonishing victory.[47]

Part 3

Amongst all his articles devoted mainly to military matters, Kennan took time to write two of a more wide-ranging nature: "Which Is the Civilized Power?" (October 29, 1904) and "The Sword of Peace in Japan" (October 14, 1905). In the first, he posed two questions: "If the whole world had to come under either Russian domination or Japanese domination, which would you choose?" He declined to answer this question unless he could reformulate it: "if I were shut up to a choice between world-domination by the present Russian Government and world-domination by the existing Japanese Government, I should take the latter without a moment's hesitation." But if both governments were "free and self-governing [he] thought he should prefer the former." However, six months later and after he had had a chance to study the Japanese, he cast his vote in favor of Japan. Why? "I should do this for the reason that Japan, as a Power, is civilized and modern, while Russia, as a Power, is semi-barbarous and medieval."[48]

How did he "support and justify" such a conclusion? Kennan contrasted the two societies by their mental-moral culture; religious enlightenment and toleration; legal respect for and observance of the security of person and property; freedom; personal-national integrity; and the virtues of modesty, morality, humanity, and fairness. Japan relied on a diffused education, out of the hands of a narrow-minded church, unlike the case in Russia. Furthermore, the tsar's bureaucracy substituted individual volition for legal prescription. Kennan cited secret ministerial abrogations of the law for political crimes and the use of an internal passport system. Then there was the defrauding by military officers and bureaucrats of their own government and vast amounts of dishonesty. He claimed: "When it comes to a comparison between Russia and Japan in the matter of political truthfulness, sincerity, and honor, the Asiatic Power stands far higher than the European." But he wanted to make it clear that his was a "comparison of systems and their results, rather than of peoples and their characteristics." Church and state oppressed and corrupted the Russian people, and the newspapers manifested the "bureaucratic spirit of intolerance, bitterness, and cruelty." Kennan ended by comparing the Tokugawa shogunate of 1616 to the Russia of Nicholas II, and he concluded that the former had been the more truly civilized.[49]

In Kennan's most cited piece in this series, "The Sword of Peace in Japan," he made assertions that President Roosevelt was at some pains to refute. The president, after all, also wrote articles for the widely circulated *Outlook* (which had more than a million subscribers) and in a few years would become a contributing editor.[50] Kennan, in his article, recounted the reception in Japan of the terms of the Treaty of Portsmouth. On September 5, 1905, the day of the signing, riots broke out in Tokyo and other Japanese cities. The reasons, he maintained, were diverse, but they issued from a "universal feeling of disappointment and dissatisfaction."[51] Kennan felt that the Japanese "expected, and perhaps had a right to expect, decisive results." They had fought "two bloody and victorious campaigns"; they had been encouraged by American and British newspapers to "believe, that they had a right to demand and exact an indemnity." What especially enraged them was the "surrender of half the island of Saghalien." It was once theirs and had been taken away when they were weak. According to Kennan, Japan was "greatly exasperated by the attitude of the Russian Government towards it, before, during, and after the peace conference."[52]

Various Japanese newspapers and leaders of public opinion claimed that the "terms of peace were humiliating; that 'the concessions of Japan amounted to a craven and discreditable surrender;' that the Government had 'bowed to Russian dictation,' and that 'such a disappointing result of a great national effort was never experienced by any other nation.'"[53] All this aroused a "storm of excitement," and the people "felt as if they had been betrayed by their own plenipotentiaries." As a result of their "Government's weakness in not pressing home the advantage it had, they were filled with indignation and wrath."[54] Hibiya Park in Tokyo became the scene of the worst rioting. Attempts were made on the home minister's life, his family compound was invaded, and fires were set there. Police boxes and stations were burned all over the city.[55]

Nevertheless, the Japanese, Kennan claimed, were not mad at the United States, though some radicals attacked the carriage of E. H. Harriman and though telegrams from Tokyo may have given that impression.[56] The government had conceded too much. Particularly, Kennan felt, the Japanese cabinet "would have been glad, no doubt, if President Roosevelt's intervention had come two or three months later." There was a fear of financial strain, of course, if the war had lasted another year. That might have imposed an "almost intolerable financial burden upon the people." It was not certain that the government could have obtained loans abroad if it had declined to negotiate.

Kennan's commentary elicited TR's strong rebuke. "It seems to me," Kennan had written, "that it would have been much better—for Russia as well as for Japan—if President Roosevelt had waited until the close of this campaign before he suggested a peace conference."[57] As Travis remarked, "Roosevelt was furious [though he acknowledged that] he regarded Kennan as an influential public spokesman whose words were weighty instruments that should therefore be wielded carefully."[58] As TR wrote to Kennan:

I do not intend to make public any of the details about this peace, because the Japanese have asked me not to make public those details which they think would in any way embarrass them, and I am anxious to do what they desire. But I do intend, privately, to keep intelligent observers sufficiently enlightened to prevent their going wrong. I think it is wise that a man of your standing who is supposed to speak with knowledge, should for his own information merely, know what the facts are. . . . I do not deem it desirable that an observer whose writings will have weight, as yours will have, should from ignorance of the facts draw totally wrong conclusions.[59]

When Kennan returned to America in June 1906, he admitted his mistake to the president because he had since learned the truth from Japanese officials. President Roosevelt also told Kennan just how much influence the journalist had exerted on official policy: the articles Kennan had written led TR to "withdraw the American legation [from Korea] and give the Japanese a free hand."[60]

Conclusion

In the short view, it is safe to say that TR was in step with American public opinion, which did not shift during the Portsmouth negotiations. That opinion, negative toward Russia, was largely shaped in the prewar years by Kennan. Furthermore, Kennan was especially critical of Russia as a Far Eastern correspondent for *Outlook* during the Russo-Japanese War. Though mostly an untapped source at present, his articles at the time attracted a wide readership, ranging from the average man in the street to the man in the White House. They constantly contrast an enlightened Japan with an unenlightened Russia—a semibarbarous, medieval European nation not even equal to the shogunate civilization of 1616. In Kennan's telling, Russian arrogance, miscalculation, and sloth inevitably led to disaster. TR's awareness of Kennan's importance in shaping his own and America's perception was indicated in the private rebuke TR gave Kennan, acknowledged by the latter in 1906. We suggest, in Kennan's case, that the power of his pen, while not mightier than TR's "sword of peace," certainly played an important role in TR's perception, by which he made U.S. policy at the Portsmouth peace negotiations.

In the long view, relations between America and Russia in the nineteenth century had been, if anything, partial and undeveloped. Russia and the United States had had only sporadic contact, and much of this had been in the form of ceremonial trips by leaders. America's first diplomatic agent in St. Petersburg, Francis Dana, received de facto recognition in 1783. The young John Quincy Adams, who accompanied Dana, was cautious about Russia. In 1809, he became America's first minister to Russia. In 1832, Ambassador James Buchanan signed the Russian-American Treaty of Navigation and Commerce, which guaranteed the terms of trading, though it expired on January 1, 1913, owing to an outburst of anti-Russian feeling in the United States over the treatment of American Jews traveling in Russia. Until Portsmouth, relations moved along with hardly a ripple. There were, of course, high points when the Russian fleets visited San Francisco and New York City during the Civil War; there was the sale of Alaska in 1867. Also, Grand Duke Alexis Alexandrovich, son of Tsar Alexander II, visited America in 1871. Ex-president Ulysses S. Grant toured Russia in 1878. In 1891–92, during the great Russian famine, Americans sent grain. Virtually all was well with America's Russian policy, notwithstanding criticism from Ambassador Neil S. Brown and, especially, from George Kennan. Therefore, TR's Portsmouth policy was the first major policy storm in an otherwise calm sea.[61]

After the abrogation of the 1832 commercial treaty in 1913, President Woodrow Wilson gave little help to Russia's Provisional Government in 1917 and refused to recognize the Soviet government. In 1920 he initiated the Colby Note, which prevented any U.S. government dealings with communist Russia. From then until 1933, the United States did not recognize the USSR.[62] President Franklin D. Roosevelt changed all that, recognizing the USSR in November 1933. Though problems arose, the new relationship held, flourishing during World War II with Lend Lease and the great wartime meetings at Teheran and Yalta.[63] But, from April 1945, with FDR's death, things severely cooled with the onset of the Cold War. Another Kennan, George Frost Kennan, won approval in 1947 of his containment policy, which morphed into Paul H. Nitze's rollback policy of the National Security Council (NSC-68) in 1950—a hard-line version of containment that culminated in President Ronald Reagan's "evil empire" or Strategic Defense Initiative (SDI) policy, often referred to as "Star Wars."[64] This arc of negativism—from the first Kennan's Russo-Japanese War perceptions and TR's policy at Portsmouth to Paul Nitze's containment perceptions and Ronald Reagan's SDI policy—defined most of America's twentieth-century relations with Russia. It was more than just fortuitous that these negative perceptions, which started with the senior George Kennan, settled into the first concrete change with TR's pro-Japanese and anti-Russian policy at Portsmouth. Negative perception had turned into negative policy and remained essentially that way for a century.

II

Legacies

Chapter 5

Lessons Lessened

The Near-Term Military Legacy of
1904–5 in Imperial Russia

Bruce W. Menning and John W. Steinberg

"That's the reason they're called lessons," the Gryphon remarked: "because
they lessen from day to day."
—LEWIS CARROLL, *Alice in Wonderland*

ilitary lessons usually come the hard way, via clear and incon-
testable defeat. By virtually any measure—save perhaps the peace terms at
Portsmouth—the Far Eastern war of 1904–5 marked a severe military set-
back for Imperial Russia.[1] Her navy paid the price of ineptitude with fifteen
capital ships, the backbone of three entire battle squadrons. Her army fared
little better, having failed to wring a single major victory from eighteen
months of grueling ground combat. The humiliation at Port Arthur and the
disasters at Mukden and Tsushima were horrifying in themselves, but they
were only the messiest blotches in the larger picture of military failure. Perhaps nothing at war's end better summed up Russian military frustration
than General N. P. Linevich's army group: it remained intact, even outnum-
bering the Japanese in central Manchuria, but it was pathetically incapable
of offensive operations.[2] In the end, the price of Russian military defeat
amounted to 270,000 casualties and 2.176 billion gold rubles, with another
3.943 billion for debt service.[3] With her naval and monetary cupboards bare
and with the empire wracked by revolution, Russia slunk ignominiously
from a conflict that was to have brought imperial glory and blessed respite
from internal strife.

Even as the war raged, the Russians sought to stem the negative tide with timely rectification of their military shortcomings. New and unexpected challenges in the dear school of combat experience yielded hard-won lessons that demanded immediate application to forestall repetitive defeat, if not simply to ensure self-preservation. With little prompting, officers and soldiers quickly learned to dye their white kepis and tunics in earth tones to frustrate Japanese sharpshooters. Infantry commanders soon learned the value of regimental scout detachments, while various higher command instances labored mightily to cover other gaps in tactical and strategic intelligence. Meanwhile, troops under fire intuitively went to ground for self-preservation, and artillerymen received crash courses on the merits of indirect fire. At Port Arthur, frantic improvisation became the order of the day as local commanders fended off repeated Japanese assaults.[4] Even in imperial St. Petersburg, government officials hurriedly applied what they understood as lessons learned from direct experience to create new structures for the coordination and formulation of higher military and naval strategy.

Once the conflict was over, the process of discerning and distilling wartime lessons and applying appropriate remedial measures assumed a more formal and broadly based character. The question now was not imminent defeat but preparation for the possibility of an even more challenging general European war.[5] Tsar Nicholas II created two special historical commissions to write authoritative military and naval histories of the war. They were to complete their work in fewer than five years, with the obvious intent to provide a generalized historical database from which the more important lessons might be extracted. Other commissions, boards, and committees sifted through the war experience and its lessons to provide recommendations that would eventually underlay a thoroughgoing reform of the Russian army and navy and their structures, means, and methods for fighting future wars.[6] Less overtly, between 1906 and 1909 higher military authorities launched a review of the army's senior leadership that resulted in a veritable purge of the officer corps. The larger reform effort even witnessed the advent of Russian Boy Scouts and patriotic organizations and celebrations that in many ways presaged their Soviet-era equivalents. By the time that Russia went to war in 1914, the application of lessons learned from 1904–5 would touch many segments of imperial Russian society and nearly every aspect of the imperial army and navy.[7]

In many ways, the far-reaching changes of 1905–12, often mislabeled as the "Sukhomlinov reforms" for the war minister who would oversee their implementation, rivaled, if not exceeded, the heralded reforms of D. A. Miliutin a half century earlier. Like Miliutin's changes, those of 1905–12 were heavily based on lessons drawn from the most recent conflict. And, like Miliutin's reforms, those of the later period also traced their justification to an altered sense of threat. However, unlike the situation in 1877–78, the reforms of 1905–14 failed to deliver victory in 1914–17. And, also unlike the Miliutin reforms, which enjoyed fifteen years to deliver on their promise—although the key transition to universal service obligation came only in 1874—those of the post-1905 period enjoyed fewer than eight years to deliver on their promise. Finally, the personalities and the primary foes were different. Miliutin enjoyed the confidence of Alexander II in ways that War Minister V. A. Sukhomlinov could never duplicate with Nicholas II, while Kaiser Wilhelm II's united Germany (along with Emperor Franz Joseph's Austria-Hungary) represented a threat of a different order from that of Ottoman Turkey in 1877–78.

There were also other important differentiating factors at work during 1905–14. For complex reasons, in key ways, and at critical junctures, the immediate post-1905 situation in Russia vitiated the impact of recent lessons learned and dulled the edge of urgency. The result was that, resources permitting, the more obvious lessons of 1904–5 found substantial reflection in military-naval structures, methods, and acquisition. Other lessons—both obvious and less than obvious—were either ignored or watered down to the extent that they produced little long-term palpable change. Still other lessons produced change that simply withered on the vine, the victim of autocratic or institutional politics or both. Many reforms based on lessons learned simply did not deliver on their promise.

Perhaps no single direct testimony better conveyed the sense of semi-fulfilled and unfulfilled promise than that of an astute contemporary observer, Rear Admiral Alexander Fedorovich Geiden. A flag officer of intellectual attainment—a rarity within the Russian navy—he was a longtime functionary at the imperial court who also served as chairman of the naval historical commission on the war of 1904–5. On the very eve of World War I, he penned a thin volume titled *Results of the Russo-Japanese War.*[8] In broad brushstrokes, this volume described the course of the war on land and at sea, summed up its more important lessons, and then assessed the degree to which these lessons had found reflection in various reform measures. Even with due circumspection, Geiden's conclusions revealed a troublesome and variegated picture. Not surprisingly, the volume was marked classified.

After his overview of the recent conflict, Geiden remarked that success in war depended on the readiness of a state's armed forces for war and on the skills and talents of senior commanders. In his judgment, readiness was a function of eight variables, among which Geiden ascribed primary importance to "unified direction of foreign and military policy, that is, of policy and strategy in peace and war." To this assertion, he added requirements for "a strong organic unity between the army and navy" and for "the fashioning in peacetime of war plans in accordance with the political situation and the resources at hand." Other requirements embraced issues of training, command preparation, and the allocation of sufficient resources to the military and naval establishments and to probable theaters of future military operations.[9] Without the same emphasis on unity of policy and direction from the top, Geiden's checklist roughly corresponded with conclusions drawn from the army's official history of 1904–5.[10] In sum, the Far Eastern experience indicated that the key requisite for success in future wars was the capacity to match scarce resources with aims through unity of overall direction, planning, preparation, and execution.

Resources remained a "red thread," to use a Russian expression, that ran through the entire period between 1905 and 1914 to dictate the material limits of Russian military transformation. And, according to the availability of resources, historians have usually divided the period of military reform between 1905 and 1914 into two distinct periods. The first, extending roughly from 1905 through 1909, witnessed limited and low-cost organizational measures that addressed some of the more obvious lessons from 1904–5. The second period, corresponding with the pre-1914 years of Sukhomlinov's tenure as war minister, witnessed dramatic change and growth in the capacity and readiness of the Russian armed forces.[11]

In a sense, the initial period of reform, though overshadowed by the sweeping organizational changes and material acquisitions of the second period, was the more important of the two. This was so for several reasons. First, under the duress of war and revolution, the tsarist government hurriedly enacted measures to stanch and reverse the flow of defeat and disturbance. Second, the prevalent and lethal mixture of autocratic, institutional, personal, and partisan politics often took backseat to the exigencies of the moment, and these exigencies usually reflected perceptions of the most pressing and immediate requirements. Thus, whether or not corrective measures were optimal, they reflected "unlessened" lessons. Finally, even though the government and its armed forces were strapped for resources during 1905–9, various commissions, committees, and institutions debated and proposed substantial and far-reaching reforms, many of which were actually realized between 1910 and 1914. Thus, the first period actually laid the groundwork for the second.[12]

With special reference to Geiden's concerns, the year 1905 witnessed the creation of two institutions, the State Defense Council (known by its Russian acronym GSO, for Gosudarstvennyi Sovet Oborony) and the Main Directorate of the General Staff (known also by its Russian acronym GUGSh, for Glavnoe Upravlenie General'nogo Shtaba, or in English simply as "the General Staff"), both of which held great promise for addressing the military-strategic lessons of the Russo-Japanese War that figured so explicitly in Admiral Geiden's overview of the conflict and its future implications. However, neither institution lived up to its initial promise, and only one, the General Staff, managed to survive the initial reform period, albeit in altered form and position. For reasons peculiar to the times and to tsarist Russia, neither institution evolved to harmonize imperial vision and resources with military strategy and foreign policy.

Like other prominent figures of his time, Admiral Geiden longed for the "good old days," in this case the predictably authoritarian rule of Nicholas II's father, Alexander III. After the internal disorders of the 1870s and early 1880s and after the foreign-policy reverses and indebtedness associated with the Russo-Turkish War of 1877–78, Alexander III had presided over two decades of stability and modest economic growth. In concert with foreign, naval, and war ministers of long tenure, he pursued a cautious imperial strategy aimed at stabilizing and securing the empire from various foreign and internal enemies. He once vowed that Russia's only true allies were its army and navy. Accordingly, he strengthened each within the limits of the state budget, managing to build Europe's third-largest navy, while avoiding confrontation with the major powers. In 1892, for strategic leverage against Germany and Austria-Hungary, he concluded a military convention with France.[13] Amid these attainments, but less evident to observers like Geiden, was a creeping military-institutional stagnation that accompanied Alexander III's rigidly conservative politics and policies.

More evident was the contrast inherent in Nicholas II's adventurous imperial policy, according to which the young and inexperienced tsar sought an outlet for Russian expansion in the Far East. As this policy unfolded between 1895 and 1904, interministerial coordination and cooperation occurred haphazardly, if at all, with various ministers behaving more like feudal satraps than custodians and facilitators of an imperial common cause. The tsar worsened the situation either by ignoring his ministers or by hurriedly cobbling together special interministerial conferences to consider more pressing problems. As ministers and favorites rose and fell, there was no harmonized, overall strategy to organize and link imperial ends, ways, and means. Ground force and fortress modernization fell hostage to naval expansion in the Pacific and construction of the Trans-Siberian Railroad. Beyond vague notions of Mahan's "command of the sea" and pursuit of elusive naval parity with the Japanese, no coherent strategy governed the deployment and employment of the newly created Russian Pacific Squadron. Indeed, a special conference of naval functionaries convened in December 1897 had determined that no plans were necessary beyond a shipbuilding program for the Far East that would produce a main battle squadron. Meanwhile, Russian ground forces were underfunded and spread increasingly thin, not only in the Far East, but also in European Russia. Not surprisingly, when war came unexpectedly in the Far East, it caught the Russians woefully unprepared and overextended.[14]

Prosecution of the war only emphasized many of the same anomalies. Beyond vague concepts and limited planning for initial ground force and naval dispositions, there was no overall war plan. War Minister A. N. Kuropatkin thought he had a strategy for waging war against Japan. With the Russian Pacific Squadron serving as a covering force, his concept was to undertake defensive operations during a prolonged ground force buildup in either central or southern Manchuria. Once he had attained ground force superiority, he would shift to offensive operations for the eventual conquest of Korea and Japan itself.[15] However, the Japanese Combined Fleet quickly bottled up the Russian Pacific Squadron in Port Arthur, while speedy Japanese ground offensives kept both Kuropatkin and Viceroy E. I. Alekseev, the overall commander in the Far East, off guard and on the defensive. Beyond consultation for initial plans, there was no genuine cooperation between Russian ground and naval forces. Meanwhile, because the tsar had not spelled out the relationship between General Kuropatkin and Admiral Alekseev, there was no true unity of command in Manchuria. In fact, rather than buying time for a Russian ground force buildup, the Pacific Squadron's primary role was to tie down one Japanese field army in the siege at Port Arthur while Russian ground forces lurched from small defeats to large defeats. Meanwhile, the tsar and official St. Petersburg attempted to provide overall guidance and support across lines of communication that extended eight thousand kilometers. Major elements of the Baltic Fleet, rechristened the Second and Third Pacific squadrons, wrote the war's final inglorious chapter when they sailed to the Far East for no viable strategic purpose.[16]

Even before Tsushima, the catastrophe at Mukden in February 1905 had prompted the tsar to consider a thorough overhaul of his apparatus and procedures for interservice cooperation and strategy formulation. The impulse for improved integration at the upper ranges of the military-naval hierarchy was scarcely new. In 1898, General K. K. Sluchevskii had submitted a brief to the tsar that proposed the creation of a Supreme Military Council under the autocrat himself (or a designated representative) to harmonize resources, policies, and objectives at the highest levels of government. N. I. Bobrinskii was to repeat this proposal at the beginning of 1904, calling his version of a coordinating mechanism the State Defense Council. These proposals went hand in hand with analogous and related recommendations to reorganize the War Ministry and its Main Staff to create a truly independent general staff on the German model. Already in September 1904, Colonel

P. N. Engalychev and General F. F. Palitsyn were floating proposals either to split off a general staff from the Main Staff within the War Ministry or simply to create a self-standing general staff outside the War Ministry. Palitsyn's proposal for the latter variant bore particular weight, both because of his reputation as a solid soldier-scholar and because of his long-standing relationship with Grand Duke Nicholas Nikolaevich, the tsar's cousin and inspector general of cavalry. Palitsyn was the grand duke's chief of staff, and, among all the grand dukes, Nicholas Nikolaevich, a graduate of the Nicholas Academy of the General Staff with a silver medal, was generally considered the leading military luminary.[17]

Desperate times seemed to call for desperate measures. Although Palitsyn often served as Nicholas Nikolaevich's stalking horse, the grand duke and the tsar evidently discussed fundamental military reform measures during a secret conference soon after Mukden. According to tsarist habit, a special conference met during May 1905 under the chairmanship of the grand duke to hammer out the mandate and organization for what would become the State Defense Council. Interestingly, in view of Admiral Geiden's later emphasis on senior command competence, one of the conferees, Assistant War Minister A. F. Rediger, proposed that the State Defense Council assume a role in command selection. Since higher command appointments routinely resided with the tsar, the grand duke dismissed Rediger's idea with the remark that appointments were outside the new council's sphere of competence.[18] With the disaster at Tsushima providing a final impulse for change, the results of the conference were announced on June 8, 1905.

The founding statute for the State Defense Council asserted that it had been established "for the assurance of state requirements and means to develop the empire's armed forces" and for the coordination of "the actions of the high military and naval administrations and their harmonization with other governmental organizations on questions related to the security of the state." In brief, the council's mandate was to debate and decide the most significant questions of state defense. These included (1) the definition of general measures that responded to the political situation for assuring the strengthening of the state's military power; (2) the debate of the most important proposals from the military and naval instances about the application of state means in the event of war and about the unification and direction of preparatory work for war; (3) the debate of changes in the activities of the military and naval instances elicited by special circumstances; and (4) the supervision of measures related to the reorganization of imperial defense. Although the council was to have sufficient authority to demand information for its deliberations, its actions were not to change the review of military questions within the State Council (at the time an appointive advisory body to the tsar), the Committee of Ministers (after October 1905, the Council of Ministers), or within the imperial ministries themselves.[19]

The State Defense Council was to be composed of six permanent members named by the tsar and a number of rotating members that included the ministers of war and navy, the chief of the Main Staff, and the inspectors general of the various service branches (infantry, cavalry, artillery, and fortresses). In addition, the rotating members might include on an ad hoc basis, as appropriate, the chairman of the Committee (Council) of Ministers and other ministers. The tsar nominally headed the State Defense Council, but the de facto chairman was Grand Duke Nicholas Nikolaevich.

On paper, the State Defense Council appeared to fulfill the requirements for overall direction and harmonization of imperial defense that were so lacking in the recent Far Eastern war. However, various realities were to hamstring the council from the outset. First, it had scant naval representation, a fact that the tsar might have rectified with judicious appointments, but which he did not. Second, its organization had been hurriedly thrown together, with little thought given to the niceties of quarters and staff. In fact, the council began its meetings in makeshift quarters with borrowed functionaries. Third, the council had no control over finances and resources. It even had to draw its budget from the War and Naval ministries, both of which were already strapped for resources in an ever-tightening cycle of state budgets. Indeed, even recommendations approved by the tsar might remain unimplemented for years because of inadequate state resources. Fourth, the council held no direct authority in itself—it could only make recommendations for tsarist approval, with subsequent implementation by the various ministries involved. Or the tsar might simply ignore the council's advice. Fifth, the way in which the council conducted its deliberations and the way that its recommendations were presented to the tsar depended entirely on the sentiment and cooperation of the grand duke. He might preclude debate on key issues, or he might quash unpleasant discussions with a display of impatience, or he might present the council's recommendations to the tsar in a way that vitiated their impact.[20]

A final important consideration was the larger governing and political context. The State Defense Council was fashioned just before the entire governing system underwent overhaul in the wake of the Revolution of 1905, which prompted the October Manifesto to grant Russia a limited autocracy with a popularly elected Duma for the lower chamber and a restructured State Council for the upper chamber. An important aspect of the new governing system was an empowered Council of Ministers, the various chairmen of which with varying degrees of success would try to impose a version of a united ministerial government on Russia and its often recalcitrant tsar.[21]

The peculiar nature of the post–October Manifesto political settlement levied its own special burden on interministerial cooperation in foreign and military affairs. By late 1907, two false starts and consequent changes in the electoral laws finally produced a Third Duma with which the tsar (indirectly) and his prime minister might work. In concert with an upper chamber, the State Council, the Duma was empowered to vote annual state budgets and to require ministers to answer questions about the activities of their respective bailiwicks. However, according to Article 14 of the Fundamental Laws governing the new constitutional order, both foreign and military policy remained the sole prerogative of the tsar. When the Third Duma created a Military Committee under the chairmanship of the Octobrist deputy A. I. Guchkov, neither the tsar nor his Naval and War ministries were overjoyed with the prospect of subjecting defense-related activities to public scrutiny. Still, the War Ministry, now headed by General Rediger, managed to work out a reasonably amicable relationship with the Duma, in part thanks to the skills of A. A. Polivanov, the assistant war minister. In contrast, neither the Naval Ministry nor Grand Duke Nicholas Nikolaevich demonstrated much patience for negotiating the political labyrinth that characterized post-1905 relations between tsarist officialdom and the Duma.[22]

In the end, the grand duke's lack of vision and unwillingness to enter the political arena even in a limited manner did much to doom efforts at harmonizing policy and strategy at the highest levels of government. His position as chairman of the State Defense Council and his easy access to the tsar in theory endowed him with the kind of power that some observers felt might lead to a military dictatorship in the event that the tide of revolutionary disturbances went unabated. In fact, during the troubled days of October 1905, the tsar purportedly offered the grand duke such dictatorial powers, which Nicholas Nikolaevich emphatically rejected (indeed, supposedly threatening suicide in the event such powers were thrust upon him).[23] As a compromise, the grand duke accepted command of the Guards and the St. Petersburg military district. Still, various conservative observers, including General Sukhomlinov, until late 1908 chief of the Kiev military district and governor-general of the southwest provinces, saw in the grand duke's position the fatal threat of "dual power."[24] However, the grand duke with rare exception remained very circumspect about wielding that kind of power. His own position paled in the long shadow of his cousin's imperial power, and instinctively he seems in the main to have consistently deferred to the tsar, acting much like a minister in presenting reports and recommendations to Nicholas II. Still, the grand duke appears to have enjoyed the highest degree of confidence with the tsar, especially during the troubled period between 1905 and mid-1907.

Thus, despite this confidence and unrivaled access, the grand duke never emerged to become the military dictator that some feared. Nor, despite the importance of the army in quelling domestic turmoil, did he become the equivalent of an all-powerful Bismarck-like chancellor, answering only to the tsar and combining in a single figure supreme authority over internal and external affairs. Instead, the grand duke seemed content with playing the role of occasional behind-the-scenes power broker and chief spokesman and defender of the interests of the army. He understood the requirements of the army and was more than a passable tactician and military district commander. However, he had no expertise in naval matters, and contemporary observers faulted him for lack of strategic vision. Worse, the grand duke apparently owed much of his influence with the tsar to a common interest in mysticism. Count S. Iu. Witte, the first prime minister after 1905, considered such proclivities "a disease," commenting that "it would be impossible to say that the [grand duke] is a lunatic and that he is either abnormal in the usual sense of the word or not right in the head." Still, Witte insisted that "he is touched, as all such people who believe in Ouija boards and such quackery."[25] These penchants, when combined with a lack of patience and staying power in the post-1905 political arena, hardly made for a titanlike figure in imperial strategy and foreign policy.

The tsar, meanwhile, after the initial shock of military defeat and revolution, seemed intent on pursuing an overall policy of "rollback." After making concessions to stem the tide of revolution, he was loath to deal directly with the Duma, and the new Council of Ministers remained legally responsible to him, not to the Duma. After the first two prime ministers, S. Iu. Witte and I. L. Goremykin, departed rapidly from the political scene in 1906, P. A. Stolypin slowly gathered the strands of power to fashion something akin to a united ministerial government. That is, between 1906 and the time of his assassination in September 1911, Stolypin succeeded in wresting the right to report directly to the tsar on behalf of his ministers. However, there were three major exceptions: the Foreign, War, and Naval ministries, all of which continued to report directly to the tsar. In addition, Grand Duke Nicholas Nikolaevich reported directly to the tsar on behalf of the State Defense Council, just as F. F. Palitsyn, the first chief of the post-1905 General Staff, had done. Since neither of these institutions enjoyed ministerial status, neither was technically accountable to anyone except the tsar. Thus, the tsar remained final interpreter and arbiter of matters affecting imperial defense and foreign policy. The only practical hold that Stolypin and the Duma held over the tsar was in the realm of resources, and Finance Minister V. N. Kokovtsov skillfully used his position at least initially to rein in the worst excesses of misguided foreign and military policies. And the Duma might fail to approve an annual budget, in which case the previous year's budget remained in effect with only a small diminution of funds.[26]

In a sense, with a few new wrinkles, coordination between foreign and military policy was not too much different from what it had been before 1905. New institutions and new political players meant that the game had grown more intricate, but overall coordination for imperial defense and foreign affairs still lay in the hands of the tsar, and his word remained law. Just as before, he still dealt with key constituencies on an individual basis. And, just as before, within the limits of resources, he retained the power to advance his own pet projects, including naval construction, against the wishes and recommendations of the State Defense Council. As Nicholas II's meeting in July 1905 with the German kaiser at Björkö had indicated, the tsar might also decide to launch his own foreign-policy démarches without even consulting his foreign minister! Or, more likely, the tsar and his foreign minister might pursue various initiatives and departures without consulting either the prime minister or other ministries. Meanwhile, during the tsar's weekly dealings with various ministers and functionaries, he often played one constituency against another, thereby retaining a large—if not near-absolute—measure of control over overall imperial domestic, foreign, and military policies. Just as in later Stalinist times, ministers were sometimes so uncertain over their standing with the supreme authority that they carried signed letters of resignation in their briefcases.[27] In comparison with the pre-1905 period, what was different was the degree of fragmentation at the top. Now, instead of two ministries reporting directly to the tsar on naval and military matters, four different functionaries reported to him: the heads of the Naval and War ministries, plus (after 1906) the chief of the General Staff and Grand Duke Nicholas Nikolaevich for the State Defense Council. Technically, the four inspectors general of the main service arms also had the right to report independently to the tsar, and the all-powerful chiefs of Russia's twelve military districts remained subordinate to the tsar and not the war minister. In an important sense this fragmentation played into the tsar's hands, for at any convenient time he might simply cite (or imply) lack of consensus or even disloyalty to impose his own decisions.

The new General Staff, or GUGSh, was a key part of this fragmentation. Unlike the State Defense Council, which owed its origins to various proposals, the proximate origins of GUGSh lay almost entirely with General Palitsyn and Grand Duke Nicholas Nikolaevich. Long a student of military administration and the German General Staff system, Palitsyn evidently used his long-term standing with the grand duke to press for the creation of a self-standing general staff on the German model. Since War Minister Miliutin's time in the 1860s and 1870s, the Russians had maintained a capital staff inside the War Ministry. It was called the Main Staff, and its activities embraced many functions of a true general staff, but they were fragmented and wholly subservient to the war minister. When inept preparation and planning for conflict in the Far East had laid bare the deficiencies of the traditional system, Palitsyn and the grand duke became the successful agents of transformation. Other arguments aside, the creation of GUGSh on the German model actually necessitated the co-creation of the State Defense Council, since some kind of central organ was now necessary to coordinate the activities of the War and Naval ministries with the new army and (after 1906) naval general staffs.[28]

Like the State Defense Council, on paper GUGSh appeared to address many of the lessons learned from the Russo-Japanese War. The new organization brought together in a single entity various functions for war planning, force structure, intelligence, military topography, higher-level military education, and the assignment and training of officers bearing the designation "of the General Staff." Essentially, GUGSh was to become the single organ responsible for war planning in all its ground-force dimensions. The object was to avoid the kind of haphazard preparation that had characterized the march to war in 1903–4. And the chief of GUGSh was directly subordinate to the tsar.[29]

However, what looked good on paper and what seemed to address the exigencies of the moment comprised another story in reality. Unlike the State Defense Council, which was created out of whole cloth, GUGSh was torn out of the side of the War Ministry. The Over–Quartermaster General sections were simply removed from the old Main Staff and reconstituted under GUGSh. This situation violated organic relationships that had evolved over more than four decades. The War Ministry, meanwhile, shorn of its planning and inspectorate responsibilities, simply fulfilled administrative, personnel, maintenance, and force-provider functions. This situation left War Minister Rediger in a difficult position: he was responsible for forces and readiness but had no direct access to resources and planning. This difficulty could be overcome with adequate coordination, but something less amenable to coordination was the exact relationship between the newly created GUGSh and the War Ministry. Elements of the old Main Staff retained control over command assignment, personnel, and troop mobilization planning. For purposes of acquisition and for maintenance of a proper balance of forces, the war minister had to have knowledge of war plans and their requirements. Yet, until early 1908, War Minister Rediger had no direct knowledge of requirements stemming from the Franco-Russian military convention.[30] Meanwhile, the relationship between the war minister and the powerful chiefs of the military districts was never spelled out. Nor was the relationship between the chief of GUGSh and the chiefs of the military districts. The whole picture looked like fragmentation run amok.

An often-overlooked aspect within the larger picture of reorganization and fragmentation at the top was the creation of the Naval General Staff, a naval entity analogous to GUGSh. Direct inspiration came from Lieutenant A. N. Shcheglov, who at the end of 1905 addressed a note to the tsar (probably via Admiral Geiden) titled "The Importance of Staff Work on the Basis of Experience in the Russo-Japanese War." Shcheglov proposed creation of a naval general staff to study naval threats, compose naval plans, and oversee measures for naval combat readiness.[31] At the urging of Admiral Geiden and over Naval Minister A. A. Birilev's objection, the tsar on April 24, 1906, ordered such a staff to be organized on the foundations of the strategy section within the Naval Main Staff. Unlike its ground-force counterpart, however, the Naval General Staff lacked both autonomy and manpower. Still, its chief, Captain L. A. Brusilov, and his fifteen officers gradually assumed overall responsibility for naval war planning. They could not hope to match the resources of the larger GUGSh, especially in the realm of threat analysis and intelligence assessment. Although the Naval General Staff's mandate included all matters related to the resurrection of the navy, the Naval Ministry possessed its share of "Tsushima-ites," as the old guard was derogatorily labeled, and they would not cede their ground without a struggle.[32]

For much of 1906, the consequences of fragmentation and institutional infighting would remain muted. For one thing, the exigencies of the moment diverted attention and scarce resources from mid- and long-term military and naval planning. The navy was still recovering from defeat and mutiny, while the army remained engaged with both redeployment from the Far East and the quelling of internal disorders. Each service worked on the basis of bare-bones continuation budgets from the previous year, and Finance Minister Kokovtsov warned that little improvement might be expected until the end of 1907. The status of each service verged on desperation. Naval losses in 1904–5 left intact only an outmoded and postmutiny Black Sea Fleet for defense of the southern littoral and some twenty recently constructed fleet torpedo boats for defense of the Finnish Gulf and the imperial capital.[33] For its part, the army returned home to demobilize its reservists; to confront depleted supplies, armaments, and equipment of every type; and to undergo redeployment to fight waves of urban and rural disorders. On the basis of wartime experience, each service required thorough reform, reorganization, and renewal. The overall military situation would later prompt Iu. N. Danilov, GUGSh quartermaster general from 1910 to

1914, to characterize the years between 1905 and 1909 as "the period of our complete military helplessness."[34]

While military and naval issues remained pressing, other priorities governed, and these priorities, including internal stability, fiscal stringency, and restoration of Russia's damaged prestige abroad, elicited a rare consensus among higher-ranking functionaries in the immediate post-1905 governing order. Restoration of Russian strength and prestige would require time to address, but after mid-1906 Foreign Minister A. P. Izvol'skii set about reorienting Russian foreign policy on requirements flowing from the Franco-Russian accord and the evolving European situation. In brief, he would seek rapprochement with Japan and England to assure Russia's eastern and southern borders and would attempt to balance England against Germany to retain freedom of maneuver on the European stage. Such freedom of maneuver was particularly significant to counter Austro-Hungarian designs on the Balkans and to garner support for Russia's own time-honored designs on the Turkish straits. Izvol'skii's initiatives would take time to develop, and while their course proceeded apace, the two general staffs and their analogous ministries would set about making their calculations for the future.[35]

Amidst these calculations and Izvol'skii's initiatives was a major make-or-break issue that laid bare the faults of the State Defense Council and the entire frail system for coordination of higher strategy and foreign policy. This issue involved quarreling between the army and navy that arose during 1907 over funding priorities. The way that this issue and its consequences played themselves out held significant implications not only for strategy and policy integration at the highest levels but also for the way that the course of subsequent military reform would unfold.

The manner in which the two general staffs set out to calculate changing geopolitical circumstance and threat was illustrative of two distinct service cultures with two distinct and divergent preoccupations with force reconstitution. Soon after his accession as finance minister in mid-1906, Kokovtsov had requested budget figures from the army and navy for 1907. Both the War and Naval ministries responded with gigantic estimates (3.5 and 2.5 billion rubles, respectively) to make good on war losses, then turned to their general staffs for baseline threat estimates and proposals for support and acquisition programs. Borrowing from a long tradition of war planning by GUGSh predecessors, General M. V. Alekseev and Colonel S. K. Dobrorol'skii fashioned a baseline threats and needs assessment that reflected the strategic primacy of the western military frontier and its requirements. Of all the various threats, they saw the Triple Alliance as preponderant. Because Russian ground forces had been so weakened by war in the Far East, the two officers saw that troop deployments in the west must be withdrawn deeper into Russia's interior and

that Russia must stand on the defensive during the initial period of any future war in the west. Further, the two officers doubted that the last prewar
mobilization schedule (Number 18, from 1903) might be reliably restored
without substantial efforts to reorganize and reconstitute the army and its
fundamental mobilization-oriented supplies, arms, and equipment.[36]

With little war-planning tradition and even less residual institutional
wisdom to draw on, Captain Brusilov of the Naval General Staff took an entirely different tack with his threat analysis. He submitted a formal query to
Foreign Minister Izvol'skii about Russia's foreign-policy objectives and possible circumstances that might require the application of Russian naval assets. When Izvol'skii answered only in general terms, Brusilov accepted
vagueness as license to propose a naval shipbuilding program based on narrowly conceived lessons from the Russo-Japanese War. Never mind direct
naval responsibilities to secure St. Petersburg and to provide seaborne flank
protection for the army on the western military frontier. Possible contention with either the Germans or the English translated into a requirement for an integrated battle squadron composed of the newest-model capital ships of the emerging *Dreadnought* class. While coastal defense was a
concern, the governing idea was that blue-water offensive capability provided
the best defense. This set of views—albeit more informed and nuanced—was
highly reminiscent of the logic that had led to construction of the pre-1904
Russian Pacific Squadron.[37]

Past mistakes notwithstanding, the argument received key reinforcement
from another quarter. Not to be outdone by the Naval General Staff, Naval
Minister Birilev had convoked in April–May 1906 a series of ten intramin-
isterial conferences to determine shipbuilding priorities. Painful deliberations over the course of these conferences foreshadowed later squabbles
over priorities for imperial defense, among them defense of the Finnish
Gulf and the imperial capital. Two issues gradually became overriding: the
English dreadnought program and the survival of Russian shipyards. Without a new shipbuilding program, Russian yards were idling on the verge of
collapse, while the appearance of the *Dreadnought*-class battleship outmoded everything that went before it. Although most participants in these
conferences conceded the coming superiority of the dreadnought, the more
experienced captains warned that such vessels were "little suited for sailing
in the restricted waters of the Baltic or the Finnish Gulf." Whatever the
more limited defensive needs for the Finnish Gulf, Birilev asserted: "We
must now build large vessels, or else all our factories will stop work, which
in any case we cannot permit." Yet there was more to the argument than
mere naval prestige and make-work for idle shipyards. For navalists of Mahanian persuasion, the new class of warships would enable Russia to steal a

march in the international arms race, since proceeding to their immediate construction would enable a post-Tsushima Russia in short order to outclass her potential naval foes. Indeed, the new Naval General Staff was of the opinion that "without special difficulty in several years we can construct a fleet suitable to fight against the Germans." It was further noted that during the recent war "we lost that which was already unsuitable for contemporary battle." Consequently, the firm conviction was that Germany's splendid prewar-style capital ships were "little suited for contemporary battle, and they will have to create capital ships anew, just like us."[38]

The rationale for skipping to the front of the naval arms race soon garnered powerful advocates from the tsar on down. Dreadnoughts translated into enhanced imperial prestige, into restored Russian international status, and into immediate shipyard utilization. For Foreign Minister Izvol'skii, a *Dreadnought*-style navy meant that Russia might again become a sought-after ally within the evolving European alliance system. In other words, a powerful and modern navy would essentially enable Russia to exert pressure on the balance between England and Germany. Unlike the land-bound army, *Dreadnought*-class vessels were mobile assets that might be shifted like chessmen among trouble spots on the global stage. With appropriate balance between the Baltic and Black Seas, the same dreadnought-strengthened navy might do wonders in addressing the problem of the Turkish straits. There was little about an enhanced navy that went against the rough consensus on Russian foreign-policy objectives. Moreover, the question of shipyard utilization united both owners and Minister of Finance Kokovtsov. He estimated that these yards would be needed in the near future, and not surprisingly he subsequently asserted "the question of naval power is almost one of life or death for Russia."[39]

Therefore, in September 1906, when Birilev requested funds at a special interministerial conference to begin construction of two *Dreadnought*-class vessels, Kokovtsov responded that funds could be forthcoming, but he qualified his approval with the proviso that no allocations might occur without reference to a complete and fully integrated program of naval construction. Still, there was the issue of the shipyards, to which Kokovtsov remained sympathetic. Consequently, the finance minister felt the entire question should be broached at an extraordinary special conference chaired by the tsar. If such a conference agreed with the request, then funds would be made available. When Admiral Birilev approached the Council of Ministers with the same request for two dreadnoughts, Prime Minister Stolypin correctly remanded the issue to the State Defense Council.

The State Defense Council met twice, on October 26 and November 10, 1906, to consider Admiral Birilev's proposal for two *Dreadnought*-class battleships. The council voted not to support the request, although in principle there was near-unanimous support for restoration of Russian naval power. The problems were how and when. Kokovtsov noted that his ministry was prepared to find at least eight million rubles for naval shipbuilding during 1907. However, he perhaps best summed up prevailing opinion when he said: "we must begin not with incidental construction of this or that type of vessel, but with the systematic implementation of a clear plan, knowing why it settles on one type of vessel and not another."[40] Under Grand Duke Nicholas Nikolaevich's leadership, the State Defense Council remanded the issue to the chiefs of the two general staffs to work out a shipbuilding program for the near term that would satisfy requirements for the Baltic Fleet, that is, defense of the Finnish Gulf. On November 29, when Admiral Birilev forwarded not one but two shipbuilding programs, the grand duke refused to consider them on the grounds that they had not been harmonized between the two general staffs.

On December 15, 1906, the two general staffs met to fashion a set of working propositions that might govern the objectives of Russia's various fleets (or their vestiges) in the near and midterm future. The conferees concluded that over the next decade or two "the Baltic Fleet cannot be looked upon as an active fleet in the broadest sense of this phrase, but must be limited by imperial ukase to a defensive role." In contrast, the Black Sea and Pacific fleets might assume more active roles, but not in the near future. To this general set of recommendations, the tsar affixed his commentary: "in complete agreement with everything asserted here."[41] Thus far, the mechanism for collegial review inherent in the State Defense Council system was working, albeit haltingly, even though the tsar was beginning to demonstrate more than a desultory interest in the proceedings.

By the end of 1906, this interest grew more evident. Apparently weary of the Naval Ministry's fumbling, Nicholas II called Admiral Birilev to a special meeting to propose a reorganization of the Naval Ministry on the German model as supported by Admiral Geiden. That is, the Naval General Staff would become fully independent of the ministry, with the chief reporting directly to the tsar. All the various fleets would be subordinated directly to the tsar through his military field chancery under Admiral Geiden. Birilev, however, objected to the German model, pointing to evidence that demonstrated the kaiser's incompetence in naval affairs. This veiled challenge to imperial authority was sufficient to bring about Birilev's replacement by Admiral I. M. Dikov, whose accession to the Naval Ministry in early 1907 was to signal a frontal attack on the army-dominated State Defense Council.[42]

In March 1907, when Prime Minister Stolypin queried Dikov about his predecessor's plan for two dreadnoughts, the admiral responded that his ministry was preparing a new proposal for the State Defense Council. That same month, the Naval General Staff presented the tsar with a comprehensive study titled "The Strategic Foundations for a Naval Plan," in which it proposed four separate shipbuilding programs, depending on the availability of resources. All variants called for one or more complete battle squadrons (each consisting of eight battleships, four battle cruisers, nine light cruisers, and thirty-six torpedo boats). The fourth variant, or "Small Program," proposed a battle squadron for the Baltic while providing for the modernization and augmentation of naval assets in the Black Sea.[43] Nicholas approved this variant in principle, after which on April 2, 1907, Dikov requested tsarist permission to forward the proposal to the State Defense Council for discussion. The proposal for the Small Program envisioned ten years of naval construction with the explicit purpose that "the Baltic Fleet defend the Finnish Gulf, in addition to comprising a flexible naval force to support the empire's interests on the high seas." Tsarist approval came with the comment: "God grant us exact implementation of the Small Shipbuilding Program." Essentially, this comment meant that the tsar had already approved the plan before its submission to the State Defense Council. However, observing the letter of institutional decorum, he instructed the council to review the Naval General Staff's proposal with an emphasis on a "fleet of the line" as the basic means for the Baltic Fleet to fulfill its mission.[44]

On April 9, 1907, the State Defense Council debated the merits of the Small Program during an extraordinarily stormy session. General Palitsyn acknowledged that GUGSh had concurred with the Baltic Fleet's mission for defending the Finnish Gulf, since such a defensive mission would permit the army to redeploy a quarter million troops elsewhere. However, the creation of "a flexible naval force" failed to correspond with discussions on December 15 of the previous year between the two general staffs. Admiral Dikov countered that such an idea had always existed since "Russia as a great power requires a fleet, and she not only must have it, but she must have it in a configuration that can be sent anywhere required by state interests." Foreign Minister Izvol'skii supported the naval contingent by asserting that Russia as a great power needed a navy, and not just for coastal defense. Rather, the navy must be "flexible," and "it must operate wherever policy directs." Meanwhile, army members of the council argued that large expenditures for shipbuilding would deprive the ground force of desperately needed resources. With an eye toward the purse, Finance Minister Kokovtsov felt that a blue-water capability was secondary and consequently "should not be pursued." Rather, he demanded a program that might satisfy two requirements: the harmonized needs of both the army and navy and the Finance Ministry's ability to provide support. War Minister Rediger called the navy's request "excessive," and "all the more so because the army required such measures without which it cannot live and be considered combat-worthy."[45]

The grand duke summarized his views by noting that in principle Russia required a fleet of the line but that its scale and time of construction could not be considered in isolation from ground-force requirements, which in themselves needed the same immediate review and resolution. Therefore, Nicholas Nikolaevich proposed that the legislative organs be presented with a unified program for the development of the army and navy. Further, such a program should feature a distribution of means between the two organizations that reflected their respective significance to overall imperial defense. With the exception of the naval officers, all members of the council voted for the grand duke's proposal. Representatives from the War Ministry unanimously added the assertion that the reconstitution of the armed forces must begin with the army and only then, insofar as possible, proceed to creation of a line fleet.[46]

Essentially, the State Defense Council's conclusions represented open defiance of the tsarist will. Not surprisingly, Nicholas II did not approve the council's journal for the meeting of April 9. Instead, he pointedly waited four months to read it, then simply appended the remark "Read" in place of "Approved." From this time to the formal abolition of the Defense Council in 1909, the tsar would simply annotate its minutes with the laconic "Read." Meanwhile, in mid-1907, the tsar approved a report from the Naval Ministry on the Small Program, with the intention that the proposal go forward with a request for funding to the Council of Ministers. In contrast with the State Defense Council, the Council of Ministers would bend to the will of the tsar, basically agreeing to support the naval program despite various misgivings. The question became one of how to present it to the Duma in the best light to secure approval.[47]

These developments meant that, not two years into its existence, the State Defense Council and its chairman had lost their credibility with the tsar. As if to punctuate the desperation of the army's situation, in December 1907 the grand duke in a second rare act of defiance uncharacteristically appealed to outside authorities, circulating a letter among Russia's high-ranking functionaries in which he urged them to support reconstruction of the armed forces with a rational eye toward the allocation of resources in accordance with the Russian situation (that is, in accordance with the primacy of the army).[48] This letter constituted abject admission that the State Defense Council was no longer in a position to fulfill its mandate.

The second shoe dropped during late 1907 and early 1908, when Foreign Minister Izvol'skii, with only limited support from the tsar and General Palitsyn, proposed to mount a preemptive war against Turkey to seize control of the Turkish straits. However, a combination of circumstances, including fear of great-power intervention, the Russian armed forces' appalling lack of readiness, and resistance within both the Council of Ministers and the State Defense Council, doomed the project. Neither Prime Minister Stolypin nor Finance Minister Kokovtsov was originally privy to the scheme, and when word leaked out, they were furious because the prospect of war over the straits would imperil the fragile domestic peace. Significantly, the forum for airing and resolving differences was not the State Defense Council but a timeworn mechanism—the interministerial special conference. Before the ill-timed and misconceived proposal died, Stolypin threatened resignation, and both Foreign Minister Izvol'skii and GUGSh chief Palitsyn suffered embarrassment and loss of credibility. Meanwhile, the State Defense Council, whose mandate included unified strategic direction, had by now clearly taken a backseat in various deliberations, meeting over Izvol'skii's proposal a week after it had already been considered during the interministerial special conference.[49]

Not surprisingly, in March 1908 the grand duke suggested to the tsar that the State Defense Council be abolished. The tsar's response was "not yet."[50] However, the State Defense Council was now living on borrowed time, especially after July 26, 1908, when the tsar formally relieved the grand duke of his duties with the council, ostensibly to free him for exclusive service as commander of the Guards and chief of the St. Petersburg military district. The council would continue to meet sporadically until August 12, 1909, when War Minister Sukhomlinov abolished it.[51]

For the sake of even-handed perspective, any conclusions about the short and often unhappy life of the State Defense Council and its fragmented constituencies should balance both the more wholly negative with the somewhat positive aspects of its activity. It did encourage planning collaboration between the two general staffs, and even Admiral Geiden admitted that such interaction was a vast improvement over the pre-1904 situation. At the urging of the State Defense Council, the two staffs also undertook serious long-term war planning that reflected Russia's changed circumstances in the post-Portsmouth world. Each of these attainments produced a generally positive and long-term effect, including lower-level committee-style collaboration.[52] In addition, late in 1905, the grand duke grudgingly agreed with War Minister Rediger's earlier suggestion to develop a mechanism to improve the process for officer promotion and assignment to significant command positions. Under the auspices of the State Defense Council, the resulting Supreme Certification Commission was responsible for relieving or pensioning off the more incompetent and superannuated officers who had failed to demonstrate their mettle either in prosecuting the war in the Far East or in quelling internal disorders.[53] Almost by accident, the council thus answered another of Admiral Geiden's requisites for future military success. The council also successfully catalyzed and coordinated several important and low-cost military reforms. They included a reduction of active service terms for soldiers and sailors, improvements in living conditions for troops, and modest increases in salaries and allowances for officers.[54]

However, the most important objective, the capacity for higher integration of strategy and policy, remained beyond the grasp of the State Defense Council and its associated diffuse planning and directing systems. In part, the failure to fulfill this promise probably lay as much with the peculiarities of modified autocracy as it did with changed political circumstances in post-1905 Russia. In a sense, Prime Minister Stolypin and his drive toward a united government under the auspices of the Council of Ministers represented as much of an integrating challenge as did the quirky and recalcitrant Nicholas II. Once the State Defense Council lost credibility, the tsar in concert with the prime minister would revert to interministerial special conferences in pursuit of policy integration. Stolypin, meanwhile, would continue his quest for a united government. That quest would elude him until mid-1909, after the Bosnian annexation crisis. Even then, the War and Naval ministries remained outside his direct purview. Perhaps what was needed inside Stolypin's government was the equivalent of a standing war cabinet to effect policy and strategy integration even during peacetime. Without such an institution, there lurked the ever-present danger of compartmentalization and politico-military fragmentation under still another guise.

More seriously for the army, naval shipbuilding requirements, subsequently supported by both the Council of Ministers and the Duma, siphoned off huge sums that might otherwise have been beneficially applied to fortress modernization, railroad construction, and heavy artillery procurement.[55] When war finally did come in 1914, these assets would be sorely missed, while the four *Dreadnought*-class vessels in the Baltic would contribute little to the overall Russian war effort. Again, just as in 1904–5, the navy would find itself off the strategic mark with its emphasis on a Mahanian-style navy, especially for the Baltic.

In the end, as David McDonald has remarked, the tsar even after 1905 retained many characteristics of a "ruler-warlord."[56] If Nicholas II chose to cultivate navalist pretensions to assert state power, then collaboration to involve other instruments and means appropriate to the task would remain problematic. It was for this reason that key "lessons learned" from the war in the Far East remained "lessons lessened" and sometimes even only "lessons observed."

Chapter 6

The Absence of Portsmouth in an Early Twentieth-Century Japanese Imagination of Peace

Sho Konishi

$\mathcal{L}$ess than a year following the Portsmouth Treaty, two of the most popular writers in late Meiji-Taishō Japan, Tokutomi Roka and Arishima Takeo, made separate pilgrimages to the homes of figures that they saw as symbols of international peace, civilization, and progress. They both had traced routes across the Middle East and Europe, visiting inspirational sites of human development, and culminated their respective travels at the homes of Russian anarchist thinkers Peter Kropotkin and Lev Tolstoi.

It was in the immediate post–Russo-Japanese War period that Tolstoi and Kropotkin appeared arm in arm on the Japanese cultural scene, to the point that we might call it a phenomenon of Tolstoi-Kropotkinism. It would be difficult to read the public prominence of these particular figures without an understanding of the impact that the war and the corresponding Non-War Movement (Hisen Undō) had on Japanese thought and culture. If, as historian Hyman Kublin has suggested, Japanese and Russians during this period provide us with one of the most successful and therefore unusual cases of antimilitarism in a time of war in modern history, then it is certainly a topic that deserves further reflection.

Historians of modern Japan have shown little interest in the puzzling fact that in the twentieth century nongovernmental cultural and intellectual relations between Russia and Japan were most intimate and intense when diplomatic relations were at their worst and the two nations at war. So how do we make sense of such a chasm between poor interstate relations and rich cultural and intellectual relations, which in this particular period revolved around Tolstoi and Kropotkin? In short, the answer to this mystery was the development of competing visions of modernity.

During the Russo-Japanese War, a body of intellectuals came to share the view that the war represented a retrogression of human progress and civilization. This perception provides the key to understanding the Non-War Movement as one of the most successful cases of antimilitarism in modern history. Participants' thinking contrasted with the modern Western mentality that sanctioned, if not heroized, Japan's entry into the community of nation-states as a result of its success in war and empire building. The Portsmouth Treaty and the Nobel Peace Prize awarded to President Theodore Roosevelt for his leadership in brokering the peace represented this understanding of international peace and a hierarchical world order that centered on state, empire, and international law.

In Japan, the war helped to clarify and concretize an alternative discourse of modernity, an internationalist vision of human progress and civilization based on the cooperative principles of anarchism. This contrasted with the familiar story and historical meaning of two imperial powers in conflict, with Japan attaining recognition as a member of the civilized community of nation-states of the Christian West. According to the Japanese anarchist vision of progress, cooperation was a key factor of civilizational development. Human society in this view had been advancing toward higher degrees of cooperation and spontaneous association among subjects. I refer to this urge to change, and corresponding actions and ideas, as cooperatist anarchist modernity.

The cultural and intellectual turn to cooperatist anarchism can be observed not only temporally but spatially as well, in that participants located themselves beyond the East-West dichotomy. Participants did not oppose "the West" or "America" per se. Rather, they opposed the particular idea of progress and temporality in which many located themselves. Indeed, perhaps no school of thought came closer to acceptance of America than cooperatist anarchism in the first half of the twentieth century, when Western-oriented cosmopolites in Japan often turned to pan-Asianism to counter the West.

This short essay does not attempt to introduce the Non-War Movement in detail. Instead, I shall focus on two developments that may serve to deepen our understanding of this phenomenon: the invention of *heimin*, "the people," during the war, and what I call a "history slide," a major shift of historical consciousness among many Japanese in the decade following the war.

Non-War participants' adherence to the cooperatist concept of progress and civilization transcended national boundaries. To interpret the phenomenon under investigation thus necessitates seeing international history not only from a nonstate level but also from nonorganizational perspectives, in this particular case by tracing the transnational interlocking networks and social thinking and practices that emerged from the Non-War Movement. In this way, an entirely new history emerges.

The existing English translations that refer to the Hisen Undō movement do not quite reflect the participants' intellectual universe. I translate "Hisen Undō", the term Japanese participants used for their movement, as "Non-War Movement." English-language references to the movement have often translated "Hisen Undō" as "Anti-War Movement," without distinguishing it from the more contemporary Japanese term *hansen undō*. This translation not only fails to reflect the intellectual universe of the movement; it may actually be misleading. For the term *hansen* as it has been used in the post–Asia-Pacific War period refers to an oppositional position against a particular war, as in the Anti–Vietnam War Movement. Hisen members, by contrast, demonstrated their unwillingness to fight or wage war as a general principle. However, at the same time, the Hisen Undō of the Russo-Japanese War did not express a philosophical position of pacifism, the absolute negation of any means of violence under any circumstance. Neither position embedded in the term "anti-war movement" accurately reflects the intellectual universe that the Non-War Movement represented.

Inherent in the language of *hisen* was a construct of civilization and progress separate from Western modernity. Imperialist wars were not a part of this construct of modernity and therefore *hi*, "absent." We may thereby conceive of this movement as an intellectual mind-set *for* a given understanding of progress and civilization, rather than *against* a particular war or *against* violence in absolute terms. *Hisen* was a term historically specific to the Russo-Japanese War, with the war being the only time that the term would ever be used. Despite this circumstance, the Non-War Movement of the Russo-Japanese War period would be an inspirational model for the various anti-war movements to follow in twentieth-century Japan.

Given a voice through the newspaper *Heimin shimbun,* participants in the Non-War Movement claimed that the idea of the international arena as one of competition and struggle for existence, or a primitive social Darwinist state of nature, was untenable because it recognized only one type of actor, the nation-state, in the practice of international affairs.[1] According to Thomas Hobbes and Immanuel Kant, the "natural" progression toward freedom and equality of advanced human beings was realizable only by means of developed nation-states, which represented the end product of a linear trajectory from originally free and equal yet violent and conflictive barbaric communities to an "advanced" state of nature in which civilized peoples maintained the natural state of freedom and equality only by guarantees of private property and legal rights under the authority of the state. It was this naturalized nature of International Relations as conceived in the West that Non-War participants would denaturalize through thought and action. In the words of Kōtoku Shūsui, one of the founders of *Heimin shimbun*, imperialism, or *teikokushugi*, was "the Monster of the Twentieth Century" *(nijusseiki no kaibutsu).*[2] In his work *Hibunmei ron* (Thesis on Non-Civilization), Taoka Reiun understood that attaining "non-civilization" was to attain progress. Like many others, Reiun had been heavily influenced by the war. He recalled: "When I saw the suffering and the misery of the war and realized the high price to pay in the process of gaining victory by shedding blood, I could not help becoming non-war."[3] While I shall not discuss it further here, it is worth noting that the intellectual practice of using *hi* or *mu* ("non-" as a prefix) to indicate an alternative to the contemporary prevalence of Western civilizational discourse was a widespread phenomenon during the war and the decade following it.

As expressed in the title of *Heimin shimbun*, the Non-War Movement revolved around the language of *heimin*, "people," as moral vocabulary. The language of *heimin* and other associated representations of *heimin*, which included the populist figure of Tolstoi himself, became a banner for the movement's ideas. During the war, the long-stigmatized term for low-class commoners, *heimin*, became a widely used new moral vocabulary for the modern subject. The wartime notion of *heimin* departed from our accepted English translation of *heimin* as "commoners," which possesses associations of an uncultured mass. The wartime notion of *heimin*, composed of the characters *hei* (plains, level, or horizon) and *min* (people), served to replace hierarchy, both at home and in the international arena, with a notion of equality (and later "democracy") embodied in a broad expanse of community that extended beyond race, ethnicity, gender, and other modern human identifiers. In short, *hei* in late Meiji came to imply that everyone was in. The modern subject was not to be defined by social status.

Moreover, the term expressed an imagining of the people in Japan without the nation-state. And, while participants considered ethnicity matter-of-factly to be one unavoidable determinant of culture, language, and society, they did not consider people to be biologically divided or hierarchically ordered by their ethnicity. *Heimin shimbun* used the term *heimin* in polemic contrast to the Japanese term *kokumin*, which defined "the people" as subjects of the imperial nation-state. Non-War participants understood "the people" instead to be smaller parts of a larger global entity.

The title of *Heimin shimbun* was similarly used in contrast to Tokutomi Sohō's famous *Kokumin shimbun* (Nation's People's Newspaper), which represented government policies during the war. In 1905, *Chokugen,* which was a successor to *Heimin shimbun,* defined *heimin* as all people outside the so-called cliques or *batsu* of elites who were representatives of the state. The article identified these cliques as being made up of six interlinked groups: the Satsuma-Chōshū clique (*hanbatsu*), the political-party clique (*tōbatsu*), the capitalist-entrepreneurial clique (*zaibatsu*), the scholar-intellectual clique (*gakubatsu*), the clique of religious leaders (*shūbatsu*), and the aristocratic clique (*monbatsu*).[4] These six cliques were conceptualized as belonging to the much larger problem of the state and Western modernity as a whole, while the people were imagined without the state. During the Hibiya riots following the war, when massive crowds destroyed police boxes and other symbols of government authority around Tokyo, a mob of up to five thousand besieged the offices of *Kokumin shimbun,* one of the first targets to be destroyed.[5] For many who had experienced the injustices of the war, *Kokumin shimbun* represented the "society of cliques" (*batsu shakai*) that was in partnership with the state and the larger international system of Western modernity. In contrast, "the people," *heimin,* who were the great majority of the population, stood outside that fold. *Heimin* had become an inclusive term embracing "everyone," except the minority of the Japanese population that belonged to these six interlocking cliques and that represented a particular modernity.

Postcolonial studies have helped to further the notion of the power that the Western imagination held over the individual as national subject in modern Japan. In keeping with this notion, one might say that the imagination of the nation itself was colonized in Japan. Yet *heimin* was the product of an active imaginary practice that was in contestation with the construction of the images of the national subject fashioned after the West. Japanese intellectuals focused on intellectual, cultural, and social ties with Russians to construct an image of a nonstate transnational community of people. During the war, the Non-War Movement formed images of a Japanese-Russian transnational community (*heimin-narod*) as an intellectual practice that denaturalized the idea of International Relations as a defining element of Western modernity.

Very early in the war, *Heimin shimbun* helped establish the idea among its readers that the enemy was not the Russian people but the elites and government that exploited the people. The meaning of the transnational community was graphically represented in a cartoon published by *Heimin shimbun* of Russian and Japanese laborers shaking hands across the sea while military officers of the two countries stand atop them with swords drawn.[6] The image was soon echoed in a cartoon printed in the Russian émigré newspaper in Nagasaki, *Volia,* in 1906. The cartoon, titled "Eternal Sleep" (*Vechnyi son*), portrays a Japanese soldier holding a cannonball looking in sympathy and wonder at a Russian soldier, who looks in shock at the be-headed ghost of French king Louis XVI. In the cartoon, the bearded Japan-ese and Russian men resemble one another, appearing as brotherly compa-triots. The figures of these two commoners stand in contrast to the royal figure of the French king. State-manufactured national uniforms and other national markers are notably absent on the Russian and Japanese figures. While the Japanese man is depicted naked from the waist up, the Russian is drawn wearing a simple peasant blouse.[7]

These images appear to suggest that Marxist ideology influenced the Non-War Movement. However, we can trace the new meaning of *heimin* to the translations of Tolstoian religion in Japan at the turn of the century, which I have treated elsewhere.[8] While I will not discuss this process here at any length, let me say that the nationwide conversions to what was called Tolstoian religion in Japan beginning in the late 1890s were essential to the unfolding of the new meaning of *heimin* during the war. In Tolstoian reli-gious discourse in Japan, "the people" came to possess a universal God-given virtue. The Japanese Russian Orthodox theologian Konishi Masutarō, with whom Tolstoi sought to work in Moscow, first constructed and translated Tolstoian religion in Japan as a modern form of Lao Tzu's philosophy, an ethical system that located a universally shared and knowable virtue in the common people. The notion of divine virtue associated with "the people" here was already inclusive of everyone. It was in this context that the word *heimin* was probably used for the first time without stigma.

In Meiji Japan, the term *shūkyō*, or modern religion, had represented a concept of a modern religious institution translated from Western Chris-tianity that served to unify and empower the nation-state by lending it the credibility of civilization. The meaning of religion itself became coupled with Western modernity in late Meiji Japan and in this way held tremen-dous authority. In response to this meaning of *shūkyō*, Konishi and Tolstoi, in their collaborative project of translating Lao Tzu, altered the notion of "modern religion" to mean virtue possessed by everyone. The dynamic phenomenon of conversion to Tolstoian religion in Japan was based on this transfiguration of knowledge and the resulting new selfhood. To convert oneself to Tolstoian religion at the turn of the century was to participate in the uprooting of some of the major tropes of the civilizational hierarchy of Western modernity as well as the imperial moral order within Japan.

During the war, the face of Lev Tolstoi became a symbolic expression of the Non-War Movement. Many of the same people who had converted to Tolstoian religion would participate in and become the core of the Non-War Movement, and, vice versa, many in the Non-War Movement would be-come converts to Tolstoian religion. It was in this context that Tolstoi became by far the most translated figure in the history of modern Japanese translation practice.

The shift in the meaning of *heimin* during the war was followed by a "sliding of history," helping to further define the widening semiotic community of cooperatist modernity. A noticeable shift in the public moral language had already occurred during this period, given inspiration by the conversion to Tolstoian religion and the forming of the image of a transnational *heimin* antithetical to the given state of nature of international relations. This shift combined with a massive slide in the making of historical narrative. History was narrated into the future, and the present became the backward past. The present as a product of Western human progress and civilization was now perceived as behind and no longer morally justified. History thus "slid" from the narratives of the past justifying the present into a narrated future vision. The "present" was now determined as the key moment in time and space in which participants were to actively create and rectify history for the future. Here, history became akin to a theory of moral knowledge and action in the here and now.

Cooperatist anarchist modernity was expressed during and following the war increasingly in terms of history, of the urgent need to "rectify" or "save" history, or *kiyome tadasu* (cleansing and morally correcting). Japanese intellectuals would appropriate the historicism in Kropotkin's anarchist writings as a coherent expression of the ideas already widely circulating during the war. As anarchist Ishikawa Sanshirō wrote in 1907 to his colleague Kōtoku Shūsui, "I felt like Kropotkin explained and clarified for me the very ideal that has been within me."[9]

The strategic use of Kropotkin's *Mutual Aid* in Japan added evolution, or time, to the transnational notion of *heimin*. According to anarchist historicity, human civilization developed from below without the need for central governance, based on the principle of mutual aid. With this radical overturning of the concept of civilization and progress, the social Darwinism and its application to civilizational progress then dominant among state intellectuals in Japan appeared hopelessly wrong.

The epistemological capacity of cooperatist anarchist modernity would provide for a variety of distinctive modern Japanese intellectual phenomena in the early twentieth century, expressed in multiple ways in the spheres of education, the women's liberation movement, the first national union of students, the Esperanto international language movement, literature, children's art, agricultural cooperatives, and just plain everyday life. It is not surprising then that cooperatist anarchism came to define a concept of *demokurashi* ("democracy") without the state by the early 1920s, symbolized by the commonly used faces of Tolstoi and Kropotkin.[10]

By repeating the narrative of Western modernity as essentially the sole historical meaning and value embedded in the story of the Russo-Japanese War for modern Japan, historians of Japan have often participated in the cultural fold of Western modernity. Along the way, any phenomena that did not fit this logic have been categorized as products of nativist or nationalist counterurges. Behind this tendency has been the cultural construct of East and West as the way to see modern Japan in the wider world. In this intellectual universe, ironically enough, the more we have expanded in recent years our methods of looking at the momentous events of the Russo-Japanese War and the treaty that ended it, the more we have solidified the importance of Western modernity as the sole intellectual foundation for modern Japanese intellectual life. While contributing tremendously to our volume of historical knowledge, this approach has also led us to overlook the phenomenon under exploration, which was neither an expression of the ideology of Western modernity nor a product of nationalism or nativism.

As articulators of a larger public imagination, Arishima and Roka expressed through pilgrimage their attempt to immerse themselves, body and soul, in an alternative historical narrative, a new temporal belonging that transcended the cultural construct of East and West, yellow and white, uncivilized and civilized, colonized and colonizer. That neither Roka nor Arishima had been a member of the Heimin Company, which was responsible for the production of *Heimin shimbun*, all the more indicates the scope of the Hisen legacy. In short, then, the "success" of the antimilitarism that united Russian and Japanese intellectuals on the nonstate and nonorganizational level was largely an expression of the unfolding of this temporal belonging, what I characterize as cooperatist modernity.

Neither the Portsmouth Treaty nor the Nobel Peace Prize, despite their sheer power as symbols of peace for the Western international community at the time, was ever mentioned in the writings of participants in the Non-War Movement. Their absence demonstrates that the peace treaty, and the definition of peace that the treaty represented, lay entirely outside the vision of progress and civilization that cooperatist anarchists imagined. This silence over Portsmouth and the Nobel Peace Prize was significant in molding the development of their modernity and its vision of a world order apart from Western modernity and cultural nationalism in subsequent decades. Here, in its weighty absence, lay the cultural legacy of the treaty for this particular history.

Chapter 7

Political Legacies of the Portsmouth Treaty

Shinji Yokote

The Portsmouth Treaty was signed as the Japanese and Russian leaders realized that they were no longer able to continue the war for their respective reasons: Japan was faced with overextension of its military power, and Russia, with the growing prospect of revolution. As if corresponding to the long, noncommittal cessation of hostilities on the battlefield, the reception of the treaty on either side was generally cool. In Japan, the terms of the treaty caused a chain reaction of incidents starting with a mass protest meeting and the police prohibition of it and culminating in a three-day riot. The government was finally forced to proclaim martial law to suppress the uprising. Likewise, when Sergei Witte, the Russian plenipotentiary at the Portsmouth Conference, returned home from Portsmouth, he found that the people tended to talk about a war of revenge; therefore, he testified, the situation was so volatile that no one could predict how long the new treaty would last.[1] As for the United States, the enthusiasm over the treaty was short-lived, changing to disappointment and then to irritation after Theodore Roosevelt left office. Most Americans could not understand what was going on in Japan and China as Japan consolidated its position on the Asian continent.

Despite all these discouraging signs, however, for better or worse the treaty survived the vicissitudes of the time. Some may claim that the treaty expired when the Russian Revolution broke out and the Bolsheviks assumed power in 1917. Others may assert that the Siberian Intervention by the external powers including Japan, beginning in 1918, terminated the effectiveness of the treaty. Certainly, each side interfered in the internal affairs of the other side either by revolutionary propaganda or by military means during these years. However, no one would deny that Japan and Russia's successor, the Soviet Union, upon restoring diplomatic relations in

1925, regarded the Portsmouth Treaty as having continuing value and agreed that it "shall remain in full force" (Article II of the convention normalizing relations). As a result, even in the latter half of the 1930s, when Japan and the USSR viewed each other as incompatible enemies, both governments treated the Portsmouth agreement as the fundamental contract binding their relations at least in the diplomatic arena.[2]

These developments raise several interrelated questions: Why did the treaty survive so many serious challenges and remain valid for so long? To what extent did the U.S. and British governments contribute to the longevity of this treaty? What about the role of the Soviet Union? Was its role as insignificant as Soviet scholars have repeatedly maintained? What were the differences between the original Portsmouth Treaty and the second one included in the 1925 convention? What replaced the Portsmouth Treaty in the end?

I have to admit in advance that it is beyond the scope of this paper to give my interpretive replies to all these questions. My purpose here is just to touch on the subtle points indicating how the powers interacted within the framework of the Portsmouth Treaty and to shed some light on the linkage among the incidents that took place from 1905 to 1945.

International Circumstances

Before going into the issues concerning the treaty itself, I will discuss briefly the problem of the international circumstances related to the treaty. I would like to limit my argument to three points. The first point concerns the vitality of the political regimes of the victim nations, Korea and China. It is clear that these regimes suffered grave damage by sticking to a policy of passive neutrality while the armies of the two neighboring countries fought in their territories. In view of their failures before the outbreak of the war, the newly added damage meant further loss of their prestige and heightened alienation from their peoples. And these outcomes, in turn, must have strengthened the Western governments' contemptuous attitudes toward both regimes. At this crucial moment, the leaders of China and Korea had to face a new challenge: Japanese encroachment on their sovereignty. In contrast to its neighbors, Japan was enjoying the best of seasons, applauded by people all over the world; in the several months immediately after the Portsmouth Conference, the Japanese regime looked attractive even in the eyes of the peoples of Korea and China.[3]

This difference in position could not but have some influence on the negotiations between the Japanese and Korean governments in November

1905 and between the Japanese and Chinese governments from November to December of that year. In the first case, the Korean government was forced to accept protectorate status under Japan, thereby losing its right to conduct its own diplomatic relations, the first step leading to the Japanese annexation of Korea in 1910. In the second case, the Chinese government gave its consent to the results of the Portsmouth Treaty pertaining to Chinese sovereignty, such as the transfer of rights and privileges from Russia to Japan.

Moreover, in the negotiations in Beijing, the Japanese plenipotentiary, Komura Jutarō, forced his Chinese counterpart to accept additional Japanese demands through a supplementary agreement and a secret protocol: Japan gained the right to improve the railway line connecting Andong and Mukden, and China pledged not to construct any line in the neighborhood of or parallel to the main railway that Japan had newly obtained under the Treaty of Portsmouth. With these supplementary concessions, Japan gained the legal ground for consolidating its continental foothold, as Komura had calculated during the negotiations at Portsmouth.

However, once the Chinese regime endured the severe ordeal of these impositions, it was placed in a considerably improved situation. The Western governments gradually turned their critical, even accusatory, glances toward the Japanese government. In parallel with the geopolitical changes, they began to sympathize with the Chinese. Needless to say, a stereotyped view of China as an incompetent, unreliable nation continued to haunt the Western powers, precluding the possibility of the formation of a new combination of powers that would include China. Nevertheless, the shift in atmosphere gave the Chinese regime a fresh opportunity to revitalize itself. In this situation, the easiest way for the Chinese leaders to restore their lost authority was to adopt a tough stance against the governments of Japan and Russia in diplomatic negotiations.

The second point is a related one. It has to do with the Korean and Chinese patriotic or nationalist movements. One could argue that around 1900 such movements emerged on the basis of broad popular support in those countries and that, at the time of the Portsmouth Treaty, very few people realized that these movements would grow to be serious enemies of the treaty in the future. The governments of Japan and Russia were gradually forced to recognize this fact. However, it is also true that, at this juncture, even the informed leaders of the United States and Great Britain were of the opinion that the Russo-Japanese conflict was partly caused by the incompetence of the Korean and Chinese governments; therefore, they thought they should support the Japanese government to bring about a lasting peace, even if it meant sacrificing the noncombatant nations. It is easy to point out today that they made a grave mistake by not distinguishing between the competence of the political regimes and the capabilities of the nations.

Ironically, the victory of Japan over Russia and the subsequent Japanese expansion on the Asian continent sent a strong message to the Chinese and Korean people that they had no other choice but to modernize their political regimes or re-create them on the model of the Western countries. Yet, in the initial years after the Portsmouth Treaty, the people expressed their patriotism and nationalism in rights recovery campaigns, small-scale resistance movements, and terrorist acts.

During this period, a symbolic incident took place at Harbin in October 1909; An Chung-gun, a Korean patriot, assassinated Itō Hirobumi, Japan's first resident-general of Korea and, at the same time, the most serious critic of Japan's expansion into Manchuria. It is well known that he strongly criticized Kodama Gentarō, the chief of the General Staff, at the interministerial meeting held on the Manchurian issue in May 1906. Itō remarked in front of Japan's top leaders that Manchuria "is no more and no less than one part of China's territory. We [the Japanese] have no right to speak of exercising sovereignty" there. Though he could not stop Japan's expansionist policy, he kept exerting a moderating influence on its policy until his death.[4]

The third point is the change in the Northeast Asian international system. Judging from the interactions of the powers after the Russo-Japanese War and the peace settlement, the Northeast Asian regional system was no longer a mere extension of European politics but had acquired a more independent status. In other words, it was the Russo-Japanese War that qualitatively separated East Asian regional politics from European tutelage; World War I promoted this tendency, which had manifested itself with the Russo-Japanese War and the Treaty of Portsmouth.

This structural change was caused by complex factors. First, the growing tensions that surfaced in Europe coincidentally with the war and the peace forced the Western powers to divert their energies more and more to their homelands. Second, Japan, with its victory over Russia, demonstrated how costly a Far Eastern war could be to extraregional states. Actually, no nation except Great Britain and the United States had a naval capability equal to that of the Japanese fleet in this region. Third, the United States entered regional politics in a new way. The U.S. government, while not prepared to wage conflict with the predominant powers, was determined to increase its economic and political engagement in China under the banner of the Open Door policy. This U.S. initiative attracted the attention of the Chinese government, which was looking for a better partner to help defend its territorial integrity against Japan and Russia.

These factors combined to end the European-dominated politics of this region and promote the collapse of the old order. The shifting balance of power enabled a relatively weak Japan to prepare the ground for aggrandizing its sphere of influence by both diplomatic and military means. This approach to foreign policy was what the Japanese leaders had learned from the "civilized" nations in the previous century. It was under these international circumstances that the Portsmouth Treaty took effect. The provisions of the treaty laid the foundation for power relations rather than establishing the rules of the game that were to regulate the participants' behavior. Then, what kind of foundation was laid by the treaty?

The Terms of the Portsmouth Treaty

As the Portsmouth Treaty was a peace settlement, most terms were of a zero-sum character. Article IX regarding the southern part of Sakhalin was a typical example. Article XI regarding fishing rights along the coast of Russian possessions in the Seas of Japan, Okhotsk, and Bering was another. These terms were clearly stipulated as if to underline which was the victor nation. Yet there were other kinds of terms stipulated so ambiguously as to puzzle the reader. Typical was Article II stipulating the arrangements for Korea. The first paragraph of this article obliged Russia to recognize that "Japan has predominant political, military, and economic interests in Korea" and to agree "not to interfere or place obstacles in the way of any measure of direction, protection, and supervision" that Japan might adopt.

Evidently, both parties avoided definitive words such as "the exclusive right to control over Korea" or "a protectorate over Korea." Though it is not clear whether this was a result of Russian resistance or was simply necessitated by the fact that Russia had possessed no clear rights in Korea before the treaty, the ambiguity gave Russia room to resist Japanese attempts to terminate Korean diplomatic independence through the above-mentioned agreement. The resistance of the Russian government was serious, as was shown by its efforts to involve the United States and Great Britain, though to no avail. The governments of those two countries had already decided to support Japan on this point. The Russian government gave up on these efforts only in July 1906, after a new foreign minister, Aleksandr Izvol'skii, had taken office.[5]

Another example of ambiguity lay in Article VI concerning the transfer of rights related to the railway. This article gave the following obscure outlines of what Russia had to transfer to Japan: Russia obligated itself to yield to Japan, without compensation and with the consent of China, "the Chanchun (Kwan-Chien-Tsi) [Changchun] and Port Arthur Railroad and all its branches, with all the rights, privileges, and property thereunto belonging within this region, as well as all the coal mines in said region belonging to this railroad or being operated for its benefit." Evidently, the Russians cared little about what they had to yield in southern Manchuria except the main railway, and the Japanese desired to gain as much as possible by obscuring the contours of the transferred rights and privileges. As a result, the article did not specify the names of the railway branches, the rights, the privileges, and so on.

There were additional ambiguous terms in the treaty: Articles III and IV concerning Manchuria and the application of the principle of the Open Door to this area. These articles were intertwined. First, with regard to Manchuria, the first and second paragraphs of Article III stipulated that Russia and Japan mutually engage, after the evacuation of their armies, "to entirely and completely restore to the exclusive administration of China" all parts of Manchuria save the leasehold on the Liaodong Peninsula. Though not containing the words "China's sovereignty," this stipulation seemed to state that both parties accepted China's demand for the recognition of its sovereignty over Manchuria. Second, as for the principle of the Open Door, Article IV contained a stipulation that "Russia and Japan mutually pledge themselves not to place any obstacles in the way of general measures which apply equally to all nations and which China might adopt for the development of commerce and industry in Manchuria." Again, this clause seemed to imply that the parties agreed on the application of the principle of equal opportunity to Manchuria, without using those words.

There must have been some reason why the parties did not specify their intentions. The third paragraph of Article II provides a clue on this point. It reads: "The Imperial Government of Russia declares that it has no territorial advantages or preferential or exclusive concession in Manchuria of such a nature as to impair the sovereignty of China or which are incompatible with the principle of equal opportunity." For what was this unilateral declaration intended? Japan's official interpretation is suggested in *Komura gaikō shi* (Diplomatic History of Komura), a separate volume of the Japanese diplomatic records. According to *Komura gaikō shi,* this paragraph was to make clear the relation between the principle of the Open Door and the rights and privileges that Russia had enjoyed through the Chinese Eastern Railway Company (CER).

In fact, Japan's plenipotentiary, Komura, taking the issue of Russia's management of Harbin (site of the CER's headquarters) as one example related to this point, posed to the Russian plenipotentiary, Witte: "If this kind of work is conducted in one part of Manchuria, it can be conducted in all areas of Manchuria." Komura's aim was not the cancellation of such rights and privileges, but confirmation of Russia's official view that it regarded such concessions as not contradictory to what Russia proclaimed as the principle of the Open Door or the principle of equal opportunity. The above-cited paragraph from Article II was what Witte declared in his response to this question.[6]

His reply must have greatly satisfied Komura, because the logical conclusion to be drawn from this paragraph was that the rights and privileges that Russia had hitherto held under the name of the CER were not of such "a nature as to impair the sovereignty of China," nor were they "incompatible with the principle of equal opportunity." And, as a corollary, the Russian government declared by this paragraph that it regarded what it would hand over to Japan under Article VI as of the same character: namely, the rights and privileges related to the railway were not contradictory to what Russia had proclaimed as the principle of equal opportunity. The paragraph was, therefore, to confirm the common front of Japan and Russia against the anticipated claimants for application of equal opportunity to the railway and other matters.

Tsunoda Jun, supporting this interpretation in principle, went on to write that the paragraph represented Komura's willingness to draw a line around Japan's sphere of interests and ensure its right to administer the southern part of Manchuria in place of Russia. Tsunoda introduced a letter sent by Prime Minister Katsura Tarō to Kodama in support of this interpretation. Katsura wrote in this letter: "As to the point that Russia managed Harbin with zeal under the name of the railway company, it is beneficial to us to abstain from examining the details . . . because we also hope to conduct a similar management in several places in Manchuria."[7] Evidently, the Japanese leaders fully understood the terms of the treaty.

In short, the terms of the Portsmouth Treaty, though ambiguously formulated, clearly expressed the intentions of the negotiators by evading definite words such as "China's sovereignty over Manchuria" or "the principle of the Open Door." Since most subjects of the bargaining were in Korea and Manchuria, the negotiators had to formulate the terms while keeping in mind the serious concerns of the third parties. But, from my point of view, what is more important is that Komura and Witte made a tacit deal and built it into the treaty: Russia and Japan acknowledged that, with regard to Manchurian affairs, they had common interests to protect and they had to maintain a cooperative relationship in order to repel the coming challenge by China or other powers.

Thus, the treaty, on the one hand, planted seeds for friction by transferring some of the possessions of Russia to Japan but, on the other hand, laid the foundation for their de facto alignment against third powers. In other words, both antagonistic and collaborative relations had their origins in the Portsmouth Treaty. Which kind of relations would come to the fore depended on the intentions of the two parties as well as international circumstances. How did these factors combine?

Intentions to Preserve and Revive the Portsmouth Treaty

First of all, it should be noted that historians of Japan and Russia have presented completely opposite views on the relations between the two countries in the period from the Portsmouth Treaty to the Russian Revolution. Yoshimura Michio, a well-known specialist in this area, for example, has written:

The near decade from 1907 to 1916 was the exceptional period in Japanese diplomatic history. During this period rapprochement between Japan and Russia took place—the first and last time in Japan's modern history. This was because the two countries found common interests in their relations with China. The delimitation of the spheres of interest in both Manchuria and the Mongolian area was indispensable to both governments, faced with the tasks of managing postwar affairs. In short, Japan's policy carried a consistently contradictory character, veiling its vigilant attitudes toward Russia while pursuing rapprochement with it.[8]

In contrast, Leonid Kutakov, also a well-known specialist in this field, has underlined the negative side of the history:

On the basis of the Portsmouth Treaty between Russia and Japan, almost ten agreements were signed. In all these agreements on various topics . . . , in Japan's postwar policy toward Russia, a clearly expressed general tendency was observed: aggrandizing its gains by making use of the conditions acquired through the Portsmouth Treaty. The more obvious the predominance of its military power became, the more rudely did the Japanese representatives act. Immersed in the problems of the Middle and Near East areas, the tsarist system was not in a position to take measures to strengthen its defense capabilities in its Far Eastern area. It was forced to give up not only its imperialistic interests in China and Mongolia, but its national interests in the Far East.[9]

Though to a lesser degree, a similar kind of disagreement is observable in studies concerning relations between the two countries during the Soviet period. The works of Sakai Tetsuya and V. P. Safronov clearly illustrate this point. Again, whereas the Japanese historian emphasizes the collaborative aspects of the relationship,[10] the Russian expert pays attention exclusively to the contentious aspects.[11] It will be sufficient to quote one paragraph of Safronov's work to grasp this point:

In the period 1925–1927, Tokyo tried to reach an understanding with Moscow on the division of spheres of interest and countermeasures against the revolutionary process in China. A sphere of interest in China was not necessary for Moscow. To the contrary, it strongly rejected it in order to inflame the revolutionary movement of the Chinese people. For them [the people in Moscow], support for the revolution was a hundred times more important.[12]

These salient differences of interpretation stem mainly from the Cold War situation or its reverberations, but to some extent they arise from the two-faced nature of the treaty that I pointed out earlier. In any event, given this state of affairs in the historiography, it would be better to limit the argument to a few crucial periods when either Japan or Russia could change or hoped to change their relationship. At such times, the intentions of those who happened to have considerable influence on foreign policy were brought to light. Here I will take up two sets of years for this purpose: 1908–9 and 1924–25.

In the case of 1908–9, the Russo-Japanese conventions of 1907 would be a good starting point for the discussion. By the secret convention attached to the treaties they concluded, Japan and Russia defined Korea and southern Manchuria as Japan's sphere and Outer Mongolia and northern Manchuria as Russia's sphere. Certainly the conventions, public and secret, presented a good opportunity to calm the bitter feelings that had lingered in both countries since the war. Nevertheless, it was inappropriate to assume that, with these treaties, the regional configuration was heading in the direction of two camps, with China and the United States on one side and Japan and Russia on the other. On the contrary, the situation was extremely fluid. This is well illustrated by the incidents that took place after the Russian government announced in early 1908 that it would establish municipal administrations in Harbin and other cities in the CER zone to cope with anomalous social conditions.

This announcement triggered China's firm protest that the contemplated step would violate China's sovereignty over Manchuria. Then the U.S. consul in Harbin followed this protest by asserting that neither the 1896 agreement between the CER and China nor the Portsmouth Treaty entitled Russia to introduce municipal authorities in the railway zone. The American consul's efforts to enlist the other powers in this campaign transformed this incident into an international dispute.

Yet the powers reacted in different ways. Whereas the governments of Germany and Austria supported the American consul, the Japanese and British governments hesitated to express their opinions. The Japanese could not decide which was better for their national interests: a wait-and-see position in order not to harm U.S.-Japanese relations or active support of the Russians to protect the foundation of their present and future collaboration. The Japanese ambassador to the United States, Takahira Kogorō, recommended the first course of action, but Foreign Minister Hayashi Tadasu took a different view. According to him, there was no problem with the Russian plan since the CER had the right to exercise police authority, and this "is not contradictory with Article III of the peace treaty." Therefore, Hayashi continued, Takahira should express the Japanese government's pro-Russian position to the U.S. government "in due time."[13] Japan's foreign minister placed the first priority on protecting the foundation of the Portsmouth Treaty.

As for the British government, Michael Hunt explains that "the Foreign Office saw little reason to offend Russia in Manchuria to the detriment of the peaceful settlement of the other issues" in areas where Great Britain had far greater interests. In addition, at the end of the previous century, Great Britain had acknowledged the northern part of Manchuria as a Russian sphere.[14]

Under these circumstances, the Russian government decided to introduce the municipal administrations in April 1908, sweeping aside the protests. But it did not hold an intransigent attitude for long. As early as October, a Russian deputy consul in Harbin completed a report recommending that Russia yield to China on this issue and rearrange the municipal administrations in a more conciliatory form. In the end, the Russian government followed this recommendation. In May 1909 it concluded with the Chinese government a new interim agreement that acknowledged Chinese sovereignty over the railway zone and stipulated the establishment of a Russo-Chinese joint organ to supervise municipal authorities in the zone.[15]

Neither the U.S. government nor the Japanese government had expected this outcome. From the Japanese point of view, the new agreement represented an epoch-making incident, as was argued by a Japanese specialist in the following way:

The characteristic features of this [interim] agreement were the adoption of the principle of equal opportunity and the acceptance of the Chinese right to control the municipal administrations in the areas belonging to the CER. This agreement contained concepts totally different from those in the treaty [*sic,* contract] providing for the establishment of the CER and raised questions about the significance of the area belonging to the CER and the administrations.[16]

Evidently this commentator was aware that Russia's volte-face of May 1909 had the potential to threaten the basis of Japan's administrative authority in southern Manchuria.

The U.S. government's position was different in character. It regarded the issue as a matter of principle: a violation of the treaty-port arrangement that Harbin was alleged to have been granted by China. In order to protect their putative treaty rights, the Americans brought pressure to bear on the Chinese government to reformulate the terms of the May 1909 agreement.[17] As a result, that agreement was suspended. The reaction of the Russian government was simple: while taking advantage of the differences among the positions of the Western governments, it put into effect its original municipal-administration plan as an expedient. Thus the American reaction created a situation that relieved not only the Russian but also the Japanese government.

According to Russian diplomatic documents quoted by S. S. Grigortsevich, the Japanese ambassador to St. Petersburg, Motono Ichirō, told Izvol'skii: "In Japan people don't understand why Russia, for example in the issue of Harbin, takes a conciliatory position toward China as well as toward the foreign powers, instead of trusting Japan and boldly defending the rights belonging to the CER by resorting to the treaty of 1896."[18] These words reflected Motono's position well.

Thus, the Harbin municipal incident reveals a characteristic feature of Russo-Japanese relations in this period: there was no entrenched policy toward Japan in the Russian government and, therefore, no regional political structure to constrain the behavior of each power. The Japanese diplomats watched Russia's handling of the problem with serious concern. For them, Russia's position in this dispute was insufficiently imperialistic for it to be a good partner. This situation poses an interesting counterfactual question: if the U.S. government had responded to the Russian concession more flexibly, would Russia's small step toward conciliation with China have served as a precedent for breaking down the wall of rights and privileges that Russia and Japan had been building around Manchuria? In any event, in this case, there was no part for the Japanese government to play in order to preserve that wall.

This fluid situation continued until November 1909 when Philander C. Knox, the U.S. secretary of state, disclosed his proposal for the neutralization of foreign railways in Manchuria. Knox's bold step, which put an end to Russia's vacillation between pro-American and pro-Japanese orientations, led to a Russo-Japanese joint veto.[19] The secret convention of July 1910 between Japan and Russia was the embodiment of their reply.[20] At least for the Japanese, by this time the collaborative aspect of the Portsmouth Treaty had overwhelmed the zero-sum aspect, and it would continue to do so until 1914.

World War I and the Russian Revolution provided Japan with a golden opportunity to expand its sphere of influence in China (the Twenty-One Demands of 1915) and in Russia (the Siberian Intervention of 1918–22). However, unexpected developments led to two difficulties for Japan: the deterioration of the U.S.-Japanese relationship and the disappearance of the Russian empire (with the establishment of the provisional government after the Russian Revolution). These two developments surfaced in the second set of years, 1924–25. Why and how did Japan and Russia revive the Portsmouth Treaty at this time? Though this question is the most important issue for this paper, it is still difficult to give a meaningful explanation of Soviet intentions. Therefore, in the case of 1924–25, I would like to confine my argument to an examination of intentions on the Japanese side.

Here, George Lensen's work presents a good starting point. According to Lensen, the following three factors pushed Japanese diplomats to take a seat at the negotiations held in Dairen from 1921 to 1922. First, Japan desired to secure economic opportunities through friendly relations with the USSR. In Lensen's words, the Japanese leaders thought: "If Japan failed to deal with the Soviets before they reestablished their strength she might find American and British nationals in commanding economic positions." Second, Japanese leaders held a fear of international isolation. They felt the rising antagonism and suspicion in Europe and the United States toward Japan. They thought these negative views were caused by Japan's prolonged intervention in Siberia. Third, Japanese leaders were concerned about Chinese efforts to acquire the CER as well as gain full control of the Sungari and Amur rivers.[21]

Lensen did not go on to examine the relationship among these factors. Yet, one can deduce from his discussion that he no doubt came to the conclusion that the Japanese government had attached greater weight to the first two factors than to the third; he emphasized that the Japanese demands centered on fisheries, oil concessions in North Sakhalin, trade, and the like. For example, in analyzing the meeting between Gotō Shimpei, former foreign minister and then mayor of Tokyo, and Adolf Ioffe, a famous Soviet diplomat, Lensen argued that Gotō advocated "renewed Russo-Japanese collaboration" and stressed that Japan's recognition would surely open great economic opportunities for the Japanese nation and at the same time help to forestall Russo-American and Russo-Chinese relations, "either of which might leave Japan dangerously isolated."[22]

Characteristically, in this analysis, Lensen, while developing his argument on Japan's interest in economic cooperation and its fear of international isolation, totally ignored the change in Japan's treatment of China—namely, whereas in the first talks in Dairen the Japanese Foreign Ministry was concerned about Chinese anti-Soviet activities, in the case of the Gotō-Ioffe talks, Gotō feared the possible emergence of cooperative relations between China and Russia. Is this reversal in Japan's treatment of China meaningless? My answer is no, because, first of all, new materials that were not used by Lensen give us more detailed explanations of the intentions of the Japanese representatives at the Dairen meeting; and, second, these explanations provide a clue as to the question of the role of the Portsmouth Treaty in the negotiations.

On the first point, note that Lensen described the Japanese intentions based on *Nis-So kōshō shi* (The History of Japanese-Soviet Diplomatic Negotiations), written by Tanaka Bun'ichirō with materials from the Japanese Foreign Ministry. This book was first published in 1942 for the use of Japanese diplomats. There is one more document, titled *Shiberiya shuppei yori Nichi-Ro kokkō kaifuku ni itaru made no keii* (The Complete Story from the Siberian Intervention to the Restoration of Japanese-Soviet Relations). This document was prepared by the first section of the Western (Ōbei) Department in July 1928 and apparently circulated in the Japanese Foreign Ministry (hereafter "the document of 1928").

This document of 1928 explained the Japanese intentions as follows. First, the "Bolshevik" government had improved its international position through interim trade agreements with Great Britain and Germany. Second, "criticism of our intervention in Siberia was gradually growing in foreign countries, especially in the United States." Third, domestic demands for the withdrawal of Japanese troops along with desires for the resumption of trade with the USSR had strengthened. Then, "in addition to these, the attitude of the Chinese toward Russia was remarkably assertive, and they put pressure on the Russian side with regard to the Chinese Eastern Railway and navigation issues in the Sungari and Amur rivers. If we neglected the Chinese desires, sooner or later the brunt of their avarice would be borne by the imperial [Japanese] special rights in Manchuria and Mongolia. Thus, the emerging situation was such that it appeared better to restrain China by establishing immediately an alignment with the de facto government in the Russian Far East."[23] Evidently, the above description, disclosing clearly what the Japanese government thought in the middle of 1921, indicates that the Chinese factor was no less vital than the other two factors in pushing the Japanese toward normalization talks with the Bolshevik government.

This document also suggests that the Japanese government considered working with Russia against China—a familiar pattern within the framework of the Portsmouth Treaty—to be an approach that could still be useful for Japan. Further, these descriptions mean that there were two calculations within the Japanese government from the start. In the first and better scenario, Japan, by reestablishing relations with Russia, would gain economic interests prior to other governments. In this case, the weaker Russia was better for Japan. In the second scenario, Japan needed a stronger but still reliable Russia as a partner to protect their common interests in Manchuria against the Chinese patriotic and nationalist movements and probably against U.S. antagonism.

Needless to say, Russia made a rapid recovery in both domestic and international spheres after 1921, pressing the Japanese government to consider the second scenario. The Japanese leaders, typified by Gotō, were increasingly concerned about the possibility that Russia might improve its relations with both China and the United States. In other words, as time went by, the framework of the Portsmouth Treaty surfaced in their minds. It should be noted here that the Japanese side referred to the Portsmouth Treaty first in the talks between Gotō and Ioffe in March 1923. And the Japanese plenipotentiary never forgot to assert that the acceptance of the Portsmouth Treaty on the Soviet side was essential for the conclusion of agreements thereafter.[24]

Thus, in terms of the Portsmouth framework, a revival of Russian imperialism was necessary and beneficial for the Japanese government. If Soviet Russia, in its revolutionary enthusiasm, had given up the CER in Manchuria and had decided to withdraw from its acquired position in Outer Mongolia, the USSR would have been not just of no use to Japan but an incompatibly dangerous enemy. On the contrary, if the Soviets' representative in Beijing had adamantly defended the USSR's rights and privileges in China, advocating the legitimacy of its position on these issues, the USSR would be an appropriate partner in the eyes of the Japanese government. In fact, as S. T. Leong and Bruce Elleman have shown, the Soviet Union revealed the latter face in its negotiations with the Chinese and Manchurian governments.[25]

As a matter of course, the Japanese diplomats and military officers followed the Sino-Soviet negotiations with the utmost care. In August and November 1923, for example, Japanese diplomats prepared reports on the issue of the transfer of the landholdings of the CER, which Chang Tso-lin, the Manchurian warlord, had raised by making forcible attempts to abolish that part of the concession and gain control of those enormous holdings. It goes without saying that in this dispute the Japanese observers sympathized with the Soviet-controlled administration of the CER, criticizing the Manchurian activities.[26]

Faced with the conclusion of a Sino-Soviet treaty in May 1924, Yoshizawa Kenkichi, who had long followed the negotiations as minister in Beijing, stayed far calmer than Foreign Minister Matsui Keishirō. Demurring from the latter's instructions, he replied as follows:

I think that, as to the influence of the Russo-Chinese establishment [sic] on south-ern Manchuria and our policy line for coping with them, careful investigation is re-quired, and we need to see how the ensuing Russo-Chinese conference on the de-tails of the treaty terms will develop. For the present, what we should consider is how to secure our interests with regard to the CER. On this point, I certainly re-ceived your instruction No. 129; yet, in the case of our claims and the problems con-cerning the linkage with the South Manchuria Railway, I don't think it [the estab-lishment] would endanger our actual interests, even if we don't make any immediate claims to both Russia and China. Rather, in view of the very delicate sit-uation, this step may have harmful effects on the feelings of both. I think the latter danger is not improbable.[27]

Yoshizawa's reply indicates that he was reluctant to follow Matsui's hasty instructions. Probably, Yoshizawa, a seasoned diplomat, thought that the Japanese government (specifically the foreign minister) should distinguish between the Soviet promise to return the CER and the actual return, which was stipulated as depending on future agreement on the amount of re-demption and so on.

Yoshizawa had at this time already been appointed ambassador plenipo-tentiary in the negotiations with Lev Karakhan, the Soviet ambassador to China. No doubt, the Japanese government realized that the Sino-Soviet ne-gotiations were closely connected with the Japan-USSR negotiations. A telegram sent by the Japanese consul general in Mukden to the foreign min-ister on July 25 disclosed the Japanese understanding that Karakhan in-tended to maintain nothing but the railway itself and regarded local nego-tiations with Mukden as the most appropriate way to reach an agreement.[28]

Keeping in mind these negotiations between China (Beijing and Muk-den) and the USSR, the Japanese government formulated its position in its negotiations with the USSR. For the Japanese, the minimum condition for the new treaty was to include an article providing for the revival of the Portsmouth Treaty in order to create a common stance on special rights in Manchuria. The document of 1928 described the Japanese position around this time as follows:

As for the old treaties, in view of the fact that not only the abolition but even the amendment of the Portsmouth Treaty will cause public protest and have grave con-sequences, we regard this [the revival of the treaty] as vital. Consequently, we de-mand the continuance of the whole [Portsmouth] treaty.

It is well known that Karakhan resisted on this point. When he signed the Basic Convention with Japan in Beijing in January 1925, he issued a declaration stating that "the recognition by his Government of the validity of the Treaty of Portsmouth of September 5, 1905, does not in any way signify that the Government of the Union shares with the former Tsarist Government the political responsibility for the conclusion of the said Treaty."[29]

Karakhan's declaration has been reiterated since then in Soviet diplomatic dictionaries. However, according to Japanese materials, the Japanese side accepted the declaration as being intended for domestic consumption in the Soviet Union. For example, *Nis-So kōshō shi* depicted the negotiations in the following way:

Minister Yoshizawa stated on 8 November that, if the Russian side intended to issue this declaration in order to explain it to its own people, the Japanese side would not continue its objection. If it were to be made in such a way as to decrease the effect of the treaty [even] in the smallest, Japan could not accept this demand. The Japanese side proposed the amendment [of the declaration], which the other side accepted.[30]

In light of developments since the Dairen conference, there is no doubt that heated debates took place on this declaration issue. In any case, the Japanese side appreciated that, however grudgingly or ostensibly grudgingly, the USSR accepted Article II stipulating the revival of the Portsmouth Treaty. Yoshizawa did not comment on this point, but he must have thought that, since the Soviets had the same kind of special rights in northern Manchuria and Outer Mongolia as Japan did in southern Manchuria, the USSR realized it needed Japan's cooperation to protect those rights, whatever revolutionary statements it might issue for public relations purposes. From the Japanese point of view, Japan and the USSR now shared a common stance for coping with the U.S.-supported patriotism and nationalism of the Chinese.

Concluding Remarks

It is often pointed out that one of the sources of the well-known Russo-Japanese territorial dispute since 1945 was the Portsmouth Treaty: as Japan had gained the southern part of Sakhalin under that treaty, the USSR was entitled to retake southern Sakhalin and gain the Kuril Islands as a result of World War II. Stalin first articulated this kind of argument on September 2, 1945. In his view, the Soviet Union had waged war against Japan in 1945 to wipe out the humiliating memory of the war that had taken place forty years earlier.[31] It was convenient for him that Japan had sent its Kwantung Army into the rest of Manchuria in 1931 and the USSR had sold the CER to

Manchukuo in 1935. There had been nothing reminiscent of the Portsmouth Treaty by the end of World War II. (The USSR had built special relations with Outer Mongolia by then, but this fact had nothing to do with the Portsmouth Treaty.) Thus, the memory of the 1905 defeat was associated with the victory of the new war and the territorial changes that resulted from it. No doubt, Stalin's argument represents one of the political legacies of the Portsmouth Treaty.

However, Stalin's speech, to say the least, ignored one salient point: the collaborative relationship between Japan and Russia within the framework of the Portsmouth Treaty. Even in the Soviet period, thanks to Japan's tacit understanding, the Soviet army could easily rout the Chinese army under Chang Hsueh-liang when he tried to take over the CER in 1929, though the Soviet Union never expressed gratitude.

This Russo-Japanese connection helps us to put the regional politics in historical perspective. In fact, the Portsmouth Treaty opened a new era in Northeast Asian regional politics. It seems to me that the subsequent history of relations among Japan, Russia, China, and the United States until 1945 still remains to be explored. The lessons of the power relations in that period, full of conflicting views, rivalries, and strategic alignments, would be instructive, especially in the post–Cold War environment, where the four powers interact more independently than in the ideologically divided world of the Cold War.

III

Contemporary Implications

Chapter 8

Riding Rough

Portsmouth, Regionalism, and the Birth of Anti-Americanism in Northeast Asia

David Wolff

The Japanese delegates wept when they read their new instructions. But Ko-
mura dutifully obeyed, accepting half of Sakhalin and forgoing any indemnity.
So it was peace after all, albeit a peace that left no one happy but Witte. When
the Governor of New Hampshire threw a grand farewell party celebrating the
Treaty of Portsmouth, the Japanese stayed in their quarters, packing their bags.
　—WALTER MCDOUGALL, *Let the Sea Make a Noise* (New York: Avon, 1993), 455

During the Russo-Japanese War, the sympathy of the United States Government and public opinion were unreservedly on the side of Japan. Besides extending diplomatic and financial assistance, President Roosevelt took the initiative in assuming the role of peacemaker and mediator. The conclusion of the
Portsmouth Treaty owes much to the great prestige enjoyed by the American
President.
　The subsequent emergence of Japan as a major power, however, aroused
anxiety among the American public. With sharpening rivalry between Japan
and the United States in various spheres, relations between the two countries
quickly began to deteriorate.
　—MORINOSUKE KAJIMA, *The Emergence of Japan as a World Power, 1895–1925*
　　(Rutland, Vt.: Tuttle, 1968), 180[1]

Without ever setting foot in Portsmouth, U.S. president Theodore
Roosevelt obtained decisive influence over the peace conference proceed-
ings. In fact, the first study to make use of the presidential papers argued:
"The last four sessions [out of twelve] may be described almost as a new

conference in which President Roosevelt had become, though not actually present, a dictator."[2] There can be little doubt that his key interventions were essential to the conclusion of peace in the span of a few short weeks in August–September 1905. The first of many U.S. presidents to garner a Nobel Prize, Roosevelt certainly earned his. At the same time, active American participation in the peace process meant that those who were dissatisfied with the terms of the peace, at least a sizable minority—if not a majority— in every country in Northeast Asia, would not remember Portsmouth to America's credit. As the two epigraphs indicate, Japanese gratitude for the peace Roosevelt brokered is often portrayed as preceding the later deterioration in relations, but in fact both took place simultaneously at Portsmouth. In this sense, 1905 signaled the beginning of a century of anti-Americanism in the region, one of the central factors driving a rapid expansion in nationalist politics on the international stage.

Of course, no country can please everyone all the time, especially once that country becomes powerful. The last hundred years have seen U.S. power increase steadily, provoking discontent in many quarters. At the same time, since World War II, America's relative power (percentage of world industrial production) has declined, suggesting that resistance is not futile, and some kind of near-term financial weakening of the U.S. economy is not completely implausible.[3] Pew international opinion surveys, released in June 2005, indicate both the breadth and depth of contemporary anti-Americanism as the result of a wide range of negative perceptions.[4] Even more recently, in a survey conducted to mark the sixtieth anniversary of the end of World War II, Kyodo News and the Associated Press found that 52 percent of Japanese surveyed distrusted the United States.

Although it is quite clear that the issue of anti-Americanism is an important one in today's world, it is less clear how hundred-year-old popular, elite, and historiographic arguments are transmitted to the present. Recent and ongoing controversies in Sino-Japanese and Korean-Japanese relations make it clear that World War II continues to play a key role in bilateral perceptions as well as in generating nationalist emotions in Northeast Asia. Therefore, in the first part of this paper I would like to focus on the linkages between the Russo-Japanese War and World War II in order to illustrate the range of ties. By transitive principles, if the 1904–5 war influenced World War II, and World War II has influenced today's world, it seems logical that the Russo-Japanese War has had an impact on the present. The second part of the paper will present the case for Northeast Asian anti-Americanism as a result of the Russo-Japanese War and the Portsmouth Treaty. Should a regional history ever be written, this perspective would serve to unite Chinese, Japanese, Korean, and Russian perspectives, while excluding that of the

United States. Finally, I would like to conclude with a discussion of regional politics in Northeast Asia, past and present.[5]

Learning Historical Lessons

In the interests of taxonomy, I would like to start by provisionally, and rather arbitrarily, dividing arguments about the linkage between the past and the present into two kinds: constructive and constructed. Constructive arguments make use of underlying principles of geopolitics to trace continuities that make learning from the past possible. Diplomats and military planners are clearly practitioners of this kind of history, although no one is specifically excluded from performing this kind of intellectual work. The hallmark of this approach is the rational belief that the proximate past influences the present and future most. In contrast, "constructed" history is less a policy than an explanatory exercise. Here, decisions already taken and events already underway are presented as the almost inevitable result of the past's heavy hand. Politicians and propagandists are the most active users of this approach. Their telltale is the equally rational belief that earliest events, by affecting all those that come afterward, are the most influential. Of course, these two approaches often overlap, and historians regularly perform both operations, often without consciously recognizing any difference between them.

At the broadest strategic level, military analysis and diplomacy converge in their basic assumptions regarding the universal applicability of geopolitics. Their vocabulary has been the "rational" language of power for over a hundred years, allowing clear continuities. For example, King Kojong, the last king of Korea, in an attempt to balance the dangerous predatory countries that surrounded his kingdom, hoped to cultivate the interest and sympathy of the distant and therefore comparatively disinterested United States as a counterweight. In 1904, as the situation worsened and the Japanese occupied the Korean Peninsula, the United States reciprocated with words of "friendship and good wishes for Korea," but nothing more concrete.[6] One hundred and one years later, in answer to South Korean President Roh Moo-hyun's new "balancer strategy," the U.S. assistant secretary of state responsible for the six-party talks on the North Korean nuclear issue, Ambassador Christopher Hill, reiterated the geopolitical logic behind King Kojong's earlier choice:

I would think if I were a South Korean, there is logic to saying that we're in a neighborhood that in the past—in the past, maybe not now—has certainly qualified as a high-crime neighborhood. You know, a lot of invasions, a lot of battles, even at times through the centuries, wars of annihilation—serious stuff, especially on the peninsula. . . . If I were a South Korean looking into the future, I would be saying to myself, "I want a special relationship with a distant power."

This discussion is meant not as a comparison of King Kojong and Ambassador Hill, but rather as an illustration of the enduring nature of certain kinds of geopolitical logic, a way of thinking shared by two men with little in common besides their calling to ponder the fate of the Korean Peninsula.

Military officers, like diplomats, are also trained to think geopolitically and to place their missions and contingencies within the context of previous experience of war. This desire to learn from battle experience is often labeled pejoratively as "fighting the last war." Nonetheless, this method makes for genuine analysis linking previous to future conflict. Present at the Battle of Tsushima where the Japanese navy sank much to most of the Russian Second Pacific Fleet, Yamamoto Isoroku, a recent graduate of the Imperial Naval Academy, drew certain conclusions that matured as he advanced to become the commander in chief of the Combined Fleet. In 1941, as he planned the surprise attack on Pearl Harbor that opened the Pacific War with America, he made the following observations:[7]

We have much to learn from the Russo-Japanese War. The lessons concerning the opening of hostilities are: (1) favorable opportunities were gained by opening the war with a sudden attack on the main enemy fleet; (2) it is regrettable, but true, although there are exceptions, that the morale of our torpedo division was not necessarily very high and its capabilities were insufficient; and (3) both the planning and implementation of the blockade operation were not sufficiently thorough. We must make efforts, based on these successes and failures, to handle the opening of the war with America much more successfully. Furthermore, we must be prepared to act decisively to secure victory on Day One of hostilities.

At the most basic level, Yamamoto was simply expressing the desire to do what worked and avoid what failed; but, as new technologies transform warfare, generations-old military lessons become moot. A maritime attack in 1904 had by 1941 become an aviation raid—not the prelude to a naval blockade, but the answer to an economic embargo. On the other hand, such issues as offensive morale as the necessary ingredient for victory and the search for a decisive battle to avoid the war of attrition that Japan knew it could not win remained strategic staples three and a half decades later.

Although eminently rational, both of these ways of linking the past and the future often stumble, even fatally, in the face of several complications.

The first of these difficulties is the different rationalities of the different armed services. What works for the army might not work for the navy, and the whole equation becomes all the more complex once the air force (and soon space weapons!) multiply the potential solutions to military challenges. In the Russo-Japanese War naval protection for army convoys won high marks for the Japanese military, but Julian Corbett's emphasis on the "fleet in being" at Port Arthur suggests that lack of naval boldness at the beginning of hostilities resulted in excessive infantry casualties during the long siege and assault. Interservice rivalry in Meiji and Taishō Japan may have had more to do with silent recriminations regarding the recent campaign against Russia than has been previously discussed. In short, different services with different institutional interests and memories are likely to have divergent prescriptions for future contingencies, that is, divergent constructive histories. Combining them is likely to be a difficult, inefficient, and thankless task.[8] By extension, we could make a similar argument for the inability of nonmilitary, or paramilitary, national services, such as the diplomatic and intelligence corps, to agree with the military on the nation's interests and choose concomitant policy. In his classic study *After Imperialism,* Akira Iriye makes this issue clear for all the main participants in Northeast Asia in the 1920s by demonstrating the "bifurcation between foreign policy and military thinking as they related to the Far East."[9]

The second problem is the role of time perception as a factor in strategic evaluations. Just as the Japanese attacked the Russians before naval and railway construction weakened their chances, Pearl Harbor was also bombed before dwindling oil reserves made war impossible.[10] In both cases, the choice to fight a country having significantly greater manpower reserves and industrial potential seems irrational, unless we assume a relatively short war in which initial advantages lead to an advantageous peace. Unfortunately, it is often difficult for military men who can calculate superiority of arms sufficient for preliminary victory to guess the degree to which the erstwhile foe will continue guerrilla warfare or other means of resistance. Over time, victory can turn to defeat, unless the diplomats can bring a successful campaign to peaceful denouement.

In *The War of the Future,* Ivan Bloch, although an industrialist, served warning to the generals that time would now alter the very nature of warfare in protracted conflicts. Appearing first in Russian in 1897, the book was quickly translated into English, French, German, Polish, and Japanese. Bloch posited that a prolonged war would be decided not by the stockpiles predating the conflict but by financial resources, industrial capacity, and public support mobilized in the course of the campaign. Failure in any of these areas could lead to defeat. This analysis proved prescient, for, in 1904–

5, Japan was quickly hobbled by financial (and manpower) restraints, and Russia was also forced to the peace table by the strike movement.[11]

Unlike elite geopolitical visions of history, premised on the assumption that geography is unchanging or at least slow to change, the politics of memory links the past and present under the assumption that human remembrance is infinitely malleable. This approach is closely linked to questions of education and propaganda with the goal of inculcating most of a "curriculum" into the minds of most members of a particular target group in order to reconstruct national memory. It is along these lines that I. V. Stalin linked the Russo-Japanese War and World War II in his famous article declaring an end to the Soviet Union's brief Pacific War.[12]

But the Russian loss of 1904 during the Russo-Japanese War left dark memories. It lay on our country like a black spot. Our people believed and awaited the day when Japan would be beaten and the black spot removed. We, those of the elder generation, awaited that day for 40 years. And that day has come.

Stalin not only grounded the victory in revanchist sentiments, ostensibly dating to his youth, but also provided a timeline of Russo-Japanese and Japanese-Soviet enmity, running from the Russo-Japanese War through the Siberian Intervention as far as the border wars at Khasan and Nomonhan in the late 1930s. A selection of conflicts creates the impression of enduring negative relations. A different choice of historical benchmarks might easily have created a different impression.

A similar kind of construction appears in Egawa Tatsuya's serialized comics (*manga*) retelling of the Russo-Japanese War. In the final August 2005 edition of *Spirits*, Egawa presents a mythic story from the childhood of Ishiwara Kanji, the architect of the Mukden incident that led to Japan's occupation of Manchuria in 1931–32, to link the Satsuma samurai rebellion of 1877, the Sino-Japanese War of 1894–95, the Russo-Japanese War, and later incursions into China. The story is somewhere between George Washington chopping down the cherry tree and the cutting of the Gordian knot, but Ishiwara emerges as the spiritual descendant of the last true samurai, Saigō Takamori, and at age five already exhibits his readiness to carry out violence against his neighbors in the name of a larger, abstract harmony. The key point is that the story contextualizes the Russo-Japanese War both chronologically and geographically by putting names and dates familiar from junior high school history courses into a new order to show the samurai spirit passing through three generations from Kagoshima to Yamagata to Manchuria.[13]

Clearly, the selection of historical events to explain the mythic formation

of a child's way of reasoning is deeply arbitrary, but the semifictional quality of Egawa's work—and its popularity—protect him from accusations of
inaccuracy. Maybe a better example of the tendentious dangers of this approach can be drawn from the rival newspapers *Asahi* and *Yomiuri,* which
during the recent historical debates with China ran different timelines.
Asahi listed the dates of Prime Minister Koizumi Jun'ichirō's visits to Ya-
sukuni Shrine. *Yomiuri* published a chart of all the times that Japanese
prime ministers have apologized for Japan's wartime atrocities in China. Both
chronologies are factually correct but make very different points. Similarly,
the Russo-Japanese War can be told as a life-or-death struggle against Russian
imperialism or as Japan's debut as an imperialist. Referring to an intellectual
environment in which people believed implicitly in law-of-the-jungle real-
politik, these two versions of the event present no contradiction. The story
lines diverge, however, as we add more data points and lengthen the timeline. Again, the crucial point is that the historical events are available to be
constructed into story lines that have a great deal of power to move people.
It is certainly no coincidence that five of the seven letters in "history" spell
"story."

The Portsmouth Treaty and Northeast Asian Anti-Americanism

During the twentieth century, the United States has had serious disagreements with every country in Northeast Asia. In fact, the United States has
fought wars both hot and cold with all the key powers in the region. Even
today, strong currents of anti-Americanism can be found in every country
in Northeast Asia. Past wars and present discontents represent two points
available for a new constructed history of anti-Americanism, should such
a history ever be written. In such a case, the role of the United States in
the Treaty of Portsmouth could well become the starting point of a *regional*
history in which the United States is portrayed as an outsider to Northeast Asia. This section of my paper will present the factual and interpretive basis on which each country could rationally empathize with such a
retelling.

Japan

Roosevelt strove to attain the role of honest broker, with his advances rejected four times in the first four months of 1905. As the French specialist on
Russia Pierre Leroy-Beaulieu perceptively wrote in *Revue des Deux Mondes*

on March 15, 1904: "If there is anything one can foresee with some certitude, it is the intervention of the neutrals at war's end to prevent the victor from pushing his victory too far." And indeed, had Witte and his entourage left Portsmouth without signing a treaty, both the French and the British were waiting in the wings.[14] In fact, the French had offered their services, but the Japanese preferred the United States, both for Roosevelt's clear professions of beneficent neutrality and for the substantial loans that had been arranged by the house of Kuhn and Loeb, presided over by Jacob Schiff.[15]

But, once engaged in the peace process, Roosevelt was remorseless. When talks deadlocked over the issue of an indemnity, Roosevelt cautioned the Japanese against creating the impression that they were willing to kill and be killed further in pursuit of money. This impression would not sit well with the public as lender, he implied.[16] At exactly the same crucial psychological moment, Schiff sent a letter to his usual interlocutor, Takahashi Korekiyo, the vice-governor of the Bank of Japan, warning that Japanese bond prices might plummet if the war continued.[17] Roosevelt defended himself vociferously from accusations of undercutting the Japanese in a powerful letter (which he never sent) to George Kennan (the elder):[18]

Let me repeat. The peace negotiations were entered into by me at the instance of Japan. The treaty of peace was finally made by Japan because it was greatly in her interests to make it then, and in the shape in which it was made. Japan was not entitled to an indemnity. . . . She was entitled to much and she gained much. . . . The peace was made on practically exactly the terms on which it should have been made. It was for the interest of Japan; it was for the interest of Russia; it was for the interest of the world.

But the Japanese people were not immediately convinced. Three days of rioting ensued in Tokyo, resulting in a few deaths and much destruction. A curfew was decreed to allow the Portsmouth delegates to reach their homes in safety. Although many sources simply blame this outburst on the lack of indemnity, something the public had come to expect following the lucrative Sino-Japanese War of 1894–95, it seems a little disingenuous to assume that there were no expectations of Roosevelt, who had endeared himself to Japan from the beginning of the war by warning Germany and France against repeating their interventionist act of 1895. In fact, books from the 1930s place the Hibiya riots firmly at Roosevelt's doorstep. For example, Griswold cites Takeuchi in saying:

In Tokyo, an uninformed populace rioted against the treaty and throughout Japan denounced the American president who had denied it an indemnity. . . . Roosevelt's picture was turned to the wall in countless Japanese homes. In Tokyo, where the outbreaks were especially violent, there were over a thousand casualties; police stations were set on fire and martial law proclaimed.

Griswold adds: "It was the Japanese Government's good fortune to have Roosevelt for a scapegoat." He even goes so far as to blame the cancellation of the Harriman-Katsura agreement on joint Japanese-American investment in Manchurian railroads of August 1905 on "hostility towards the United States stirred up by the Portsmouth treaty terms."[19]

Not surprisingly, Japanese writers treated Theodore Roosevelt in an exclusively positive light during the American occupation after World War II, but the U.S. president's concern in 1905 that Japan might finish the war with Russia too strong has recently found voice in slightly right-wing Japanese books with such chapter headings as "If Japan wins too well, it will be inconvenient for the United States."[20] A 2005 version tries to separate popular and elite reactions, with "the people of Japan" condemning the Portsmouth peace as "miserably poor" and "an outrageous betrayal." The blame, however, is placed, not on the United States or Roosevelt, but on the Japanese government for not preparing the Japanese people for a realistic peace.[21]

In 1906, the United States formulated its first war plan (Orange) against Japan, and conversely for the first time America became Japan's hypothetical naval opponent in the 1907 Defense Guidelines.[22] Whether Roosevelt's hints about what public displeasure at Japanese bloodthirstiness might do to Tokyo's credit rating were actually understood as financial blackmail is unclear. What is certain is that Tokyo did not return to Wall Street as a borrower until the Great Kantō Earthquake of 1923. By then Wall Street had taken over from London's City as the center of world finance.

Russia

From the beginning the Russians were quite sure that the Americans as well as the British had pushed the Japanese into war, and the diplomatic record certainly has no lack of clear statements expressing indignation regarding Russia's violation of the "Open Door" principle by keeping troops in Manchuria after the agreed withdrawal date. John Hay, the secretary of state at the time, famously remarked: "Sometimes I think it will be a valuable lesson to them [the Russians], if Japan does fly at their throat." Shortly, after the war began, the president wrote approvingly to his son that Japan was "playing America's game in Manchuria." Nonetheless, Roosevelt, as peacemaker, would soon write to the tsar: "I earnestly ask Your Majesty to believe that in what I am about to say and to advise [that] I speak as the earnest well-wisher of Russia, and give you the advice I should give were I a Russian patriot and statesman." Roosevelt then went on to argue for the cession of Sakhalin, which had been in Russian possession only since 1875, while conjuring up the specter of further Russian losses leading to a Japanese occupation of East Siberia as well. Furthermore, the American ambassador to St. Petersburg, George Meyer, was provided with information regarding how much unspent loan money the Japanese still had on deposit in the United States, a simple way to suggest that the Japanese were prepared to fight on, at least for a while.[23]

By early October Roosevelt was already receiving reports that the Russians felt betrayed. A dispatch from Ambassador Meyer quoted a high official as saying: "war would never have taken place but for England and America," which also provided money and ships. Although Witte had clearly made efforts to convince the press of Russia's and his own great negotiating success, the tsar was soon telling his confidants: "If I had only known that the Japanese were ready to give up on the indemnity, I would never have agreed to give away half of Sakhalin."[24] We can be sure that Witte was most blamed, for the tsar continued to find him essential and intolerable, all at the same time.[25] At the Russian court's 1905 New Year's reception, the tsar told Meyer that "he would never forget what the American president had done and repeated it with feeling." There is absolutely no reason to assume that the sentiment was a positive one.

In bilateral summation, Norman Saul writes:[26]

The treaty was initially greeted by outcries of opposition in both countries. Japan felt cheated by being denied Russian largesse to help repay its war loans, while Russia was incensed by the first voluntary loss of territory in its modern history, half of a large but remote island. The tendency was to blame the interference of other powers, especially the United States.

This shared sentiment would soon result in joint policy when, in 1909–10, Russia and Japan banded together to block the American plan for the neutralization of Manchuria. At that time, the Russian foreign minister wrote to his Japanese counterpart: "If there is a possibility that Russia and Japan which are most deeply interested in this matter, may present a united front, the two governments will enter into discussion in advance before replying to the American government."[27] Needless to say, antipathy toward America and a willingness to ascribe "imperialist" motives to Roosevelt became a staple of Soviet historiography on the Russo-Japanese War.[28]

China

Millions of inhabitants of the Chinese Northeast were unwillingly en-
meshed in the hostilities as foreign soldiers turned their homes into the first
proving ground of twentieth-century warfare.[29] The Chinese casualty count,
the value of destroyed property, and the toll of human suffering rose as the
months passed. The informality of Chinese participation makes statistical
accuracy difficult, but here are some estimates: Rosemary Quested cites
Chinese Maritime Customs in giving the number of Chinese dead as twenty
thousand, while fixing the capital losses at seventy million taels, concentrated in the "swathe of devastation" where the armies had passed.[30]

Probably, the anecdote most widely known in China about this war is
how Lu Xun (Hsun), the father of modern Chinese literature, drew inspiration from it. At the time, Lu was a medical student in Sendai, Japan. Later,
he recalled in the preface to his first book of short stories:[31]

One day in a [glass-lantern] slide I suddenly came face to face with many Chinese
on the mainland, and I had not seen any for a long time. In the center of the group
there was one who was bound while many others stood around him. They were all
strong in physique but callous in appearance. According to the commentary, the
one who was bound was a spy who had worked for the Russians and was just about
to have his head cut off by the Japanese military as a warning to the others, while the
people standing around him had come to watch the spectacle.

Before the term was over I had left for Tokyo, because after seeing these slides I
felt that medical science was not such an important thing after all. People from an
ignorant and weak country, no matter how physically healthy and strong they may
be, could only serve to be made examples of, or become onlookers of utterly meaningless spectacles. Such a condition was more deplorable than dying of illness.
Therefore our first important task was to change their spirit, and at the time I considered the best medium for achieving this end was literature.

This concern over China's weakness is the bitter central root of twentieth-
century Chinese literature, which lends itself so well to the nationalist cause.[32]

Although it is well known, if understudied, that most of the Russo-
Japanese War's casualties fertilized China's soil with their blood, the Qing
court's desire to participate in the Portsmouth deliberations is almost unknown.[33] Like King Kojong, the Chinese assumed that American distance
would work in their favor. In February 1905, Prince Qing, the foreign minister, and Yuan Shikai, the powerful governor of the area surrounding Beijing and the commander of China's new modern army, went to visit the de-

parting American ambassador, Edwin Conger, to request America's good offices in support of Open Door principles. Conger replied that "the US government could in the future, as in the past, be relied upon to do whatever, as a friend of China, she might properly and legally to secure her fair treatment, save her people from spoliation, and to protect the international right which she, together with other Powers, had acquired in the Empire."[34]

Four months later, Prince Qing revisited the American embassy, where Conger's successor, William Rockhill, had taken up residence, specifically to ask to participate in the recently announced negotiations. Rockhill dissuaded him by stating that "matters involving Chinese sovereignty" would not be settled at the peace conference. Keeping in mind the previous visit, Rockhill also telephoned Yuan Shikai to encourage China to remain quiet during the Portsmouth proceedings. China's acquiescence only provoked negative comments from Rockhill, who concluded his dispatch to Washington about this episode with strong words:[35]

The lack of any settled policy among the high officers of Chinese government, I refrain from using the word statesman, as I fear there is not one to be found in China at the present day, is terribly evident. Indecision and a determination to drift with any current is shown on every side. It is manifest to the most casual observer that China is quite unable to manage her international affairs without strong support and constant pressure from without.

Nonetheless, believing in the sincerity of American professions, the emperor sent a message to Washington requesting that "the President will exert his influence for the protection of the territorial rights of China in Manchuria and all China's interests, preserving her sovereignty without loss."[36] No further mention of participation was made.

Given the nearly universal belief that China was unable to formulate and carry out its own policies, the request for participation and the emperor's telegram merely aroused suspicions as to whose original idea the initiative was. The Russians suspected that Roosevelt had prompted the Chinese request to attend Portsmouth while Roosevelt was equally suspicious that it was a Russian ploy.[37] Roosevelt had, in the meantime, informed the Japanese of the Chinese request, the American dissuasion, and his suspicion that the Russians were behind it all.

In fact, however, it appears that the failed appeal to the Americans emerged from a Qing court request for opinions from court, local, and foreign affairs officials that circulated in June 1905, at the same time that participants in a boycott of American goods were protesting anti-Chinese immigration practices being carried out by state-level officials on the American West Coast. Roosevelt took active measures to curb these immigration abuses, but not to invite a Chinese delegate to Portsmouth. For this nonaction, he, too, would share blame when the Russians transferred rights in Manchuria to the Japanese. In December, the same foreign minister Komura who had negotiated these privileges from Witte would force "consent to all the transfers and assignments made by Russia to Japan by Articles 5 and 6" from unwilling Chinese negotiators at Beijing. Prince Qing and Yuan Shikai were among the signatories. Their faith had been misplaced, and the Treaty of Portsmouth brought no benefits to China.

Korea

Ironically, it was America, which in 1882 had been the first country to recognize Korean independence, that would take the lead in removing diplomatic representation from Seoul in November 1905, signaling the disappearance of an independent, united Korea until the present day. Unlike China, which both Japan and the United States encouraged to declare and observe neutrality during the war, Korea received no support for its attempt to do the same.[38] When war became visibly unavoidable in late January 1904, King Kojong notified both the United States and Japan of his intention to remain neutral, but the note was simply "acknowledged" rather than "approved," since it seemed likely that Japanese wartime control in Korea would be a logistical prerequisite to victory in Manchuria. Nonetheless, the Korean king still seemed to think that the United States would "do something for him." According to the American envoy, Horace Allen, when the royal palace burned in April 1904, the king moved to a building adjacent to the American legation, seeking either protection or at least its semblance.[39]

A year later, Japan had captured Port Arthur, and Roosevelt began to consider the nature of a peace he might broker. He wrote to Secretary of State John Hay: "We cannot possibly interfere for the Koreans against Japan. They could not strike one blow in their own defense." Two days later, Hay responded in agreement: "I entirely agree with you about Korea. We have no business interfering." A month later, Roosevelt communicated this belief directly to Prime Minister Katsura Tarō via George Kennan, working as *Outlook* correspondent in Japan.

In mid-2004, Che Mun-hyon, the chairman of Korea's History Association, published *A Global History of the Russo-Japanese War* simultaneously in Korean and Japanese. The final chapter is "Japan's Annexation of Korea," and previous chapters lead to this topic by presenting Korean perspectives on the war.[40] The discussion of the Portsmouth peace negotiations is con-

tained in a section called "'The Portsmouth Peace Treaty' and Japan's Protectorate over Korea." The first three parts of this section reveal the step-by-
step causation that Che sees leading to Korea's loss of independence.

The first subsection is "'The Katsura-Taft Secret Agreement' and Japan's
Protectorate over Korea," the second is "'The Second Anglo-Japanese Alliance' and Japan's Protectorate over Korea," and the third is "'The Portsmouth Peace Treaty' and Japan's Protectorate over Korea." The final subsection covers the United States' "voluntary" closure of its mission in Seoul. The
logic of the section is quite clear: U.S. initiative before the peace conference
began assured the Japanese of dominance in Korea, with the British
confirming Japan's "special position" on the peninsula even as the delegates
gathered in Portsmouth.[41] All that remained was for the Russians to follow
suit to seal Korea's death warrant. In this narrative, all the key steps, so detrimental to Korean pride and position, took place under American auspices.[42]

The Open Door in Manchuria turned out to be a myth, with the
Harriman-Katsura agreement for joint financing of the South Manchuria
Railroad evaporating as soon as the Portsmouth Treaty was concluded. Although the American minister in Beijing, William Rockhill, had hoped that
Korean annexation would be Japan's "final step westward," it turned out
that the minister to Seoul, Horace Allen, was closer to the truth, as Japan
took additional steps to the north, west, south, and finally east, fulfilling his
1903 prediction that "Japan . . . would make us increasing trouble until we
might have to cross swords with her." When the United States withdrew its
representation to Korea, one American firm lamented Washington's short-
sighted policy and the resulting loss of U.S.-Korean trade opportunities:
"The Japanese have got what they have been planning for these many
moons and it is clear that Roosevelt played into their hands when he posed
as the great peacemaker of the twentieth century."[43]

Continuing Echoes of Portsmouth: Regionalism and Instability

On May 24, 2005, Harvard University professor Akira Iriye delivered a keynote speech to the World War Zero conference, outlining the way in which
five crucial "Isms" were reflected in the Russo-Japanese War's brief and
deadly passage.[44] I add below my own parallel observations of events that
took place a century later to the five "Isms" that Iriye observed in the events
of 1904–5. At this level of analysis, the continuities are startling.

(1) One hundred years after Portsmouth, in language reminiscent of
1905, Imperialism's failure to keep the peace was lamented on August 14,

2005, by a Caracas stadium filled with a very international crowd "Against Imperialism and War." Anti-Americanism was all too evident.

(2) In 1905 the world's powers had difficulty coming to terms with the new Nationalisms they had provoked both in their colonies and at home. In Northeast Asia, the robust nationalism of China and Korea, dating from their exclusion from international society—and from Portsmouth—at the beginning of the twentieth century, is still regarded by many as a sign of "immaturity," but in 1905 it was already regarded with fear as well as condescension. Of even greater concern now is the potential for Japanese, Taiwanese, Russian, and American nationalisms to increase, leading to further echoes of Portsmouth's anti-Americanism as well as other forms of xenophobia.

(3) In 1905, Regionalism failed when the two rising powers in the Pacific—Japan and the United States—failed to cooperate, choosing instead the path of conflict. If we substitute China for Japan in this sentence, we will arrive at the central theme of Asia-Pacific affairs in 2005 and a clear potential for anti-Americanism to spread among 1.3 billion people.

(4) Theodore Roosevelt's intervention in favor of an early peace, regardless of his multiple motives, was a brilliant exhibition of Internationalism from a man whose vision and vitality seemed to offer bright vistas for the emerging century. Who today has the status and stature to take powerful action in favor of humanitarian goals? President Jimmy Carter's trip to Pyongyang appeared to produce results, but in hindsight it is unclear how the Agreed Framework he brokered should be evaluated. It may indeed be the fate of all brokers and balancers to be maligned by those they serve, but who can substitute for American authority in Northeast Asia, where bilateral and multilateral cooperation is often blocked?[45]

(5) Transnationalism has multiplied many times over since 1905, but it remains unclear if increased cross-border flows really lead to higher levels of understanding. Positive influences need to be enhanced, and negative exposures minimized, if this "Ism" is to work for a more peaceful and prosperous world. Although Americans travel much, enjoying the leisure and resources to indulge in world (and self-) discovery, the image of America is not always improved by direct, often glancing, exposure.

Going through this list, we see that none of the major forces shaping our world is necessarily working to advance peace, stability, and cooperation in Northeast Asia or to avoid the growth of anti-Americanism. With some frustration, academic analysts have observed the inability of countries in the region to build on a wide range of contacts, including impressive economic growth fueled by China, to create regional institutions. Edward Lincoln has focused on the economies of East Asia to reach pessimistic conclusions that might be labeled with Gilbert Rozman's suggestive title, "Stunted Regionalism."[46]

The core complaint is that no regional institution comparable to ASEAN has emerged to referee regional disputes and develop denser regional ties. Indeed, it is hard to imagine on what basis such an organization could exist, since for China, Japan, and Korea regional relations are paramount, whereas for the United States and Russia they are but one among several high priorities. Furthermore, both Russia and China are ambivalent about strengthening the Russian Far East and the Chinese Northeast, respectively, for transnational and subnational regionalism go hand in hand. Neither country feels strong enough to risk another bout with separatism. Similar concerns motivated Russian and Chinese approaches to Portsmouth.

Both Rozman and Lincoln focus on the post–Cold War era as an opportunity to enhance Northeast Asian security and wealth, while blaming the region's inability to unite on a range of Cold War "legacies." I would like to suggest two other perspectives on the lack of progress in building regional cooperation. First, in evaluating the shift away from the Cold War in Northeast Asia since the 1990s, one can say that the glass is half empty rather than half full. It is true that the Chinese economy is essentially capitalist. South Korea has developed full relations with China and Russia, and the Soviet Union's main military capabilities in the East have rusted away. On the other hand, if 1991 with the collapse of the Soviet Union is considered the end of the Cold War, in Asia three communist parties continue in power, wielding control over more than a billion people. If you considered the fall of the Berlin Wall the decisive moment, then divided China and partitioned Korea remain the telltales of the Cold War. Finally, if, as in the Soviet definition, the arms race was the key attribute of the Cold War, today's rocketing defense budgets in Northeast Asia are undeniable. Even with some new alignments, the key issues borne of the Cold War in the region—Taiwan, Korea, and the U.S. military presence—remain unresolved. With that presence, anti-Americanism continues among the populations of both potential enemies and allied nations.[47]

Secondly, to the extent that the Cold War has given way to a thaw, long-frozen trends have resurfaced. The striving of Koreans worldwide for unity and independence is almost a century old, with no clear end in sight. Old nationalisms have resurfaced as communism has been put to rest, for, even where the parties are still in power, the ideology is almost universally disbelieved. The "security dilemma" that to some extent was curbed under the umbrella of Soviet-American nuclear enmity and guarantees has now reemerged as a multipolar arms race, in which defensive measures can be just as destabilizing as offensive additions to the arsenals of the region. Finally, the economic relations that were deemed secondary to alliance considerations have now come to the fore in a struggle for regional resources not seen since the dangerous days of the 1930s.

In short, it is all too easy to create a constructed history that starts with the anti-American experience of Portsmouth, builds on negative U.S. acts of commission and omission in the interwar period, before iterating readily available complaints about sixty years of U.S. military presence, either inconveniencing, even as it protects, American allies or threatening foes with instant and total destruction. This layering of historical events could be all the more effective for the many similarities between past situations and the present, as frozen in time by the Cold War. A sense of historical flow as well as a clear feeling that the events of the past are repeated mutatis mutandis in the present can be the strongest motivation for individuals looking for the meaning of their individual actions in a longer chronological framework.

Finally, it is worth mentioning that, although many old bilateral hostilities can be conjured up, anti-American feeling is most likely to prevail as long as Asia-Pacific does not coalesce as a region. Until the United States is fully incorporated into such structures, there is a lingering sense, built on distant geography and unshared culture, that Americans are in the region, but not of it. In order to prevent isolation, the United States must continue to promote the vision of Asia-Pacific rather than the more exclusive Northeast Asia. The narrative of Theodore Roosevelt's willingness to break the American taboo on avoiding foreign entanglements in order to volunteer his good offices in the name of peace can be a story in favor of Asia-Pacific unity rather than the source from which anti-Americanism flows toward the creation of Northeast Asia.

Chapter 9

Economic Engagement

Coping with the Realities of the Globalized World

Vladimir I. Ivanov

In 2005 Japan and Russia celebrated the 150th anniversary of the establishment of bilateral diplomatic relations. The peace treaty signed 100 years earlier in Portsmouth as well as the 60th anniversary of the ending of World War II also require assessing both past events in the two neighbors' relations and considering the paths that they may henceforth choose. This essay attempts to review briefly the existing currents in bilateral economic ties and to highlight some potential building blocks for a long-term economic partnership between Japan and Russia.

An Encouraging Geopolitical Context

At the Japan-Russia Summit held in Bangkok, Thailand, in October 2003, the leaders agreed to establish a policy-oriented, expert-level framework to exchange views on a broad range of bilateral issues as part of an effort to improve the environment for the conclusion of a peace treaty. Indeed, Japan and Russia are the only major powers that are short of complete normalization owing to the lack of a treaty with agreed borders. Nonetheless, one must also recognize that the bilateral interface is now qualitatively different and more positively focused than ever before.

Certainly, this interface is not perfect: there is significant room for improvement. Further advancement requires leadership and a working institutional framework. Whether we like it or not, the role of politicians and their supportive bureaucracies is becoming less dominant. The world is changing, and global competitive pressures require that both countries respond to groundbreaking economic trends and geopolitical shifts. It seems that burning economic needs and changing interests as well as emerging nonmilitary concerns will define the transformation of the bilateral agenda for decades to come. Factors unimaginable just two decades ago have created a demand for innovative approaches, including those suited to steering the policy dialogue, making investment decisions, and dealing with rapidly increasing grassroots-level interactions.

The reality is that the role of the United States in Japan-Russia relations has changed dramatically. Since 1991, Russia's political leadership has never defined its security priorities in terms of confrontation with Washington or its allies. In general, Moscow seems to be free from openly antagonistic relationships with other countries and does not threaten any other state. The military forces on both sides of the Cold War divide have been downsized, and the risk of large-scale war has practically vanished. The new relationships with NATO are guided by the idea of partnership. Military-to-military exchanges with Japan are also developing quite rapidly, contributing to the policy dialogue.

Since 2001, personal bonds among the leaders of the United States, Germany, Italy, France, and Britain have become stronger and more meaningful than at any point during the last century. New geopolitical interests are now supportive of closer economic ties. Links with the West appear so much different today, when Moscow is a full-fledged G8 partner. Actually, other members of this group compete more with Japan, promoting their own trade and economic interests.

Still, there are numerous specific areas in which strengthened cooperation could distinctively serve the interests of both Tokyo and Moscow. One such area is North Korea. Japan and Russia agree that North Korea must be prevented from developing nuclear weapons. Both countries, however, need to envision how and under what specific conditions they could support the reform process, providing economic and technical assistance in rebuilding infrastructure and normalizing the energy supply in the north of the peninsula. Provided that the nuclear issue is resolved through diplomatic means and an agreement on a nuclear-free Korean Peninsula is reached, trans-Korea infrastructure projects could become physically possible, including a power grid, railroad, and pipeline for transporting natural gas.

Yet another opportunity for a close link is assistance for the dismantlement of the old nuclear submarines. Under phase two of the bilateral "Star of Hope" project, five Russian nuclear submarines are to be dismantled, four of them in the town of Bolshoi Kamen, near Vladivostok, the other in the town of Vilyuchinsk in Kamchatka. The first eighteen-month stage involved dismantlement of *Viktor-3*-class submarines. The full plan envisages dismantling about forty nuclear submarines by 2010.

In the realm of international organizations, Japan assisted Russia in joining the Asia-Pacific Economic Cooperation (APEC) forum. Tokyo has supported Moscow's bid to join the World Trade Organization and expressed
its readiness to endorse the application formally. In the context of the reform of the United Nations, Russia reiterated support for Japan's bid to become a permanent member of the U.N. Security Council, giving broad consent to the draft framework resolution of the G4 countries.

Investment Climate

Obviously, economic limitations, particularly those on the Russian side
over the last decade, have been mostly to blame for sluggish progress on the
investment front. Russia, however, has attained macroeconomic stability
and made progress in repaying its foreign debt. In 2004, Russia's annual
GDP growth was above 7 percent, while industrial production expanded by
6 percent. Investments from all sources were estimated at approximately
$100 billion, and capital expenditures increased by 11 percent.

By 2005, accumulated foreign investment in Russia exceeded $82 billion,
including $40 billion attracted in 2004. The share of foreign direct investment
(FDI) was 23.3 percent, while portfolio investment accounted for 0.8 percent
of the total volume. About 80 percent of the entire inflow, including 78 percent of FDI, originated from Cyprus, the Netherlands, Germany, the United
Kingdom, the United States, and France. Most of the foreign funds were
flowing into the industrial sector, retail trade and catering, and commercial
operations. Russia's economic image was changing, influencing its credit
rating. In 2003–5, Moody's, Fitch, and Standard & Poor's awarded Russia an
investment-level credit rating. According to the A. T. Kearney international
consultancy, Russia occupies the eleventh position on the list of economies
most appealing to foreign investors, equaling China in that respect.

Since 2004, Russia has been undergoing fundamental changes in its system of state management. This reform is aimed at reducing the excessive in-
volvement of the state in economic affairs, dismantling barriers to entrepre-
neurship, and protecting the rights of economic entities. Part of the effort is
related to the protection of property rights, including intellectual property
and copyrights.

The tax pressure on businesses has been reduced considerably, contributing to the investment capacity of enterprises. In 2004, the tax rate for
operations with stocks and securities was reduced from 0.8 percent to 0.2
percent of the nominal emission volume. The value-added tax was reduced
to 18 percent. A law signed in July 2004 reduced social tax rates and ex-

panded the list of activities covered by simplified tax regulations. Amendments adopted in 2005 sought to promote competition in the context of antimonopolistic regulations.

In July 2004, the government adopted a strategy for developing the banking sector, aimed, among other things, at nondiscrimination toward foreign investors. Then, in September 2004, the government took up a plan aimed at promoting financial infrastructure development and enhancement of the financial system as well as reduction of risks for participants in the financial markets. The government has initiated new legislation to prevent money laundering and improve the transparency of banking institutions.

The government is also set to introduce international accounting standards by listed stockholding ventures. The maximum foreign share allowed in insurance companies has been raised to 25 percent, and some regulations have been abolished for firms with foreign shares under 49 percent. In addition, a law was adopted that liberalized the currency market. New legislation will soon be introduced to establish transparent rules for companies operating in natural-resources-based industries.

The Economic Links

For Japan, Russia is a marginal trading partner. In 2004, it occupied the twenty-fifth position on the list of Japanese export destinations, following Vietnam. As far as Japanese imports from Russia were concerned, Russia was in twenty-first place, between Kuwait and Switzerland. In absolute terms, the bilateral trade volume constitutes only about 10 percent of Japan's trade with South Korea and 5 percent of that with China.

Although trade and economic links are not sufficiently developed, for Russia, Japan is an important trading partner. In 2002, however, it was not on the list of the top ten export destinations or the top ten sources of imports. Surprisingly, in 2004, bilateral trade reached a record-high $9 billion, doubling the figure for 2003. Nonetheless, these official figures are incomplete. The Russian State Statistical Service registers only direct exports and imports. Exports by Japanese companies via third countries would add another $3–4 billion, making Japan the fifth-largest trading partner of Russia.

In addition, by 2004, Japanese investment in Russia had reached almost $2 billion, making Japan the eighth-largest investor there; but, again, counting the Sakhalin projects and investment via third countries would add another $3 billion, mostly in direct investment, raising Japan to the fifth-highest position among foreign investors in Russia. The leading Japanese companies now put Russia on their lists of strategic markets. There are more than eighty Japanese representative offices registered in Moscow alone. Furthermore, according to a 2005 survey by the Japan Bank for International Cooperation, Russia was then on the list of the top ten geographic destinations for business expansion—a remarkable progress compared with 2001, when it was not among the first thirty countries attractive to Japanese businesses. The point is that bilateral economic ties represent part of the entire relationship. The larger picture reflects the impact on bilateral links of megaprojects such as those on Sakhalin as well as the influence of globalization.

At the same time, the institutional framework that supports bilateral ties needs to be improved along the lines of public-private partnerships. In this context, the efforts of the U.S. government aimed at supporting private-sector operations in Russia deserve attention, including the BISNIS framework (Business Information Service for Newly Independent States, which helps U.S. firms do business in former states of the Soviet Union), the Commercial Service representation offices established in ten locations in Russia, and the three offices established under the Regional Initiative Program—all funded by the U.S. Department of Commerce. Moreover, the two nations' leaders established the Commercial Energy Summit, a public-private framework that elevated the U.S.-Russia bilateral dialogue at the ministerial level and the level of the leading energy companies. The European Union established similar institutions that support the activities of the private sector.

Economic cooperation between Japan and Russia must also rely on the proactive role of governments, following the model of the public-private partnership and promoting a dense and multilayered supportive net for trade and investment links. In reality, the current situation is quite far from this model, considering that on the part of both Japan and Russia the state and the private sector act independently, using parallel channels. There are no government-funded entities that support the activities of the private sector in either country.

Coordination is lacking among the existing government-level bilateral frameworks and national organizations. In other words, the national and bilateral "lobbies" that would promote bilateral economic links and closer interaction are both weak and unorganized or do not exist at all because of the lack of coordination at the bureaucratic level. Such entities would be important software-type building blocks for promoting a new bilateral economic agenda, particularly if the goal of such an agenda was to restore Japan's leadership in trade and investment links with Russia and its eastern regions. Another priority could be the initiation of large-scale strategic projects similar to those on Sakhalin, which could have a significant spin-off effect on bilateral economic relations.

Subnational Relations

It is well known that countries do not trade; businesses and companies do. In Japan-Russia relations, however, activities at the subnational level could play a very important supporting role. As Ambassador Nomura Issei noted, "contacts between regions boil down to nothing but relations between people. Russians and Japanese who have been to each other's regions can play an active role promoting regional exchange between our countries." On the other hand, Nishimuro Taizō, vice-chairman of the Japan Business Federation (Nippon Keidanren) and chairman of Toshiba Corporation, raised the issue of a resolute shift from the system of centralized government control in Japan to one of regional decentralization in order to sustain a balanced nationwide development through local initiatives and autonomous decision-making.

Local regions across Japan are now moving in this direction. A law on establishing Special Zones for Structural Reform was enacted. By 2005, the authorities had approved over one hundred Special Zones, granting exemptions from regulations in education, urban renewal, distribution, agriculture, medical care, industry-academic cooperation, and other areas. Over time, this trend could enhance the competitiveness of local regions and municipalities and provide Japan with the means selectively to test new policies that enhance competitiveness and promote region-to-region links.

For Russia, the Far Eastern region represents the strategic border area. The challenges are the weak economic and transportation links between this part of the country and other regions in Russia as well as difficult climate and economic conditions. It seems that a strategy for responding to these problems could be found in strengthening infrastructure connections, including transport, telecommunications, and energy-delivery systems. These measures could provide incentives for regional development, supporting at the same time closer economic links with neighboring states.

Far Eastern Russia is the traditional source of interest on the part of Japan and Japanese companies. From the early 1990s the economic situation of several Far Eastern provinces depended on trade with Japan and other neighbors. In 2003, bilateral trade transactions of Far Eastern Russia totaled close to $7.7 billion, with exports consisting mostly of oil and oil products (32 percent), timber (15 percent), fish and shellfish (11 percent), coal (4 percent), metals (9 percent), and machinery (5 percent). By 2004, in terms of its share in the foreign trade volume of the Far Eastern region Japan accounted for almost $1.7 billion, or 22 percent of the total, following China (37 percent), but ahead of the Republic of Korea (15 percent).

In 2003 Japan's imports from the Far Eastern region were approaching $880 million, including oil and oil products (25 percent), timber (21 percent), coal (20 percent), and fish and shell products (15 percent). The smuggling of fish and shellfish from the Pacific provinces to neighboring countries is perhaps the most notorious part of the underground economy in eastern Russia. According to official statistics, in 2003, such exports to Japan were estimated at about $102 million. In reality, this figure represents only a fraction of the actual exports.

Japan's exports to the Far Eastern region of Russia consisted mainly of passenger cars and trucks (35 percent), steel pipes and rolled steel (20 percent), and construction and earthmoving machinery (9 percent). By province, the leading trading partners of Japan were Sakhalin ($438 million), Primorskiy ($377 million), and Khabarovskiy ($247 million). Sakhalin was far ahead in terms of Japanese investment ($784 million), followed by Primorskiy ($26 million) and Khabarovskiy ($2 million).

It seems unlikely that a conventional expansion of trade and evolutionary accumulation of Japanese investment in Russia would suffice to change all these important but minuscule economic exchanges. Rather, we should anticipate some megadevelopments that could affect both the scale and the quality of economic links. The Sakhalin oil and gas projects are quite representative in this regard. At the 2005 summit meeting with Koizumi Jun'ichirō at Gleneagles, Scotland, Vladimir Putin expressed his appreciation that Toyota Motor Corporation had decided to construct an assembly plant in St. Petersburg, promising maximum support for this venture. The leaders discussed progress in implementing the "Japan-Russia Action Plan." They agreed that Putin would pay a visit to Japan from November 20 to 22. The leaders also affirmed the strategic importance of an oil pipeline to Russia's Pacific coast.

The Oil Pipeline Impasse

The Pacific oil pipeline project is now a part of Japan-Russia and Russia-China policy dialogues. Initially, the project was not designed to gain support from Japan, but Japanese energy planners became interested. Supportive remarks made by Koizumi when he visited Moscow in January 2003 paved the way for high-level exchanges, working-level discussions, and technical visits. This activity ignited hopes that Japan could become a partner in the project. The expectations of an agreement were initially high on both sides, but especially in Russia. The process, however, has been stalled, leading to disappointment among its proponents, including Transneft Company.

To understand the sources and mechanisms of such disappointment on the part of Russia, one has to review the role of Putin in the decision-making process concerning the Pacific oil pipeline and other critical infrastructure issues. It seems that he is strongly convinced that the eastbound pipeline infrastructure is vital to Russia's economic well-being, political integrity, and international posture. Beginning with his service in St. Petersburg, Putin gave priority on his agenda to transportation routes and related infrastructure, which partly defined his long-standing personal links. For example, in 1996–99, Alexei Miller, currently Gazprom's chairman of the board, served as director for development of the Sea Port of St. Petersburg. In 1999–2000, with Putin taking over the reins of government, Miller was given responsibility for the Baltic Pipeline System (BTS). This project then became the top infrastructure achievement.

Putin believes in state control over the trunk pipelines, including projects such as BTS and the Pacific pipeline. Despite some differences in approach related to investment mobilization,[1] the cabinet members have no choice but to follow his view. Putin discusses pipeline infrastructure issues on a regular basis with Miller of Gazprom, Transneft's chief executive officer Semen Vainshtok, and others. He does not shy away from chairing cabinet-level meetings on pipeline infrastructure development. He also discusses with the minister for natural resources the prospects for exploring and developing oil and natural gas reserves in eastern Russia. On the other hand, he likes sharing his ideas with the leaders of Germany and France as well as other G8 members, including Japan.

Putin's overall position in defining the pipeline routes could be perceived as Russia-centric. The earlier drafts of *Energy Strategy to 2020* stated the need to avoid transit of oil and gas via the territories of "third" countries. Before visiting China, Putin explained that a decision regarding the destination point of an oil pipeline would be based on Russia's national interests, including the development prospects of the Far Eastern provinces. On the other hand, he alluded to a comprehensive energy partnership with China.

Japan presumably had a lack of confidence in the project's economics, including available reserves of oil in eastern Siberia, which are currently estimated at about 1,000 million tons (Mt). In total, about forty new fields were projected to be licensed in 2006–7, with an additional thirty fields to be auctioned soon thereafter. As of 2005, the discovered oil and gas fields, including Talakanskoe (Yakutia), Urubcheno-Tokhomskoe (Evenk District), Verkhnechonskoe (Irkutskaya Oblast), and smaller fields, could have allowed production of 50 Mt of oil a year.

The long-term plan envisions an increase in oil reserves of about 1,500 Mt by 2010 and a similar expansion of resources estimates. The cost of the program to allow this increase is close to $25 billion. By 2030, the estimated cost of the geological exploration and development of new oil reserves could amount to $50 billion.[2] On the other hand, the plan envisions an initial supply of about 30 Mt of oil from western Siberia. Moreover, the funding for geological exploration and development of new reserves will be supported through the federal budget, but an international exploration-and-development consortium that could help alleviate investment risks could be established with the participation of Japan. There was a strong expectation that President Putin's planned visit to Japan would bring about more good news regarding this oil pipeline megaproject and related activities.

In this context, it is important to envision the demand for Siberian and Sakhalin oil on the part of Japan. In 2005, the capacity of the United States to absorb oil from eastern Russia was estimated at 15–25 Mt a year. A similar estimate could be applicable to the Republic of Korea and Taiwan combined. The remaining 30–50 Mt should find their way to China and Japan. A commitment on the part of these two countries to certain volumes of oil imports from Russia could be important for the overall design and commercial success of the project.

An Energy Partnership?

In a broader sense, extensive energy links could make Japan and Russia economically interdependent, promising significant benefits but requiring closer policy coordination. The war in Iraq has only reasserted Russia's vital position in meeting global energy needs. According to the Japan Business Federation, the Achilles' heel of Japan is energy. A stable energy supply must be secured, consistent with both environmental and economic concerns. Sources should be diversified to avoid the risks of overconcentration.[3]

Similarly, Russian energy planners propose to diversify energy exports, accessing new oil and gas markets in the Asia-Pacific region, Northeast Asia in particular. As of 2005, Russia's energy exports basically had only one predominant destination—Europe. The Russian government also proposes to diversify energy supplies in the "north, east, and south," promoting energy production in new, capital-intensive environments, including eastern Siberia, the Far Eastern region, the Arctic, and the continental shelf of the northern and Caspian seas.

The economies of Northeast Asia and possibly of the United States are emerging as potential new targets for Russian oil producers and exporters of natural gas. Recent policy developments support this trend. In May 2002, Moscow and Washington launched their "new energy dialogue." China, for its part, has been successful in lobbying for an export pipeline. Energy cooperation became part of the Japan-Russia Action Plan adopted in January 2003. The Russian Energy Ministry held high-level consultations with counterparts in Japan.

On the other hand, Russia is not planning to expand its energy exports to Europe in physical terms. Contrary to expectations, including projections by the International Energy Agency, the main provisions of Russia's *Energy Strategy to 2020*, adopted in August 2003, basically reflect this change in priorities. The Russian government says that in a favorable scenario crude oil exports to the Asia-Pacific region could reach 105 Mt a year—a little more than two million barrels—including 25 Mt to be produced by the Sakhalin offshore fields. These huge amounts will constitute about one-third of projected Russian oil exports in 2020.

The plan includes building a 4,200-kilometer crude oil pipeline linking an oil terminal built on the Pacific coast with fields in eastern Siberia and Yakutia as well as with the existing trunk oil pipeline in Taishet, near Lake Baikal. The estimated cost of this project is close to $12 billion. If materialized, it could divert as much as 15–20 percent of Russia's total oil output and 25–30 percent of its oil exports to markets in Northeast Asia. Japan's trade minister, Nakagawa Shūichi, stated that Japan was willing to help "in every way possible" if Moscow gave priority to building a pipeline to the Pacific coast, but plans to divert part of the oil exports to China upon completion of the first phase of the project appear to be a problem.

The situation involving natural gas is less urgent and has not created political turbulence thus far. In total, the share of Northeast Asia in Russia's gas exports could reach 15–20 percent by 2020. Russian gas exports to China and the Korean Peninsula via pipelines could reach 25 billion cubic meters (Bcm) by 2020. This amount is above the volume of natural gas that South Korea currently imports in liquefied form (LNG). Technically, a gas pipeline to South Korea could be routed via North Korea, but a more viable transit option would be through China. Exxon Mobil has proposed a submarine gas pipeline between Sakhalin and Sendai or Niigata, Japan. Also, the Sakhalin-2 LNG project could annually export about 13 Bcm of LNG by 2015, and Japan was intending to contract half of this volume.

To sustain domestic demand, expand exports, and modernize domestic energy industries, Russia needs between $620 billion and $850 billion of investment over the next two decades, including $260 billion to $300 billion mobilized before 2010–12. Most of these funds should originate from private sources and loans. Only the Sakhalin-1 and Sakhalin-2 international consortia, in which Japanese companies are involved, plan to invest as much as $25 billion over the next decade or so, but several other oil and gas projects on the Sakhalin shelf are in the formative phase, promising to generate another $30 billion to $50 billion in investment.

All these funds needed to support energy-sector and infrastructure development would create huge business opportunities. Investors and equipment manufacturers could benefit from the construction of new power plants and the modernization of existing facilities as well as a broader reorientation of the Russian energy sector toward increased efficiency and added value. More generally, the Russian government sees the development of energy industries in the context of technological advancement and high-tech research and development that would reduce project costs and enhance energy efficiency. Russo-Japanese technological cooperation in the field of energy, fuels, and emission reduction could benefit both countries, but these issues have yet to become part of the bilateral agenda.

Also, cross-border power interconnection is on Russia's list of long-term priorities, with forecasts of electricity exports to China and the Koreas. Regional electricity markets and power-grid interconnections have already been considered. Eastern Russia's unique hydroelectric power potential presents an opportunity for projects that are efficient in both economic and environmental terms.

Indeed, energy-sector development contains significant potential for investment and trade, including new business opportunities for companies and investors from Japan, South Korea, the United States, and China. It seems, however, that a new conceptual framework is needed to integrate these new investment and infrastructure decisions and physical developments into the long-term policy agenda. For example, the concept of "Asian Energy Partnership" publicized in April 2004 by Japan's Ministry of Economy, Trade, and Industry mostly aimed at promoting cooperation among ASEAN+3—Japan, Korea, and China—and avoided explicit mention of the new sources of energy located in eastern Russia.

On the other hand, it seems that the interests and capacities of Japan's leading companies could go far beyond bilateral and regional needs. For example, a number of leading Japanese firms were set to partner with Gazprom in producing liquefied natural gas from the offshore Stockman field in northwestern Russia and delivering it to international markets.

The Kyoto Protocol

It is important to mention briefly the Kyoto Protocol,[4] which recently came into force as a result of ratification by Russia. Under the Kyoto Protocol, the volume of CO_2 emitted in 1990 became the "base" level for Russia as well as for many other countries that adhered to the agreement. Contrary to some emotional observations,[5] the Russian government tends to view the protocol not as a "money bag" but as a "pilot agreement" designed to launch innovative economic mechanisms aimed at emissions reduction and improved energy efficiency. Foreign Minister Machimura Nobutaka said that Japan welcomed Russia's decision to ratify, indicating that his government had been approaching Russia on this issue on many occasions and at various levels.

In general, the agreement could stimulate both bilateral and subregional energy-environment cooperation, contributing to the promotion of renewable energy sources and energy-saving technologies and lifestyles. Defining the links among climate change, economic development, and energy security would help enrich the agenda for regional cooperation. Among possibilities for transborder projects are various options for power-grid interconnection, natural gas pipelines, hydroelectric power, and biomass energy. By investing in these environment-friendly ventures, Japan and other Annex II countries would increase the range of options available to them for meeting their Kyoto targets. To justify investment in projects of large capacity, however, the authorities must assure market access to such ventures.

Russia needs vast improvements in energy efficiency and new investment in the modernization of energy facilities. In eastern Russia, in some cases, renewable energy can replace obsolete thermal capacity. Japan is the world's leading nation in terms of energy efficiency, but it faces immense challenges in meeting its Kyoto targets. It is also conceivable that the Kyoto process would require active participation at the prefectural level. There are many opportunities to benefit from the Kyoto process. One option for managing international emissions trading while ensuring "environmental integrity" is through a Green Investment Scheme (GIS). This concept is designed to channel proceeds from international emissions trading into environmentally efficient projects. Energy efficiency improvements, renewable energy development, and biofuels could be priorities for GIS application.[6] For example, small hydroelectric power stations represent a very promising source of renewable energy.[7]

In addition, Russia has more than 20 percent of the world's forests, and three-quarters of these forests are located in eastern regions. With two million rivers, the country has the second-highest level of river runoff after Brazil. More than three-quarters of these water resources are in eastern regions. The economic hydro-energy potential is above 850 billion kWh/year, including 350 billion kWh/year concentrated in eastern Siberia and 294 billion kWh/year in the Far Eastern region. It is worth noting that the life-cycle CO_2 emissions from projects based on hydro and biomass energy match those from wind projects as the lowest among renewables.

Given the extremely rich resources of renewable energy in eastern regions of Russia and the very large markets for cleaner energy in neighboring countries, growth in renewable energy production could be significant. With ninety-eight large hydropower stations (HPS) of 44 gigawatt (GW) installed capacity, hydroelectric power accounts for 18 percent of total power generation in Russia. These stations generate approximately 170 billion kWh of electricity per year. By 2005, whereas Canada and the United States had developed more than half of their economic hydroelectric power potential, Russia had come to utilize only 23 percent of such potential nationwide and only 33 percent in eastern Siberia and 6 percent in the Far Eastern region. These two areas had sixteen HPS with 9 GW installed capacity under construction, including the largest Bureiskaya HPS project in Amurskaya Oblast. To serve customers beyond national boundaries, HPS projects would require transborder power-grid interconnection, allowing a "seasonal diversity exchange" between systems. For example, north-south interconnectors would allow a flow of hydropower from eastern Russia to China in the same fashion as that between southwestern Canada and the northwestern United States.[8] As far as biomass energy is concerned, the pulp and paper industry in Russia relies on biofuels to meet only 20–30 percent of its energy needs, while in Europe this share is above 50 percent.

A Geoeconomic Complementarity

Russia needs much closer links with the economies of East Asia. Japan has been a key player in helping to promote Asian integration. It has done so through investments by private firms as well as government grants to develop regional infrastructure, service operations, and production capabilities. It now invests approximately 10 percent of its outbound FDI into ASEAN and Asia's newly industrialized economies. At the November 2004 ASEAN+3 summit in Laos, economic ministers decided to set up an expert group to study the possibility of forming an East Asian Free Trade Area.

In 2005 Japan was still the second-richest country in the world, surpassing all the rest of Asia combined. Japanese imports from East Asia surged from 31 to 43 percent between 1992 and 2001, while exports to East Asia rose from 33 to 42 percent over the same period. It was estimated that more than 70 percent of the largest Asian companies on an annual turnover basis were Japanese.

Moreover, Japan plays a special economic role in East Asia in terms of trade, investment, market access, and innovation. Japan's Ministry of Economy, Trade, and Industry estimates that by 2020 Asia will have a 25.5 percent share of world GDP versus 19.3 percent in 1990. As a result, the region is now seen as a huge market for commodities and consumer goods. Less widely appreciated is that Asia is quickly becoming a hub for advanced research and development as well as higher-end products.

Japan serves as a major customer for Asian products. China became Japan's largest trading partner, supplanting the United States, while trade with ASEAN represented about 15 percent of total Japanese trade in 2003. In addition, India is attracting more attention from economic planners. It is interesting to note the significant presence of India in the Sakhalin-1 project, which initially was solely dependent on the participation of Japanese companies. The rising regional economic interconnectedness requires Russo-Japanese support, which potentially could lead to investment projects that do not just cover a single market but create a production and export platform that serves as a springboard into several regions.

Building Human Networks

In their bilateral relations, Russia and Japan have reached a point where the feelings of "remembrance and reconciliation" should prevail. The "Portsmouth contract" did not really work out well for various reasons, including revolutions and conflicts that broke out after 1905. The post-1945 alliance obligations changed the geopolitical currents further, completely altering the intermediary role of the United States in Tokyo-Moscow relations. Today, relatively loose trade and industry links continue to reflect these century-long upheavals as well as the limited capacities on both sides to interact economically.

The bottom line is that the new trade and economic links cannot be a part of policy bargaining any longer, but appear to be mutually reinforcing promoters of national interests, prosperity at the regional level, and international stability. It seems that globalization intertwined with decentralization offers new opportunities for development and cooperation.

In conclusion, economic interaction between Japan and Russia is moving ahead, promising significant mutual benefits. First, the real level of bilateral economic exchange is much higher than official statistics suggest. Second, megaprojects, including the Sakhalin oil and gas ventures, the Pacific oil pipeline, and similar projects, could further motivate bilateral trade and investment cooperation. Third, the relationship with China has become one of the most important bilateral links for Japan and Russia alike. China's demand for commodities, energy, and manufactured goods represents a golden opportunity for both Japan and Russia, particularly if they can somehow complement one another on a long-term basis. Fourth, cross-border energy cooperation in Northeast Asia, focused on energy-sector development in eastern Russia, would enhance the energy security of the economies of this area, contributing to the international competitiveness, environmental sustainability, and overall political stability of the entire region. Fifth, Japan and Russia should carefully examine opportunities for business links with support coming from the provinces and prefectures, keeping in mind that central bureaucracies in both countries are still in control and will likely remain the key channel for business-related communications. Finally, both the expansion of grassroots contacts, including those between the business elites of Japan and Russia, and the mutually beneficial geoeconomic positioning of the two nations are among the goals that are long term in nature but highly dependent on the overall international environment and leadership.

Over the last hundred years, each country has demonstrated an ability to survive without depending on the other. But the truth is that geographically Russia is the closest country to Japan: the distance between the northernmost cape of Hokkaido and Sakhalin is forty-two kilometers. Traditionally, each society was keenly interested in the culture of the other. Recently, private travel and business exchanges have been developing rapidly, contributing to an increasing number of border crossings. In particular, owing to positive changes in the domestic economic situation and relaxed regulations, Russians have been provided with a unique opportunity to visit Japan in relatively significant numbers.[9] Russian citizens, females in particular, have been joining the growing number of international marriages registered in Japan. It is worth noting that Russian-speaking spouses residing in Japan have organized a "club for mothers" with a website in Russian.

It would seem that the wide human segment of bilateral connections could promise tangible benefits on the economic, humanitarian, social, and political fronts. For example, Niigata Prefecture and Niigata City, known for pioneering good-neighbor relationships with Russia, maintain multiple partnership-type links with the Far Eastern area, including the cities of Khabarovsk and Vladivostok. In the summer of 2005, a large delegation organized by the Niigata business association visited Khabarovsk and Vladivostok, exposing a significant number of its members to Russia for the first time. Some of them were quite impressed by the fact that Vladivostok, which is only ninety minutes away from Japan by air, strongly resembles a European city! This reaction demonstrates that even the elites of Japanese localities that strongly favor the development of bilateral contacts with Russia may be unfamiliar with their closest regional neighbors. The same is true of the Far Eastern provinces and the rest of Russia. The good news is that this whole situation is now changing fast and that new relationships based on the concept of partnership are emerging.

Chapter 10

The Contemporary Implications
of the Russo-Japanese War

A Japanese Perspective

Kazuhiko Togo

The year 2005 marked the centennial of the Russo-Japanese War and the conclusion of the Portsmouth Treaty. Many symposia have been held on this occasion, and many academic papers have been published with a view to enlarge the historical knowledge of this war, to analyze the impact it left on international relations of the twentieth century, and to examine the consequences for military history, nationalism, national identities, and so on. Many publications appeared in Japanese but also in other languages including English, Korean, and Russian. Yet, given the great significance of this event for Northeast Asia and its continued relevance for mutual understanding in our time, one more examination should prove justified. This paper aims to assess the impact of the Russo-Japanese War on contemporary international relations, particularly among Japan, Russia, China, Korea, and the United States.

The war was waged between Japan and Russia but actually fought in China (Manchuria). Moreover, the Japanese army landed in Korea and went north to Manchuria, while Korea was probably the most important casus belli for Japan and Russia. The United States played a key role in mediating the Portsmouth Treaty and, after the war, became closely involved in the geopolitics of East Asia. So this war implicated all five major players in contemporary international politics in Northeast Asia to an unprecedented degree and with consequences that still are varyingly perceived in these countries.

The impact of the Russo-Japanese War on contemporary international relations is considerable. The war left a direct imprint on the historical discourse between Japan and Korea. In the case of China, the impact of the war was indirect, but in the wake of the conflict international relations centering on the Open Door policy and respect for the territorial integrity of China became an important theme in the decades leading to World War II. The United States became deeply involved in Northeast Asian geopolitics after the Portsmouth Treaty, and Japan's failure to cooperate with the United States in Manchuria in the wake of the Russo-Japanese War ultimately led the two countries to a collision course in the Pacific. The Portsmouth Treaty may be considered one origin of the territorial problem between Japan and Russia, and viewing this issue through the lenses of both the Portsmouth agreement of 1905 and the 1945 Yalta Conference may yield a better understanding of the present difficulties between these two nations.

This paper analyzes the historical relations among the five countries at the time of the Russo-Japanese War and their impact on international relations in its wake from the perspective of international relations theory. Analysis reveals a classic case where we can distinguish three layers of international relations: state-to-state relations, the domestic situation in each state, and the role of individuals. We can observe from an eclectic perspective how three schools of contemporary international relations apply: realism (centered around the analysis of power), liberalism (around ideals), and constructivism (around identity).[1] Since the potential coverage of this paper is so large that it could require an entire book (or books) to complete all the analysis in detail, the author narrows the focus by presenting the broad historical context of the war and its aftermath for the five major countries in the region and by concentrating on one issue that has contemporary implications for Japanese foreign policy in relation to Korea, China, the United States, and Russia.

Japan

Japanese historiography on the Russo-Japanese War before World War II was very positive. The war was a major success in that it established Japan as a modernized, civilized power in line with European and American nations.[2] After the defeat of World War II, leftist-Marxist historians argued that the war was a manifestation of Japanese imperialism and militarism against Asia and analyzed it from only a negative perspective that did not try to comprehend mixed motives and historical complexities. But the main trend in recent historiography has been to see it in the spectrum of the overall East Asian history of the early twentieth century and analyze its consequences as objectively as possible. In 2005, the centennial of the war, many books were published in Japan, some of them recapturing exclusively the honorable victories and heroic courage and patriotic devotion displayed by Japanese soldiers, but at the same time serious efforts to grasp the overall impact of the war in an objective manner were also made.[3]

A majority of historians may probably concur that, for Japan, the Russo-Japanese War was the culmination, beginning with the 1868 Meiji Restoration, of thirty-five years of national effort to create a strong country. Being surrounded by imperialist powers, the Meiji government determined that its major objective would be to reject colonization and develop Japan as an independent state capable of rivaling those advancing imperialist powers. The first of several popular slogans to rally the country was *fukoku kyōhei* (rich country and strong army). The second slogan was *datsu-A nyū-Ō* (departing from Asia and entering Europe). The Meiji government viewed Asia as hopelessly backward, compared with civilized and powerful states in the West, and believed that Japan, in order to become strong and rich, should follow the path of Europe. Thus, the key considerations for the Meiji government were realism and power. But in order to settle the issue of Japanese identity, the third slogan of the era, *wakon yōsai* (Japanese spirit and Western intellect), appeared. From 1868 to 1905, the Meiji government negotiated its place in international politics with this basic recognition of the world and Japan's place in it.

Japan's initial foreign-policy objectives were to determine the border with Russia, China, and some of its southern islands. By the 1890s, the Meiji government had established not only its "cordon of sovereignty" but also a "cordon of influence." Keeping Korea under Japan's influence became the major objective of the latter. The Sino-Japanese War in 1894–95, for example, was fought over the question of influence in Korea. The unexpected Japanese victory in this confrontation had several important consequences. First, Japan emerged as a military power capable of winning a war against a much larger and more populous China, which was characterized at the time as a "sleeping lion." Second, China lost its international credibility, and as a result European colonization, which began with the Opium War (1841–42), expanded to the entire country.[4] Third, seeking opportunities in this new round of imperialism in Asia, Russia led the Triple Intervention against Japan to have the Liaodong Peninsula returned to Chinese control. From this point onward, the Meiji government's primary foreign-policy objectives focused on repulsing the Russian threat from the north—more concretely, shutting out Russian influence in Korea and balancing the two countries' influence in Manchuria while avoiding international isolation. Internally, under the slogan of *gashin shōtan* (bear hardship for future revenge), the Japanese expanded their industrial and military power.

Russia did not hesitate to expand its influence in Manchuria. In 1896, when the Chinese statesman Li Hongzhang visited St. Petersburg on the occasion of the coronation of Nicholas II, the two countries concluded a confidential agreement to put the Chinese Eastern Railway under Russian control.[5] In 1898, when European powers began successively encroaching on Chinese territory, Russia leased Dairen and Port Arthur for twenty-five years, the territory it had asked Japan to relinquish after the Sino-Japanese War. In June 1900, just after China declared war against the West during the Boxer Rebellion, Russian troops occupied Manchuria from the end of July to October. Russia's November 1900 demand for control of Manchuria was withdrawn in April 1901 under harsh Japanese protest. On April 8, 1902, immediately after the conclusion of the Anglo-Japanese alliance, Russia signed an agreement with China to withdraw its troops from Manchuria in three stages. The first stage of the withdrawal was implemented but not the second, which was due to begin on April 8, 1903. Furthermore, in November 1903, Russian troops crossed the Korean border at the Yalu River and established a garrison under the guise of timber exploitation. Despite the Korean government's objection, made with guidance from the Japanese government, a lease agreement was concluded between a Russian timber company and the local Korean agricultural authority.[6]

While Russia's physical presence expanded through Manchuria, Russian diplomats preserved substantial influence in the Korean court. Korean reformers, who saw a model in Japan's modernization, began to exert some influence after the Kanghwa Treaty of 1876, when the Japanese government succeeded in opening ports in Korea through gunboat diplomacy. Japanese influence in Korean domestic politics decreased after the Kapsin Coup of 1884 failed. The Japanese government could not send adequate help to the reformers and concluded the Tianjing Treaty of 1885 with China.[7] Japan's intervention in the Tonghak Rebellion and eventual victory in the 1894–95 war with China renewed Japanese influence in Korea. But when Japanese radicals assassinated Korea's Queen Min in October 1895, King Kojong sought protection from Russia and stayed in the Russian legation in Seoul for about a year (from February 1896 to February 1897).[8] From this point, Russia and Japan both sought to expand their influence over the Korean court.

As threats from the north rose year by year, a broad consensus among Japanese leaders suggested that Korea had to be kept under Japanese influence whatever the cost, even at the expense of war. Two schools of thoughts emerged. *Man-Kan kōkan* (exchanging Manchuria and Korea) sought an agreement with Russia that would sustain Japanese influence over Korea and leave Manchuria to Russia. Itō Hirobumi and other elder statesmen who were cautious about waging war against Russia supported this position. *Man-Kan ittai* (unify Manchuria and Korea), favored by Komura Jutarō and the younger generation of Meiji leaders, sought to retain Japanese control over Korea and expand Japanese influence in Manchuria. Three arguments informed the thinking of this faction: (1) Any southward expansion of Russian influence would not stop in Manchuria, and sooner or later Japan would inevitably clash with Russia. (2) The capacity for a Russian military buildup through construction of the Trans-Siberian Railroad was adding to Russian power. Time was running against Japan; therefore war should be waged before it became too late. (3) Japan should first secure international support by aligning with Britain, which was the world's strongest naval power and which shared concern over Russian expansion into India and China. The two factions agreed on a coordinated and simultaneous approach to Britain and Russia. By early 1902, Britain had acknowledged Japan's special rights over Korea but Russia had not. The choice became clear as the first Anglo-Japanese alliance was signed on January 30, 1902.[9]

Japan's ultimate position was decided on June 23, 1903, at an imperial conference that included nine top Meiji leaders. It was agreed that under no circumstances would Korea be allowed to fall under Russian influence. This decision did not mean immediate war, but six months of negotiations with Russia based on the *Man-Kan kōkan* model yielded no progress.[10] Thus, on February 5, 1904, the Japanese government decided to terminate the negotiations and break off diplomatic relations with Russia. Japan's ultimatum was transmitted to Russia on February 6. The Japanese fleet attacked the Russian fleet on February 8. A formal declaration of war was made on February 10.[11]

Thus far, the logic and structure of the Russo-Japanese War are straightforward and simple. It was a war between imperial states based on power. The stronger country brings more territory under its influence. Foreign policy had its role in achieving national objectives through negotiations and agreements, but military power was ultimately the decisive factor. In order to strengthen a country's position in international politics, alliances with other imperial powers were an essential factor. Under this classic world of realism and based on its alliance with Britain, Japan fought a war with Russia, won, and got what it essentially wanted at Portsmouth: dominance over Korea (Article II), the right to lease the Liaodong Peninsula from Russia (Article V), and rights over the South Manchuria Railway from Russia (Article VI).

Beyond those gains, the Meiji leadership was realistic and flexible. Unlike its aims in Korea, Japan was not seeking absolute dominance in Manchuria, and the Russian right to the Chinese Eastern Railway was basically preserved

(Article VII). Likewise, China's sovereignty over Manchuria was confirmed, but the treaty was worded carefully to leave leeway for the preservation of Russo-Japanese influence in Manchuria (Articles III and IV).[12] Furthermore, the Meiji government knew that after its impressive but costly victories in Mukden (March 2005) and Tsushima (May 2005) it did not have the power to drive the Russians out of Manchuria, and peace was necessary as soon as possible. Tokyo was prepared to renounce both reparations and territory. Last-minute intelligence from Britain suggesting that Nicholas II was prepared to cede the southern part of Sakhalin enabled the Japanese delegation in Portsmouth to insist on having southern Sakhalin transferred to Japan (Article IX), but otherwise the Meiji leadership was ready to compromise.[13]

For the Japanese public in general, the Russo-Japanese War and the Portsmouth Treaty were inseparable. Despite initial public outrage against the treaty because of the perception that Japan had obtained less than it deserved, the Meiji leadership's decision to terminate the war at Portsmouth while Japan was still a victor is now viewed as the correct choice because it established Japan as one of the great powers of the twentieth century. The war was remembered as proof that even an Asian state could defeat one of the strongest European powers if the Asian country persevered and tried hard to catch up with the West.[14] But after Portsmouth, when Japan had basically achieved its fundamental objectives of *fukoku kyōhei* and *datsu-A nyū-Ō* and emerged as one of the great powers, it faced a new situation with wider options and further complexity. Not only realism and power but also national identity and idealistic liberalism began to play a greater role in international relations. After exploring several foreign-policy options through the 1910s and 1920s, Japan chose a path of rigorous autarkic imperial expansion that finally led to collision with the United States and complete defeat in 1945. In that sense, Portsmouth was the starting point for Japan to face a new world of greater complexity. Korea, China, the United States, and Russia were the objects of Japanese policy at Portsmouth and, in its wake, became the subjects of future contention.

Korea

Korean history leading to the Russo-Japanese War may be summarized as a tragic narrative of failed desire for modernization and independence. King Kojong reigned from his youth to abdication (1864–1907), but it was Kojong's father, Taewongun, who ruled as prince-regent in the initial decade of extensive contact with the West (1864–74). Taewongun adopted a strong anti-Western policy. Looking down on all Western powers as barbarians, he succeeded in fighting back against France in 1866 and America in 1871. Tae-wongun's extreme anti-Westernism was replaced with a policy of openness and modernization in 1874 when Kojong began his own rule. Over the next three decades Korean politics faced many hurdles. The court endured constant tension because of the strife between Taewongun, who kept power among his supporters, and Kojong's politically active wife, Queen Min, who was supported by reformists. Public unrest also erupted, in many instances to protect traditional values, as in the Tonghak Rebellion (1894) or the Righteous Army Movement (1895), but in others to support reformist initiatives such as the Independence Club (1896–97).[15] The Korean court, government officials, and opinion leaders sought support from foreign powers. Conservatives looked to China, while reformers sought support from Japan, Russia, and America, depending on the circumstances. But their pleas did not bring about what the Koreans expected.

In February 1897, King Kojong ended a year of residency in the Russian legation and moved to the Kyong'un Palace. In October he named himself emperor, promulgating the Empire of Great Korea. Kojong started a new process known as the Kwangmu reform, aiming to modernize the political, military, industrial, and educational structures of Korean society. But a lack of capital led Korea to grant many concessions to foreign powers in order to develop modern industries. Russia and Japan actively expanded their interests in Korea, causing a rift in the Korean leadership between supporters of Japan and Russia.[16]

When the Russo-Japanese War broke out on February 8, 1904, the Korean government declared its neutrality. But the Japanese army landed in Inchon on February 16, advanced to Seoul, and eventually reached the Yalu River in April.[17] The Japan-Korea Protocol of February 25 guaranteed Korean independence in Article III but allowed for Japan's military use of Korea while restricting Korean diplomatic power.[18] Korean writings emphasize that Korea's agreement to the protocol was coerced: "[Japan], intimidating the Korean government into renouncing its declaration of neutrality . . . ,"[19] or "Japan coerced Korea with pressure to conclude the Protocol."[20] Korean writings also indicate that the Japanese government cleverly grouped Koreans who were sympathetic to Japan into the pro-Japanese *Ilchinhoe* (Society for United Progress), and it was this specific group that actively supported Japan.[21]

However, in his book *The Tragedy of Korea*, F. A. McKenzie highlights a different aspect of Koreans' initial reactions to the Japanese presence.

I travelled largely throughout the northern regions in the early days of the [Russo-Japanese] war, and everywhere I heard from the [Korean] people during the first weeks nothing but expressions of friendship to the Japanese. The coolies and farmers were friendly because they hoped that Japan would modify the oppression of the native magistrates. A large section of better-class people, especially those who had received some foreign training, were sympathetic, because they credited Japan's promises [to strengthen the Korean nation] and had been convinced by old experience that no far-reaching reforms could come to their land without foreign aid.[22]

This account is credible in that McKenzie later described in detail the ruthlessness of Japanese colonial policy. His book is known to have "told the world about the fact that the Koreans bore a deep-rooted grudge against the Japanese for their aggressive attitudes, and he fiercely criticized the Japanese colonial policy in Korea."[23]

But the most stunning description of the Korean people's reaction at the initial stage of the war was made by the hero of Korean patriots, An Chunggun, who assassinated Japan's first resident-general of Korea, Itō Hirobumi, on October 26, 1909. After the assassination, An was arrested and transferred to a prison in Port Arthur, where he was detained until his execution on March 26, 1910. Judging from many Japanese records, An gained genuine respect among the prison guards and judicial officials in Port Arthur. He was permitted to write an autobiography and left many stunningly beautiful calligraphies. He also began narrating his worldview in a work titled "Thesis on Oriental Peace," but this was never completed, because Japanese authorities, acting on instructions from Tokyo, refused to postpone his execution.[24] In this unfinished thesis, An wrote about Koreans' initial reaction to the outbreak of the Russo-Japanese War and to the early success of the Japanese forces:

In the Declaration of War promulgated by the Japanese emperor, it was written that Japan would maintain peace in the orient and consolidate the independence of Korea. This great cause was superior to the white sunlight under the blue sky, and people of Korea and China, whether intelligent or not, agreed and supported it with unified hearts. Another point was that the Russo-Japanese War was a reflection of the competition between the whites and the yellows, and momentarily yesterday's animosity disappeared and a bondage of one race emerged. That was also a natural reflection of human sentiment. Such fun, such courage! A bridgehead of the whites, who continued to do wrong for several centuries, collapsed by a single drumbeat. . . . At this moment, spirited Koreans and Chinese rejoiced [at Japan's initial victory] as if the victory was our own.[25]

Current Korean scholarship also confirms that, at least at the beginning of the Russo-Japanese War, Korean people were friendly to Japan, believing that Japan would honor its promise to maintain Korean independence.[26] But this rejoicing and the hopes inspired by Japan's victory did not last long. Japan's victory over Russia initiated Japan's annexation of Korea. In Article II of the Portsmouth Treaty, Russia "acknowledged that Japan possesses in Korea paramount political, military, and economical interests." After the end of war in November 1905, Japan and Korea concluded the Protectorate Treaty, which gave Japan the right to conduct Korea's foreign policy. From the Korean point of view, even if the Japan-Korea Protocol of February 1904 might be acknowledged as a necessity of war, this second agreement cannot be seen as anything but Japan's intrusion into Korea's sovereignty. It was, moreover, a direct consequence of war and the Portsmouth Treaty. Kim Djun Kil quotes a *Hwang-song sinmun* (Imperial Capital Newspaper) editorial expressing profound indignation against the Protectorate Treaty.[27] Lee Ki-baik describes how this treaty was coerced against King Kojong's will and says: "Korea's standing in the international community as an independent nation was all but destroyed."[28] A third agreement in July 1907 deprived Korea of the right to supervise not only its external policy but also its internal policy, giving it instead to the Japanese resident-general.[29] In August 1910, Korea's annexation by Japan was formalized in a fourth agreement, the Treaty of Japan's Annexation of Korea.

It would be incorrect to assume that the Meiji leadership was unified from the beginning on the policy of annexing Korea. There were periods when the model of British attempts, in the case of Egypt, to preserve at least outward independence was pursued. Itō, who was chosen as the first resident-general in December 1905, stated in a speech given in Seoul in July 1907: "why should Japan destroy Korea?" and "Korea must gain autonomy."[30] He tried swiftly to enact the benefits of protectorate status through the construction of "roads, hospitals, schools, and an increase in agricultural production."[31] But even Itō eventually gave his consent to annexation. Okazaki Hisahiko argues that, though Itō, in his strategic thinking, was firm that Manchurian sovereignty could not be infringed on, the annexation of Korea fell within his range of acceptability.[32] From the Korean point of view, all four agreements with Japan are understood as one package. The Russo-Japanese War and the Portsmouth Treaty, moreover, gave a great push to this process.

For Koreans, the international assent to leave Korea under Japanese control was all the more painful and outrageous. The Korean court sought support from the international community, but even before Russia agreed to Japan's dominance over Korea at Portsmouth, America and Britain acknowledged Japan's rights in Korea. The Katsura-Taft agreement of July 29, 1905, mutually recognized Japan's dominance over Korea and America's dominance over the Philippines. This was, after all, a period when the U.S. government acted in a typically imperialist manner, colonizing Hawaii and the Philippines in 1898. President Roosevelt was known to be enormously supportive of Japan's fight against Russia and, within the context of imperialist realism, had no objection to Japan's managing of Korea. In the first Anglo-Japanese alliance, Britain had already acknowledged Japan's special rights over political, trade, and industrial matters in Korea. The second Anglo-Japanese alliance, signed on August 12, 1905, further acknowledged Japan's right to take measures to guide, control, and protect Korea. Che Mun-hyon argues that the Katsura-Taft agreement, the second Anglo-Japanese alliance, and the Portsmouth Treaty should be regarded as a unit that became the basis for the Korean annexation five years later.[33]

Through Syngman Rhee in August 1905 and through Reverend Homer Hulbert in November–December 1905, Emperor Kojong sought America's "good offices" based on the 1882 U.S.-Korean Treaty of Peace, Amity, and Commerce, but President Roosevelt did not respond favorably.[34] International recognition that Korea constituted a part of Japan was more rigorously imprinted in 1907, when Emperor Kojong sent officials to the second International Peace Conference held in The Hague. The delegation was not recognized as the official representative of Korea, thus inducing Kojong's resignation (forced by Japan). When the annexation came in 1910, there were no international forces to stand against Japan.

Thus, for the majority of Japanese, the Russo-Japanese War and the Treaty of Portsmouth are remembered as the culmination of their nation's half-century endeavor to become a civilized, modern state. But for Koreans, even though they hailed Japan as the first Asian victor against Euro-American imperialism at the initial stage of the Russo-Japanese War, Portsmouth became the symbol of their humiliation, indignation, and abandonment by Euro-American civilized powers.

The historical discourse between Japan and Korea today is naturally not limited to Portsmouth. After Portsmouth, the issue of Japanese annexation and rule deeply offended and angered Koreans. Retrospectively, serious questions remain valid: "Even if the Korean protectorate was thought to be necessary, why could Japan not respect Korean culture and tradition, prohibit Japanization, prohibit the influx of *furyō Nihonjin* (unworthy Japanese), and respect Korean rights to land and other property?"[35] Through the initial years of occupation, Korean indignation against ruthless Japanese rule, especially its brutality and destruction of traditional values, gradually established a profound sense of national identity in Korea. And yet, even in the post–World War II period, such questions as "Why did it take fourteen years for Japan to resume diplomatic relations with South Korea?" or "Why is the history issue still creating such tension and emotion in contemporary relations between the two countries?" remain unanswered. It may be worthwhile remembering that the origin of this ongoing historical discourse lies in the Russo-Japanese War and the Treaty of Portsmouth, which leads to the question: "Why did An Chung-gun, who described so eloquently Koreans' rejoicing in the initial Japanese victory against the Russians in 1904, assassinate Itō Hirobumi five years later?"

China

In the years preceding the Russo-Japanese War, the Chinese government was having no less difficulty than the Korean government in managing its domestic politics. The reign of Empress Dowager Cixi was closing but not entirely. Grand Councillor Yuan Shikai was in command of the government. But a series of failures in government policy such as the defeat in the Sino-Japanese War of 1894–95; the encroachment by Germany, Russia, Britain, and France in 1898 and 1899; the reformist coup by Emperor Guang Xu, assisted by Kang Youwei and Liang Qichao; its collapse in 1898; and the failed Boxer Rebellion in 1900 all contributed to weakening the Qing dynasty. The Russian occupation of Manchuria and Russia's continued presence after April 1903, despite a commitment to withdraw, naturally irritated the Qing court.[36] The Russo-Japanese War broke out amid these circumstances. China was at the center of the conflict because, other than short periods when General Kuroki's army moved across the Korean Peninsula toward the Yalu River at the beginning of the war and when Japanese troops occupied Russian Sakhalin near the end of the conflict, the war was fought almost exclusively in China (that is, in Manchuria).

In 1896, Russia and China concluded a confidential agreement dictating that the two countries should cooperate in case one was attacked by Japan, but the Chinese government was not prepared to side openly with Russia. Yuan Shikai's reaction to the war was typically realist: "if we take the side of Russia, the Japanese navy will attack our south, but if we take the side of Japan, the Russian army will attack our northwest."[37] The Chinese government took a position of neutrality, paying particular attention not to violate its neutrality with a view to its agreement with Russia.[38] Neither the Russian nor the Japanese armies felt obliged to show mercy toward locals who happened to be on the enemy's side. In fact, a contemporary Chinese scholar stated that "China's memory of the Russo-Japanese War is victimhood, because the war was fought inside China and had its consequences."[39] When Lu Xun saw a picture of a Chinese crowd smiling joyfully around a compatriot

being beheaded by a Japanese soldier for spying for the Russians, he decided
that his primary work was to reform Chinese people's mentality.[40] Nevertheless, the Manchurian inhabitants seem generally to have been sympathetic to
the Japanese side. "The atrocities [by the Russians] merely intensified Chinese
support for the generally less destructive, better-organized and disciplined
Japanese. . . . In Japanese-occupied areas Chinese authorities generally co-
operated with the Japanese 'civil governors.'"[41] As in the case of An Chung-
gun, Sun Yat-sen, who in August 1905 established the Chinese Revolutionary
Union in Tokyo, stated the following in a speech titled "Great Asianism":

From the day when Japan won the war against Russia, all Asian people thought to
beat Europe and began their independence movement. The independence movement began in Egypt, Persia, Turkey, Afghanistan, Arabia, and India. As a result of
Japan's victory over Russia, great hope for the independence of Asia emerged.[42]

But here again the initial Chinese support for Japan did not last long.
After the conclusion of the Portsmouth Treaty, the situation began to change
rapidly. In Manchuria, the Japanese government tried to capitalize on what
it had gained in Portsmouth: the right to lease the Liaodong Peninsula (Port
Arthur, Dairen, and adjacent territorial waters) (Article V) and the South
Manchuria Railway (between Changchun and Port Arthur) (Article VI). Komura Jutarō went to Beijing in November–December 1905 and obtained the
necessary Chinese consent to what had been agreed in Portsmouth concerning Manchuria. But in addition, through supplementary agreements, Komura "gained the right to improve the railway line connecting Andong and
Mukden, and China pledged not to construct any line in the neighbour-
hood of or parallel to the main railway that Japan had newly obtained under
the Treaty of Portsmouth."[43] There is no reason to presume that the Chinese
government was happy to see Japan replacing Russia in maintaining and
enhancing imperialist rights over China. Nor is there any reason to presume
that the Chinese government was happy with the four conventions Japan
and Russia concluded in 1907, 1910, 1912, and 1916, of which one of the major
objectives was to keep Manchuria under their respective influence in order
to shut out American interests in the region.

After Portsmouth, China's domestic political turmoil worsened. The
fundamental political structure was shaken to the degree that even the
emergence of a Russo-Japanese alliance in Manchuria looked secondary.
Both Empress Dowager Cixi and Emperor Guang Xu died in 1908. Yuan
Shikai was ousted from power after the death of Cixi. The Nationalist movement led by Sun Yat-sen began to gain momentum. Led by the Guomindang, the revolutionary movement exploded, and in October 1911 the Nanjing

provisional government was established with Sun Yat-sen as its head. The Nanjing and Beijing governments were on a collision course, but after internal and diplomatic maneuvering, particularly by Britain, the Qing dynasty fell, and Yuan Shikai returned to power in February 1912 as the first president of the newly established republic. But Yuan's program for modernization financed by gigantic loans from abroad clashed with Guomindang policy. Yuan crushed the Guomindang opposition, began his dictatorship, and created a deep rift with widespread opposition before he died in 1916.

While China was engulfed by the political turmoil resulting in the fall of the Qing dynasty, an important change in the international climate was taking place. Under the presidency of William McKinley, the United States colonized Hawaii and the Philippines in 1898. Secretary of State John Hay declared the Open Door policy in September 1899. Amidst the Boxer Rebellion the following year, the U.S. policy to preserve Chinese territorial integrity was declared in the July Third Circular to other Western powers. Okazaki argues that this circular had strong domestic policy implications because it was issued one day before the Democratic Convention.[44] The major characteristics of the new U.S. policy could be summarized as follows.[45] European reaction to China's defeat in the Sino-Japanese War of 1894–95 had been quick and vigorous: in 1898–99 four countries (Germany, Russia, Britain, France) had expanded their colonial territories in China in a striking manner.[46] Hence, U.S. policy in 1899–1900 was designed to protect America's rising economic interests against that expansion. The United States tried to ensure those interests while not challenging the vested interests that the Europeans and the Japanese had acquired before 1899. Instead, the gist of the U.S. Open Door policy was that all future rights regarding trade with China should remain open to all outside powers including the United States. "Equal opportunity" was the key. The United States inherited this policy emphasis from Britain, which had developed it to monopolize close to 80 percent of the trade with China.[47] However, the principle of "equal opportunity" was applied together with the principle of "preservation of China's territorial integrity." As we will see below, the U.S. vision on this point was much conditioned by the existing reality among the imperialist powers. And yet the idealism of "respect for China's sovereignty and territorial integrity" gradually became an integral part of U.S. policy toward China. It provided the guiding principle for the Washington Conference in 1921–22, and it dictated the U.S. position in the 1930s against Japan's expansion in China.[48] Most important, in this liberal vision of respect for the sovereignty and territorial integrity of China, Chinese leaders from Sun Yat-sen to Chiang Kai-shek to Mao Zedong found a perfect justification for their policy to recover China's honor and identity.

Two possible foreign-policy directions emerged in Japan in response to this dramatically changing situation inside China and the Asia-Pacific region in general: to respect Chinese sovereignty including Manchuria or to put Manchuria under Japanese control and eventually make it the basis of an autarkic sphere of influence. Some Japanese politicians and opinion leaders before the Russo-Japanese War thought that the Open Door policy and respect for China's sovereignty in Manchuria suited Japan's interests. Ogawa Heikichi, a member of the Japanese Diet, argued on June 4, 1903, that "Manchuria must be opened to all countries for their trade and commercial interests, as supported by America or Britain."[49] After Japan's victory in the Russo-Japanese War, the Japanese military began to assert the necessity of introducing military rule in Manchuria, but the Ministry of Foreign Affairs strongly opposed it. In a well-known episode in May 1906, Itō Hirobumi firmly rejected the military's view and dictated that China's sovereignty should be respected in Manchuria.[50] In fact, Japanese foreign policy made a serious turn in that direction in the 1920s. Japan became a signatory of the nine-party treaty on China at the Washington Conference in 1922, agreeing to the principles of equal opportunity and respect for China's sovereignty and territorial integrity.

But those who saw in Manchuria, and later in northern China, the basis for Japanese imperialist development were no less influential. Ultimately imperialist policy got the upper hand. When World War I broke out in 1914, many political leaders in Japan perceived it as a "heavenly opportunity of the Taishō Era," as was stated by Inoue Kaoru.[51] So the Japanese government took advantage of the situation and, in January 1915, presented its Twenty-One Demands to force China's acknowledgment of Japan's rights in Manchuria, Mongolia, and the Shandong Peninsula (which Germany had leased from China) as well as its right to dispatch counselors in financial and military administration on behalf of the Chinese government. The Beijing government leaked Japan's demands to the international press and, with support from the UK and the United States, successfully rejected Japan's requests for a voice in China's internal matters.[52] The Japanese government could agree with the Chinese government only on fourteen clauses in May 1915. The Japanese delegation at the Paris Peace Conference in 1919 succeeded in having the Shandong Peninsula transferred to Japan, but that decision ignited strong protests among students and intellectuals in China in the form of the May Fourth Movement. After the 1920s, Japan's turn toward establishing an autarkic empire became increasingly clear. The Manchurian Incident (1931), the establishment of Manchukuo (1932), and the war with China from 1937 set the course for eventual collision with the United States.

Counterfactual historical analysis poses the following question: In the early 1900s, could Japan have agreed to the Open Door policy and respect for Chinese sovereignty and territorial integrity, and, if so, what would have been the consequences? Even if Japan had accepted both, that path probably would have been little more than a compromise between the existing imperialist order and the eruption of national sentiments for Asian liberation. As the result of its victory in the Russo-Japanese War, Japan became a member of the civilized, modern imperial powers. The requirements of that position were probably inescapable. In accordance with the Anglo-Japanese alliance, Japan began oppressing expatriate members of the Indian independence movement in Japan. The Taft-Katsura agreement of 1905 resulted in the departure of Philippine nationalists from Japan. The Franco-Japanese accord of 1907, agreeing on mutual recognition of respective spheres of influence in Indochina, Manchuria, and Korea, resulted in the expulsion of Vietnamese nationalists from Japan. Sun Yat-sen was also expelled in 1907, and his journals were banned.[53] Japan was no longer the vanguard of Asian liberation, as had been expected after its victory in the Russo-Japanese War.[54]

But, even within that limitation, could the Japanese government have sided with the policy of preserving China's territorial integrity? In fact, that policy, as advanced by the American government, had many limitations that probably would have made it easier for the Japanese government to follow. Okazaki writes that, despite all policy promulgations, the nature of U.S. imperialism did not differ much from that of other nations, because John Hay tried to obtain a bay in Fujian Province as a naval storage area in December 1900 but was cordially discouraged by the Japanese government, which claimed that this action would be against the U.S. policy of preserving China's territorial integrity.[55] Regarding Russian troops stationed in Manchuria after the Boxer Rebellion, John Hay told the Russian envoy on March 28, 1901 that the United States acknowledged Russia's right to take measures necessary to prevent attacks against its interests, such as had occurred the previous year, so long as American trade was not jeopardized and the Open Door was observed.[56] In a memorandum to Roosevelt on May 31, 1903, Hay stated that the United States was not objecting to the Russian position in Manchuria, whose exceptional nature it recognized, and that, whatever happened in North China and Manchuria, the bottom line for Washington was not to be subjected to an inferior position than it had under the Qing regime. This stance virtually meant that, so long as its commercial interests were preserved, America did not care whether Manchuria was governed by the Qing or by Russia.[57]

Nevertheless, respecting China's sovereignty and territorial integrity gradually became the principle that attracted international consensus in the

1920s and the 1930s. The May Fourth Movement of 1919 ignited "nationalist agitation" among Chinese students and intellectuals.[58] Through the period of warlord rule in the 1920s, the Guomindang and the Chinese Communist Party began to share a common urge for reunification and a common anti-colonialism, above all, against Japan. Had the Japanese government respected China's sovereignty and territorial integrity along with other imperialist powers and responded to the Chinese urge for national identity, Japan's position in East Asia would have been very different toward the middle of the twentieth century. In 1905, Japan faced a historic opportunity to become the vanguard of liberation in Asia. Because Japan itself was becoming an imperialist power, full Japanese support for Asian liberation might not have been realistic. But was not the policy of respect for the sovereignty and territorial integrity of China within the reach of the Japanese government? The American government had already advanced this policy, at least pro forma, for five years. The Japanese government failed to grasp that the new U.S. policy, which began as a moderate, economy-oriented Open Door declaration, then gained strength through its correspondence to China's urge for national identity. Eventually this idealism became a guiding power in East Asian international relations. Instead, the Japanese government moved toward autarkic imperialism. This counterfactual historical perspective does not engender self-mesmerizing defeatism or self-righteous justification of the past. It shows the full extent of Japan's past activities together with their limitations, and it raises an important question as to what is the best policy for a twenty-first-century idealism that would incorporate the major requirements of our era in East Asia.

The United States

The late nineteenth century marked the rise of American imperialism, with the Spanish-American War of 1898 being its most symbolic incident. By the end of the century, American sugar investments had become sizable in Cuba, where an independence movement against Spanish rule was in progress. The American government declared war in April 1898, began operations against Spain the following month, and occupied the Philippines in August. The Spanish garrison in Guam had surrendered to the American fleet in July. Germany, with gunboats, and Russia, without, objected most to the U.S. conquests; France took a neutral position; Japan and Britain were most conciliatory.[59] After the United States won the war in Cuba (June to July), a peace treaty was concluded in Paris the following December. The treaty "established the independence of Cuba, ceded Puerto Rico and Guam to the

United States, and allowed the victorious power to purchase the Philippine Islands from Spain for $20 million."[60] In 1898, President McKinley signed a resolution to annex Hawaii as well.[61] But colonization of the Philippines met strong opposition inside the United States, with Democrats and free traders arguing that colonialism was imperialistic and against democratic principles. Yui Daizaburō argues that the U.S. Open Door approach to China arose partly from this public backlash against a military approach in the Philippines.[62]

President Theodore Roosevelt, who succeeded President McKinley in September 1901, thus inherited two aspects of the U.S. policy of imperialism: to protect the vested interests in U.S. colonies and to advance the Open Door policy in China. Roosevelt was already a strong supporter of colonization of the Philippines and, as assistant secretary of the navy from 1897 to 1898, paved the way for eventual occupation.[63]

When tensions rose between Japan and Russia, Roosevelt's position was based on the geopolitical interests of the United States. On the issue of Korea, Roosevelt was willing to let Japan dominate, provided Japan would agree to U.S. preponderance over the Philippines. Rising Japanese power, the relative inability of Korea to assert itself, and the proximity of Taiwan (by then a Japanese territory) to the Philippines resulted in this delineation of spheres of influence. On the issue of China (that is, Manchuria), Roosevelt's official position was to seek equal access while preserving China's territorial integrity. As noted above, securing equal opportunity for American economic interests was Roosevelt's primary objective. The objective of preserving China's territorial integrity was far more ambiguous. The bottom line of U.S. policy on Manchuria, therefore, might have been to acknowledge the Russian presence provided that U.S. commercial interests would not be affected. Russia's high-handed approach, however, raised discomfort and anger among Americans, including President Roosevelt. He expressed to John Hay that he wished to go against Russia to the extent that public opinion allowed.[64] In July, Roosevelt also published an official statement saying that Russia had taken several measures that went against U.S. goodwill toward St. Petersburg regarding Manchuria. Some analyses indicate that Roosevelt's position reflected American anger against oppression of Jews in Russia in April.[65]

Thus, when war began, Roosevelt's sympathy toward Japan was clear, and his possible role in mediating a peace treaty was understood. But, when the war ended and the Portsmouth Treaty was successfully concluded, a series of new issues emerged and became the origin of future tensions between the two countries. These include the Open Door policy in Manchuria, the status of Japanese emigrants in America, and naval competition, among

others. The Open Door issue, which probably had a lasting impact, concerned Edward Harriman, an American railroad magnate who was eager to
create a global railroad network. He arrived in Japan on September 1, 1905,
with a view to purchase the South Manchuria Railway. The Tokyo leadership welcomed his proposal: Harriman had the financial resources that
Tokyo lacked to run the railway, and America could become a buffer in coping with Russia. An agreement was almost ready for signing in early October 1905, but when Komura Jutarō came back from Portsmouth on October
16, he categorically refused to support it. Komura's long-term strategy was
to keep Manchuria under Japanese influence. The railroad was critical to
achieving this objective and could not possibly be sold to the Americans. He
also argued that public opinion would explode (protests were already underway against concessions made at Portsmouth) if people knew that one of
the few tangible gains from the war would be transferred to America. He
further consolidated his position through legal arguments that any transfer
of the South Manchurian Railway needed Chinese approval.[66] Komura won,
and the agreement formulated between Prime Minister Katsura Tarō and
Edward Harriman was revoked.[67]

Okazaki agrees that Komura's decision met Japan's short- to midterm interests: Japan's control of the railway furthered its domination of southern
Manchuria. But Okazaki strongly criticizes Komura's decision for its consequences in the long run. Okazaki's view is not based on a moral or idealistic argument that Japan should have sided with the Open Door policy. In
fact, Che agrees that "the principle of equal opportunity did not apply to investment opportunities such as the railroad management, and Japan had
good reason to oppose Harriman's proposal."[68] Furthermore, American
foreign policy at the time was based on the Monroe Doctrine, designed to
establish U.S. dominance in the Americas but not intervention in matters
outside the Western Hemisphere.[69] The Japanese government thus had a
solid basis from which to argue that it had legitimate reasons to expand its
influence in Manchuria.

Okazaki's view is based exclusively on power considerations. He argues
that Japan's success in expanding and protecting its special interests in
Manchuria over a period of forty years is attributable largely to luck. The international situation in East Asia was fluid. Had there not been war in Europe, and had Russia regained its power to threaten Japan's interests in
Manchuria, or had there not been a power struggle in China, and had a
united Chinese government urged America to pressure Japan to abandon its
claims to Manchuria, Japan's position as an imperialist in Asia would have
become shaky much earlier than it eventually did. "It was not that difficult
to foresee such an eventuality just after the Russo-Japanese War. Japan's cor-

rect answer should have been the acceptance of Harriman's proposal. Komura's tactic derailed Japan from its long-term national interests."[70]

Rather than seeing America as a future ally in the wake of the Russo-Japanese War, the Japanese government chose a different path. Although defeated militarily, Russia remained Japan's greatest potential threat. The 1907 Imperial Defense Directive defined "Russia as the first potential enemy, to be followed by the United States, Germany, and France."[71] But, in the area of foreign policy, the Japanese government moved quickly to establish close relations with Russia. The future possibility of a Russian threat, combined with the immediate necessity for cooperation in the face of rising pressure from the United States, brought the two countries closer. The first Russia-Japan convention was concluded in 1907 in order to clarify and confirm what was achieved in Portsmouth. Under the attached confidential agreement, Japan's dominance in Korea was reaffirmed, and Manchuria was divided in half, with Russia retaining influence in the north and Japan in the south.

The second convention, concluded in 1910, was designed to protect Japanese and Russian interests in Manchuria from outside forces. The primary motive was defense against American action. In 1909, Russia oscillated between America and Japan. Minister of Finance Vladimir Kokovtsov argued that Japan's expansionist threat could best be prevented through an alliance with Washington and proposed to sell the Chinese Eastern Railway to America. Foreign Minster Aleksandr Izvol'skii argued that, because Japan was the most dangerous actor in the region, Russia must strengthen its alliance with Japan. But, when U.S. secretary of state Philander Knox proposed to let the Chinese Eastern and South Manchuria railways be bought back by the Qing, with Western powers bearing the financial responsibilities and joint administration of these railways, Izvol'skii's views prevailed. Japan and Russia agreed in a confidential attachment to the 1910 convention that, "if special interests are threatened, the two countries will take joint action to protect them and assist each other."[72]

Political turmoil in China in 1911 resulted in the independence of Outer Mongolia and an increase of Russian influence there. This development raised suspicions in Japan about the extent of Russian influence in Inner Mongolia. The third Russia-Japan convention, concluded in 1912, defined their respective spheres of influence in Inner Mongolia. After war broke out in Europe in 1914, the Russian government desperately needed a stable front in Asia and assistance from Japan in the supply of weapons and ammunition. The Japanese government saw an opportunity to gain Russian support for Japan's expansive China policy and receive some direct gains from Russia such as the portion of the Chinese Eastern Railway connecting Harbin and Changchun.[73] Thus the fourth convention was concluded in 1916. But Japan-Russia ties were broken with the Russian Revolution in 1917 and Japan's intervention in Siberia from 1918 to 1922.

After the revolution had weakened Russia, Japan's natural move was to consolidate its position in Manchuria by displacing Russia and bringing the entire region into its own sphere of influence. This policy eventually led to the Manchurian incident in 1931, followed by the establishment of Manchukuo as a Japanese client state in 1932. Japan's autarkic sphere of influence expanded from Manchuria to northern China, to southern China, and eventually to Indochina, leading to the Pacific War and Japan's defeat. Retrospectively, history shows that Japan's choices in power politics proved to be wrong. Power politics in East Asia in 2005 differ from those in 1905. While the participants are the same, the game they are engaged in is different. But it may well be useful to look back in history and ask once again, from the point of view of power and realism, what is Japan's best choice for a partner in contemporary Northeast Asian international relations.

Russia

The Russo-Japanese War left a grave impact on the Russian domestic situation. In fact, the defeat signaled the need for internal reform and ultimately led to the Revolution and the demise of tsarist Russia in 1917. Tsarist Russia in the late nineteenth century was a gigantic state, rife with contradictions. On the one hand, it underwent astonishing modernization under the leadership of Peter the Great and Catherine the Great in the eighteenth century, became one of the strongest military powers in Europe after the Napoleonic Wars in the early nineteenth century, and thereafter developed an amazing level of intellectual and cultural capacity. On the other hand, Russia still comprised an underdeveloped rural society where serfdom was the norm until the emancipation initiated by Alexander II in 1861. Small circles of exclusive aristocrats, rich farmers, and merchants constituted the ruling class; the bourgeoisie that led Europe to industrialize was not formed. Deep frustration among idealistic intelligentsia often led to terrorism, which was reprised by more oppressive rule. Sergei Witte's attempts at industrialization from above with the introduction of foreign capital had barely begun in 1892. The autocracy remained immensely powerful when Nicholas II succeeded his father, Alexander III, in 1894.

Russian policy in Asia can be summarized as a constant drive for eastward expansion. Whether we attribute this drive to an inherent urge to seek sunlight and warmth, to a subconscious desire to expand the frontiers as a buffer for security, or to a missionary spirit to disseminate Christianity to barbaric easterners, expansion dominated Russian policy. It started with Ermak Timofeyevich's Siberian expedition in the sixteenth century and the demarcation of the East Siberian border with China in the seventeenth century.[74] Russian explorers finally reached Vladivostok in 1860. Two border agreements were concluded with China that gave Russia the area northwest of the Amur River (Treaty of Aigun, 1858) and east of the Amur and Ussuri rivers (Treaty of Beijing, 1860). Construction of the Trans-Siberian Railroad began in 1891 and represented another dynamic eastward push. The 1896 confidential agreement with China to build the railway across northern Manchuria to Vladivostok furthered this initiative. Meanwhile, all this expansion eastward, and particularly the construction of the railway, brought Russia into conflict with Japanese interests in Northeast Asia.

While the Russian court and government unanimously supported rapid construction of the Trans-Siberian Railroad, the question remained of how to deal with Japan. Traditional historiography suggests that two schools of thought existed at the time. Moderates, such as Finance Minister Sergei Witte, Foreign Minister Vladimir Lamsdorf, and Minister of War Aleksei Kuropatkin, preferred nonmilitary, economic means and tried to avoid conflict with Japan. Hard-liners, such as former Guards colonel Aleksandr Bezobrazov, Interior Minister Vyacheslav Plehve, and Rear Admiral A. M. Abaza, preferred political and military solutions. The moderates prevailed until the spring of 1903, but from May of the same year the hard-liners gained greater influence over Nicholas II.[75] Recent scholarship contends, however, that this distinction between personalities is too simplified, concluding instead that "the war resulted from the irreconcilable ambitions of two aggressive states in an age of great power rivalry over the entire globe."[76]

Russia was ready for war at the beginning of 1904, fought the war, lost it, but still had ample forces left in Manchuria. However, the Russian domestic situation reached a boiling point and exploded on Bloody Sunday, January 3, 1905. Mass demonstrations and national strikes followed, resulting in the establishment of the first soviet in May, to the north of Moscow.[77] By August 1905, the Russian court had good reason to terminate the war with Japan.

From the Russian perspective, the most difficult points for agreement at Portsmouth were reparations and territory. Instructions to the delegation in Portsmouth stated that cession of territory, payment of reparations, partial cession of the Chinese Eastern Railway, and deprivation of the right to keep a Pacific fleet were unacceptable. Nicholas II told Witte: "not a *kopeika*, nor an inch of territory can be ceded."[78]

But the Japanese public expected sizable reparations and cessions of territory befitting Japan's victories at land and sea. From the Meiji leaders' point of view, however, the combination of their shrewd realism, strong alliance with Britain, accurate intelligence, and effective conduct of the negotiations in August 1905 resulted in the cession of southern Sakhalin at Portsmouth. After the victory at Mukden in March 1905, the supreme command in Tokyo had considered that further victory in Manchuria was necessary, but the military command in Manchuria strongly objected and sent General Kodama Gentarō, chief architect of the Manchurian operation, to Tokyo to convince the supreme command that the war could not be prolonged. His views were accepted, and after the victory at Tsushima in May, Foreign Minister Komura Jutarō instructed his envoy in Washington to ask President Roosevelt to mediate peace treaty negotiations. In order to give Japan more bargaining power, Japanese troops occupied Sakhalin in July 1905, just before the negotiations began on August 9.[79] The Tokyo government instructed Komura Jutarō, who now represented Japan in Portsmouth, that the absolute minimum conditions for a peace agreement were Japan's dominance over Korea, withdrawal of both armies from Manchuria, transfer of Russia's lease of the Liaodong Peninsula to Japan, and Japanese control of the South Manchuria Railway; reparations and territory were only relatively necessary conditions, without which the negotiations could still be concluded.

When it became clear that monetary compensation and cession of land were the key difficulties, Komura made a compromise proposal on August 18: Russia could keep the northern part of Sakhalin and, instead of ceding that territory, would pay Japan an indemnity of 1.2 billion yen. The Japanese ambassador, Kaneko Kentarō, conveyed this proposal to President Roosevelt, and on August 21 Roosevelt sent a message to Nicholas II advising him to accept. On August 23, Nicholas II told the American ambassador in St. Petersburg that he was prepared to cede southern Sakhalin to Japan but could not accept having to pay any reparations. Nicholas II's position was conveyed to Japan not by President Roosevelt but by the British envoy to Tokyo on August 27. Tokyo had already instructed Komura that Japan was prepared to agree to a peace treaty without any territory or reparations, but having heard this information, Tokyo instructed him to postpone the last meeting for one day. On August 29 agreement was reached, with the cession of southern Sakhalin to Japan. The Treaty of Portsmouth was signed on September 5, 1905.[80]

Why did Nicholas II think that the cession of southern Sakhalin was acceptable to Russia? U.S. ambassador George von Lengerke Meyer, who spoke with him on August 23, maintained that the tsar made his decision soon after Meyer convinced him that under an earlier treaty that land had temporarily become Russian territory, just like Port Arthur.[81] Indeed, when

Japan and Russia concluded their first border agreement, the Treaty of Commerce and Friendship in 1855, the frontier was established between Etorofu and Urup in the Kuril Islands, but Sakhalin was left without border demarcation. In reality, there were settlers on the island from both countries, with Russians occupying the northern part and Japanese residing in the south. An undetermined border did not suit the interests of either side, and in the second border agreement between Japan and Russia in 1875, the Treaty of Exchanges Concerning Sakhalin and the Kuril Islands, Russia ceded eighteen islands of the Kuriles north from Urup. In exchange, Sakhalin fully entered into the Russian empire. So in fact, at the time of the Portsmouth Treaty, it was only thirty years since Sakhalin had formally come under Russian sovereignty. Forty years after Portsmouth, however, Japan realized that the consequences of the treaty might have cost it dearly. The Soviet Union evened the score by inflicting on Japan much more damage than Japan thought it had a right to inflict. Naturally, the complexity of the situation in 1945 went far beyond the legacy of 1905.

If the world in 1945 had been governed by only the criteria of power, realism, and the decisive role of military strength, it would have been much simpler for Japan. Japan lost the war—the victor had a right to gain territory, and the Soviet Union took away southern Sakhalin and the Kuriles. Someday, Japan could rebuild its military and take back what it lost. If Japan could not become strong enough to achieve this objective, then its lost territories would not be regained. Under the criteria mentioned above, this situation resembled that of the period between the Sino-Japanese War and the Russo-Japanese War (1895–1904). But in 1945 the world was changing, and additional criteria other than power politics began to make an imprint on interstate relations.

First, there emerged the question of identity. Stalin defined the USSR's August–September 1945 war against Japan as an opportunity to redress the shame Russia had incurred in the Russo-Japanese War. He stated: "For forty years, we the elder generation have been waiting for this occasion."[82] The Yalta agreement and the transfer not only of southern Sakhalin but also of the Kuril Islands were a realization of Russian irredentism. Naturally, the reasons for Stalin's heated emotions in 1945 were not limited to the events that took place in 1904–5. Allied intervention after the Russian Revolution was another cause of wounded Russian pride. But, seen from the Russian perspective, these issues originated at Portsmouth. Aleksei Bogaturov, a Russian political scientist, argues that "Japan's acquisition of Sakhalin was the decisive factor that fuelled Russia's mistrust of the Japanese."[83]

Second, the resolution of territorial disputes became entangled with the norms of righteousness and justice. In 1945, the Allies and Axis were not fighting as equals among civilized nations. The Allies' logic was that they were fighting against evil. But, in proclaiming justice against evil, the Allies had issued several principles to govern postwar international relations. The Atlantic Charter, promulgated by America and Britain on August 14, 1941, and joined by the Soviet Union on September 24, 1941, declared that "their countries seek no aggrandizement, territorial or other." The Cairo Declaration signed by Britain, America, and China on November 27, 1943, stated that the signatories "covet no gain for themselves and have no thought of territorial expansion." The Potsdam Declaration of July 26, 1945, prescribed that "the terms of the Cairo Declaration shall be carried out." The Soviet Union joined the Potsdam Declaration on August 8, 1945, thus promising to abide by it.

Despite these principles, the Yalta agreement of February 1945 prescribed that not only southern Sakhalin but also the Kuril Islands should be returned to the Soviet Union. From the point of view of the above-mentioned principles, Soviet rights to the Kuril Islands could in no way be justified. Southern Sakhalin might be understood, from the Russian point of view, as a territory "which Japan had taken by violence" (Cairo Declaration). But as for the Kuril Islands, exchanged peacefully for Sakhalin in 1875, it is difficult to argue that they constituted a territory "which Japan had taken by greed" (Cairo Declaration).[84]

If one looks at Yalta from the point of view of the idealistic post–World War II principles, the handing over of the Kuriles was a crude violation of the principles to which the Allies had committed themselves. But if one looks at Yalta from the point of view of realism and power, in which the winning party's right to gain territory is still respected (as it was in 1895 and 1905), the result is hardly surprising.

In fact, China also suffered substantially at Yalta because Franklin D. Roosevelt agreed to give back to Stalin practically everything that Russia had lost in 1905, including Russia's preeminent interests in Dairen, the lease of Port Arthur, and control over the Chinese Eastern Railway and the South Manchuria Railway.[85] Later, these Soviet rights over China were acknowledged by both Chiang Kai-shek and Mao Zedong. Eventually, both railways were returned to China, in December 1952, but it took until September 1954 for Nikita Khrushchev to agree to Soviet withdrawal from Dairen and Port Arthur.[86]

In subsequent territorial negotiations between the Japanese and Russian governments, the Japanese side has long been overwhelmed by victim consciousness inflicted by Russia and based on a sense of territorial injustice, the atrocities Russians committed against Japanese civilians and military personnel in Soviet-occupied areas, and the USSR's betrayal of the Soviet-

Japanese Neutrality Pact in August 1945. In San Francisco in 1951, moreover, the Japanese government had to agree to renounce the Kuril Islands. Japan took it as an inevitable consequence of war. But, feeling betrayed by Yalta's double standards, the Japanese government coalesced around a new position in the 1955–56 negotiations with the Soviet Union. It asked for the return of four islands, which had been recognized as Japanese territory by the 1855 Treaty of Commerce and Friendship.[87]

In order to understand the nature of current difficulties in Japan-Russia relations, one might find it helpful to enlarge the scope of analysis. If one could look at Yalta through the prism of Portsmouth and understand it not solely from the perspective of betrayed justice but also from the perspectives of identity (that the Russian side as well might have emotions that need to be considered) and of power (that, in reality, the idealism proclaimed was too weak to govern), it might remove emotional issues from future negotiations and lead to a breakthrough.

Conclusion

Post–World War II history in Northeast Asia developed with a dynamic different from that described above. The Cold War, Sino-Soviet rivalry, détente in the first half of the 1970s, the second Cold War in the early 1980s, the demise of the Soviet Union and the end of the Cold War, 9/11, U.S. unilateralism, and the economic rise of China continue to affect Northeast Asia. Meanwhile, Japan took a different course defined by pacifism, concentration on economic development, efforts to build democracy, and remorse for atrocities committed in Asia. In the latter half of the twentieth century, Japan on the whole succeeded in achieving its objectives. And yet Japan's Asian policy is still fraught with difficulties, the greatest being how to cope with a rising China and U.S. global power supremacy.

In analyzing the Russo-Japanese War and the Portsmouth Treaty, one can draw clear lessons concerning contemporary issues facing Japan and its Northeast Asian neighbors. From the Meiji Restoration to its victory in the Russo-Japanese War, Japan's sole purpose was to reject colonization and ensure its independence. It achieved that objective. But the manner in which Japan parted from the war left contradictions in practically all of its major relations in Northeast Asia. Japan-Korea relations leave us to reflect that from Portsmouth onward, albeit with some oscillation, Japan went straight ahead to annex Korea and crush Korea's urge to preserve its independence and national identity. Japan-China relations leave us pondering that, even within the accepted norms and practice of imperialism in the early twentieth century, idealistic respect for China's sovereignty and territorial integrity, as advanced by the United States, exactly matched China's desire for reunification, independence, and national identity. The inability of Japanese leaders to grasp this trend ultimately pushed Japan to build a closed autarkic regional order that led to a collision with the United States. Japanese-U.S. relations leave us wondering how, in the very wake of victory in the Russo-Japanese War, Japan failed to create cooperative relations with America, which eventually became the real power in East Asia. Japan's failure to choose the appropriate geopolitical partner ultimately led to its defeat in the Pacific War forty years later. Identity, idealism, and power are key factors that transcend the century between the Russo-Japanese War and Japan's current relations with Korea, China, and America. Furthermore, Japan-Russia relations leave us thinking that, if Japan can look at the difficult history that has governed the two countries for sixty years since 1945 with a more holistic approach to identity, power, and idealism, current obstacles could be confronted with less emotion.

As we face the many foreign-policy issues in the early twenty-first century, what is the best combination of power, idealism, and identity required to maximize Japan's national interest? The centennial of the Russo-Japanese War and Portsmouth Treaty offers either directly or indirectly many relevant lessons to bear in mind when we attempt to answer this question.[88]

Summary of Conference Discussions

Participants at the international conference Dartmouth College hosted on September 8–10, 2005, to commemorate the centennial of the Portsmouth Peace Treaty participated in four roundtable sessions. Eight papers, revised versions of which appear in this volume, provided the focal point for discussions. Authors offered brief summaries of their work; formal comments and queries from preappointed discussants opened the discussions that followed. This appendix, drawn from the conference report,[1] summarizes the main themes that emerged from each roundtable session as well as the open discussion that concluded the program.

Session 1: Diplomatic and Military Aspects of the Russo-Japanese War

Two coauthored papers provided the focus of this roundtable session. The first, by David Schimmelpenninck van der Oye and Yasutoshi Teramoto, examined Russo-Japanese relations before and after the 1904–5 conflict, and the second, by Bruce W. Menning and John W. Steinberg, addressed the lack of unity and coherence in Russian military strategy during and after the war.

Jennifer Siegel (Ohio State University), the first of two discussants in this session, observed that one clear theme common to the two papers was confusion and lack of coordination within ministries and across governments: incoherence marked both Russia's prewar diplomacy and postwar military planning and Japan's postwar diplomatic strategy. The Russians were incapable of formulating and implementing a discernible foreign policy in the early years of the twentieth century partly because of the conflicting personalities and agendas of those who were in charge or were competing to be in charge, men who produced, in Foreign Minister Komura Jutarō's words, "a curious diversity of opinion in the councils of Russia." With top officials clashing over strategy, all trying to gain the confidence of the "pathologically indecisive" Nicholas II, Russian policy was perhaps doomed to disorder. Similarly, in postwar Japan, competition among several lines of diplomacy prevented that nation from presenting its friends and potential foes with a discernible position. In the prewar period, Japan had clear aims and demands in East Asia; its policy was focused and determined, its methods more diplomatic than military: an alliance with Great Britain was Komura's solution to the Manchurian-Korean question. But a real shift occurred either during or immediately after the war, as Japan's postwar diplomacy was much more muddled. Meanwhile, although Russia's prewar policy was conflicted and ambivalent, its postwar policy was relatively consistent. Siegel then speculated on what factors led to these shifts from focus to confusion and vice versa. Did the specific experiences of the war itself for victor and loser alike produce these shifts? Were the shifts the result of more general wartime experiences or simply the natural response to the outbreak and challenges of war? Did the details of the peace treaty produce the rather marked reversal in methodological orientation of both combatant governments? Or did the experience of the diplomatic game played out in Portsmouth affect the future policies of Japan and Russia?

Siegel remarked that the picture Menning and Steinberg presented of Russian military planning in response to the war was painfully similar to the picture of Russian diplomacy before the conflict. Defense strategists lacked a long-term understanding or concept of Russia's needs, the greatest of which, according to one contemporary observer, was "unified direction of foreign and military policies." Menning and Steinberg showed that Russian authorities could not even agree on structures that would allow for the making of those policies, let alone agree on the policies themselves, and found that the fault lay in exactly the same place as did Schimmelpenninck: Nicholas II and his appointments. The result was a short-lived, ineffectual planning apparatus. Neither of the two examples of Russian efforts to devise and implement policy—the prewar diplomatic instance and the postwar military one—produced a unified, discernible, and effective policy. Again, Siegel asked, what explains these outcomes? Did Russia continually fail to draw the right lessons from its military and diplomatic experiences? Did it fail to ask the right questions, or did it fail to implement the correct policies in response to the answers to those questions?

Siegel concluded with comments on the importance of perception in the making of foreign policy as well as in military planning. She underscored the dangers that policy makers face when their perceptions of others don't coincide with others' perceptions of them. Russia's view of Japan as non-Western and therefore, in its eyes, inferior and backward kept the Russians from negotiating with the Japanese in earnest and from seeing them as credible rivals who could play by the rules of the "diplomacy of imperialism." After the war, Japan's growing perception of the United States as its principal competitor for East Asian hegemony hinged on the Japanese view of America as an increasingly Pacific rather than Atlantic power. This perception would greatly affect geopolitical maneuvers to follow, no matter what long-term agenda the United States actually had in East Asia.

The second discussant, Kaoru Iokibe (Tokyo Metropolitan University), stressed that time is an important factor in diplomacy leading to war. Further, he noted that, at the end of the war, Japan enjoyed a short-term military advantage but faced underlying deficiencies; for Tokyo, the victory was a temporary one, and the postwar challenge was how to make the most of the nation's short-term advantage. Iokibe also wondered whether the war and its aftermath prompted a change in awareness on the part of Nicholas II and pointed out that Japan and Russia differed greatly in their conceptions of constitutional monarchy: it was unthinkable for the Japanese emperor to play a role such as the tsar did, even after the creation of the Duma.

Teramoto agreed that a major cause of the war was the perception gap between Russia and Japan. In the end, he noted, Japanese officials concluded that their country had to resort to war in view of Russian moves in Manchuria and on the Korean border. Following the conflict, even though Japan emerged as the winner, it felt insecure and feared isolation, mindful of when the European powers had forced it to return the Liaodong leasehold to China a decade earlier. After Portsmouth, Tokyo decided to strengthen ties with St. Petersburg; relations with Russia improved as ties with Washington deteriorated.

On the question of whether the war brought about a change in the tsar's thinking, Steinberg observed that after the conflict, in important budgetary decisions, Nicholas always sided with the Russian navy, despite his training as an army officer and pride in his army background; at some point he became a "navalist." Menning added that imperial culture, specifically the tsar's drive to restore Russian prestige abroad, explains much of the willingness to take shortcuts on integrating policy and strategy, as in the short-sighted postwar naval building program.

Kazuhiko Togo (Princeton University) addressed the notion of Japan's "treacherous attack" on Port Arthur as a precedent for Pearl Harbor. Before the attack, Komura had officially informed the Russians that Japan was going to break off diplomatic relations. Togo wondered whether, in terms of then-existing international law, breaking off relations was tantamount to declaring war: was the attack really "treacherous" if it followed a rupture in diplomatic relations? He also questioned the distinction Teramoto drew between coherence in Japanese foreign policy before the war and confusion afterward. Togo's understanding was that postwar Japanese policy was not that confused, especially after Komura rejected the tentative agreement with U.S. railway tycoon E. H. Harriman on joint management of railroads in southern Manchuria. Thereafter the main line of Japanese policy basically followed the thinking of Komura: Japan would keep southern Manchuria in its own sphere of influence and, to that end, would cooperate with Russia and shut out the United States. Japan essentially sought to establish that situation by entering into four accords with Russia from 1907 to 1916, the fourth one being tantamount to an alliance. In that sense, Japanese policy was fairly consistent.

Teramoto responded that Russia had carried out a similar surprise attack against Turkey some decades earlier. Before 1907, no explicit convention existed on how to declare war, so by conveying that it was breaking off diplomatic ties Japan met at least minimum standards of conduct at the time. Article 1 of the 1907 Hague Convention, "Relative to the Opening of Hostilities," appears to have been the first treaty to set rules for the declaration of war: "The Contracting Powers recognize that hostilities between themselves must not commence without previous and explicit warning, in the form either of a reasoned declaration of war or of an ultimatum with conditional declaration of war."

On Togo's second point, Teramoto agreed that no major confusion characterized postwar Japanese policy. Officials differed in their opinions on how to treat Manchuria; but, once the government put an end to the military regime the army had set up in southern Manchuria immediately after the war, Japanese diplomacy did not exhibit a great deal of inconsistency.

Wayne Merry (American Foreign Policy Council) commented on the lessons Russia failed to learn in terms of naval tactics and fleet design. Both Russia and Japan had built their fleets according to Mahanian big-ship doctrine, but the Japanese were also extremely innovative in weapons and tactics, and by the start of the war most experts considered the Japanese navy the world leader in torpedo and cruiser tactics and in night fighting. In watching the war, a number of other navies noticed that until the Battle of Tsushima Japan scored its major victories not with battleships but with a more balanced fleet, and several of them subsequently reflected this observation in their own fleet designs. The one navy that reflected these lessons the least was that of Russia. This outcome is curious not only because Russia experienced the most immediate lessons but also because it should rationally have moved in a more balanced direction based on its geography. Of necessity the Russians had three separate fleets that operated in narrow, shallow bodies of water; yet their reaction to losing two battle fleets in East Asia was to try to build another such fleet for the Baltic, probably the least appropriate body of water for *Dreadnought*-type ships. Rather than learning from the small-ship tactics and new technologies Japan had pioneered and used against it, Russia was in some ways the least innovative participant in the naval arms race leading to 1914. Why did Russia, unlike some of its competitors, not learn the correct lessons?

Menning replied that the answer is simple: the leading apostle in Russia of basing fleet design and tactics on geography, Admiral Stepan Makarov, had been killed early in the war. After the conflict, the argument that Russia needed to build *Dreadnought*-size ships to keep domestic shipyards afloat won out over calls for a balanced fleet. Steinberg added that military planners were dealing with a fractured system in which the tsar had the final say on all matters, and in the midst of budgetary battles the idea that, in order to be an imperialist power, Russia must have a blue-water navy became dominant in the tsar's mind.

David Wolff (Woodrow Wilson International Center for Scholars) stated that one point Tatiana Filippova (*Rodina*) had made at a conference on the Russo-Japanese War held at Keiō University in May 2005 was at variance with the panelists' views: Filippova had suggested that the Russian perception of Japan before and during the war was actually quite mixed rather than uniformly disparaging. Top Russian attachés, for instance, recognized that Japan was a potent force and sent warnings to that effect directly to the tsar and his military commanders.

Session 2: The Making of the Portsmouth Treaty

A coauthored paper by Eugene P. Trani and Donald E. Davis concerning the role of George Kennan (1845–1924) in shaping U.S. policy during the war and peace negotiations and I. V. Lukoianov's exploration of Russian perspectives on the treaty negotiations provided the focal points for the second roundtable session.

The first discussant in this session, Andrew Gordon (Harvard University), noted that the strengths and weaknesses of both papers lay in their uniarchival and unilingual foci. He conceded that their method remains a valid means of studying diplomatic history but suggested that multiarchival work is ultimately more valuable. He stated that collaborative research and conferences can provide the means to get around this limitation but also argued that one scholar's overarching multiarchival view has tremendous value. Gordon offered specific comments on each of the papers. He commended Lukoianov's detailed analytical approach to the pretreaty tensions in Russia and the diplomatic efforts of Witte to resolve them. In responding to Trani and Davis' paper, he noted that Kennan largely subscribed to Japan's view of itself as Asia's most modern nation at the time.

Gordon closed his comments with some general observations about the treaty and its long-term consequences. Looking at the treaty purely from the perspective of that time and without the benefit of hindsight, one would have to say that it was a remarkable achievement given the very real possibility (brought out in several papers) that the peace process could have easily unraveled at several points. He added that the settlement left unresolved or even exacerbated most of the tensions overshadowing twentieth-century Asia. These tensions included strains in the bilateral relationships between America and Russia and between Japan and each of its neighbors—Korea, China, and Russia—particularly, in China's case, as Japan's new foothold in Manchuria that resulted from the treaty provided the blueprint for Japanese colonial activity throughout the early twentieth century.

Tatiana Filippova opened her remarks by observing that the broad cultural legacies of the Russo-Japanese War point to its having been the first "image" war of the twentieth century. She suggested that a key issue of the conflict centered on the mutual images of these new empires, specifically the perceptions they held of their relative modernity or backwardness. Based on her own research and the papers delivered so far, she concluded that the Russian image of the Japanese empire was not racist but rather "ageist." In other words, Japan was too young to participate in the concert of world powers. Filippova contended that this attitude strongly influenced Russian behavior at Portsmouth and noted that the comparatively young power, America, sided with the very young imperial power, Japan.

Filippova posed questions to both presenters. She asked Trani: What was American public opinion concerning the Russo-Japanese rivalry? Was it seen as a rivalry between old and new imperial projects, between different political projects, or between different trajectories of modernization? Trani felt that the U.S. public's view was that the Russian bear had been tamed and would sign on to whatever was dictated to it. The American public and press remained solidly behind the Japanese throughout the war and the treaty negotiations. Even Witte's attempts to manipulate U.S. opinion had little effect. Americans were apprehensive about emerging Japanese power, but they were even more fervently anti-Russian, and this sentiment was one of the legacies that lasted throughout the twentieth century.

Turning to Lukoianov, Filippova remarked that Russian historiography has sometimes unduly stressed the relationship between the Russo-Japanese

War and the Russian Revolution. She was particularly interested to know whether the war and peace treaty had any direct effect on Witte's thinking. Lukoianov replied that Nicholas II decided, as a result of the war with Japan, that Russia should prioritize East Asian foreign policy over domestic policy. Lukoianov also stated that, during Russia's postwar reforms, Witte surveyed the constitutions of several European countries and asked for a translation of the Japanese constitution. Although Lukoianov did not know Witte's views on the Japanese constitution, he suggested that Witte was a realist and recognized the success of the Japanese imperial project. In general, however, the war primarily affected Russian foreign policy as opposed to domestic policy. St. Petersburg became far less aggressive and far less expansive in its diplomacy.

In the discussion that followed, Lisbeth Tarlow (Harvard University) questioned Lukoianov's contention that Witte used Portsmouth to reassert himself in Russian politics. She wondered what sources support this claim, in view of Witte's comment that he was only called upon to "clean up the dirty work." Lukoianov responded that some of Witte's unpublished private correspondence suggests that his desire to return to power drove his interests in Portsmouth.

Ronald Edsforth (Dartmouth College) critiqued both papers as being locked in the narratives of later twentieth-century nation-states that focus on the two world wars and the ensuing cold war. He suggested that historians have generally ignored the development of the world peace movement that grew out of the Hague Peace Conference and the Portsmouth Treaty negotiations. The Nobel Peace Prize and the Carnegie Endowment for Peace were also created in this period. The Inter-Parliamentary Union gathered at the St. Louis International Exhibition during the Russo-Japanese War and persuaded Roosevelt to issue a call for another Hague conference. Edsforth noted that, because of the increasing mechanization of war and the extensive coverage of the 1904–5 conflict by new media, especially photography, two ideas emerged: (1) war is no longer an option for civilized nations, and (2) when war breaks out it needs to be restrained by international law. He posed two questions: Did the wartime images of slaughter have any impact on the decision makers in Russia and Japan? And can we frame the Russo-Japanese War and the Portsmouth Treaty as marking the beginning of an emergent international order that runs contrary to the notion of competing nation-states?

Responses to these questions were varied. According to Lukoianov, some Russian scholars at the time suggested that modern war cannot solve problems, only peace can. He also believed that images of war influenced public opinion but did not directly affect political decision makers in autocratic states like Russia. The main legacy of the conflict was the conclusion that war was especially dangerous to existing governments in that it could lead directly to revolution. Kaoru Iokibe noted that the Japanese press also articulated general goals for the war and peace, especially the idea of a permanent peace for East Asia. Japanese expressed dissatisfaction with the treaty in the form of the Hibiya riots, but in general the press argued that the long-term consequences of the peace were favorable not only for Japan but also for the possibility of a permanent peace.

Naoko Shimazu (University of London) remarked that images of the war were censored in Japan and ultimately mattered little because tens of thousands of bodies of war dead were brought back to Japan, with numerous public funerals. The mounting casualties led to an emerging sensibility known at the time as *ensen kibun,* not "antiwar feeling" but an "unwillingness to fight war." Trani responded to Edsforth by suggesting that he look to Roosevelt's Nobel acceptance speech in which the president supported The Hague and urged powers bent on international peace to band together and form a league to enforce it. John Steinberg commented that, despite Roosevelt's Nobel acceptance speech, despite the threat of destabilization that wars posed to governments, and despite media portrayals of mass slaughter, the twentieth century is a history of more wars and more mass slaughter; in effect, it is a history of making mass slaughter acceptable. David Schimmelpenninck added that most nations got the entirely wrong idea from the war: one needed hypernationalistic sentiment to win modern wars.

Edward Miller (Dartmouth College) observed that hostility toward a foreign nation can have a general dimension, for example, antagonism stemming from fear of the Yellow Peril or the Slavic peril, but he wondered whether hostility toward Russia was more specifically directed toward its form of autocratic government. The distinction is important because the more specific form of hostility holds out the possibility that the enemy can eventually become civilized. He asked Trani whether this distinction is applicable to twentieth-century Russian-American relations and specifically to Roosevelt's attitudes toward Russia in 1904–5. Trani replied that, based on the evidence, America has not been, nor will it ever be, happy with Russian governments, irrespective of what Russia does to comply with American wishes.

Lisbeth Tarlow questioned Roosevelt's role in the treaty process. Citing Trani's claim that Roosevelt did not change his opinion of Japan throughout the negotiations, she asked whether his position really had any effect on the treaty itself since we generally recognize that Roosevelt's importance was primarily in bringing the combatants together. Trani responded that Roosevelt supported Japan mainly with China in mind: he wanted China preserved intact. His views mattered because they tempered American public opinion toward Japan. Following this line of inquiry, Togo wondered how we should understand American imperialism at the time. How did the Open Door policy toward China differ from American attitudes toward Russian and Japanese control of Manchuria? Lukoianov suggested that American imperialism has specific economic characteristics that distinguish it from earlier forms of imperialism and that the Open Door policy in China was a reflection of those characteristics.

Session 3: Cultural and Political Legacies of Portsmouth

Discussion in the third session revolved around papers by Sho Konishi and Shinji Yokote. Konishi explored the transnational implications of Japan's Non-War Movement (Hisen Undō) while Yokote examined postwar instances of cooperation between Russia and Japan in order to protect their mutual interests in Manchuria.

The first discussant, Naoko Shimazu, began her comments by noting that the two papers represent radically different methodological approaches to international history. Yokote takes a more traditional approach, looking at interstate relations; Konishi is "revolutionary" in that he provides an alternative to traditional discourse by focusing on nonstate actors and issues—individuals, nongovernmental or nonprofit organizations, and non-state-driven concerns such as ecology and demography. While their approaches differ, both authors share an interest in relationships of collaboration and cooperation. More specifically, the relationships Yokote explores are dynamic and collaborative because Russia and Japan had vested interests in continuing a dialogue. In that sense, a peace treaty ends a conflict but also regenerates a relationship between two players. From this perspective, peace treaties become analogous to living organisms: they change shape, and they evolve over time. In other words, peace treaties are as much political frameworks as they are legal frameworks. Konishi, on the other hand, explores a parallel discourse—cooperative anarchism, which challenges the dominant Western discourse on modernity. These two discourses present conflicting accounts of human progress and civilization: in the alternative one, war is retrogressive, whereas, in the dominant discourse, war is a positive force.

Shimazu suggested that we study the legacies of the peace treaty from the perspective of historical memory in the sense that historical memory is a strategy for understanding or historicizing the present. Stalin, for example, utilized the historical memory of the Russo-Japanese War to frame his policy toward Japan. Meanwhile, Japan saw the Russo-Japanese War as obsolete, that is, historically useless in a general sense, and only selectively used heroic narratives from the war for martial education. The historical memory of the Sino-Japanese War of 1894–95 was much more useful for Japanese foreign policy in the 1930s.

Shimazu posed questions to both presenters about socialism as an ideology, which she felt neither fully addressed. She asked Yokote about the importance of socialism in determining the relationship between Japan and Russia. And she asked Konishi to explain his labeling as cooperative anarchists people we normally refer to as socialists.

The second discussant, Matthew Ouimet (U.S. Department of State), noted that, according to both papers, the Portsmouth Treaty sowed seeds for a productive relationship between Russia and Japan that were actually better than most would have imagined at the time, but he wondered how realistic are the possibilities that the authors lay out and how "alternative" are the interpretations they articulate. Referring to Konishi's thesis, he observed that the Japanese Non-War Movement contained two conflicting ideologies, both from Russia: Tolstoi's preindustrial utopian ideology and Kropotkin's technological utopian one, though both represented antiviolent revolutionary discourses. Ouimet also pointed out that, as Russia moved toward violent revolution, the Japanese did not act on these conflated ideologies with a real-world agenda. Moreover, in the 1920s Japanese Non-War activists advocated peoples' movements that had been popular in Russia in the 1860s. He wondered what the utopian anarchists in Japan thought of the Russian Revolution and how these transnational cooperative movements resulted in two entirely different approaches.

Ouimet asked Yokote why the Portsmouth Treaty went down in Russian memory as yielding little more than a territorial loss and why Russian scholars have not recognized the cooperation he portrayed as being a direct result of the treaty. He offered an alternative explanation: post-treaty Russo-Japanese cooperation was the product of a weak China and international competition with the United States. Ouimet also suggested that Yokote overestimated the level of Russo-Japanese cooperation after the Siberian Intervention. Russian historiography is quite clear on this point. Is it really true that in 1924 Japan was pushing the Portsmouth Treaty as a model for cooperation with the new Soviet state in the continued mutual exploitation of Manchuria?

Konishi replied to the discussants by contextualizing his work more broadly as an effort to depart from the accepted teleological narrative of socialism, hence its absence in his paper. He noted that Russian studies of Japanese Tokugawa-era society influenced Russian cooperativist thinking prior to its formulation by Kropotkin. Konishi stated that his view of modern Japanese intellectual history is not bounded by the Japanese nation-state. Rather, it is inherently international from the outset. Against this background, notions of East and West—especially where socialism is concerned—quickly lose their relevance.

Yokote responded by stating that historical memory is always politicized. Regarding the legacies of the Portsmouth Treaty, he noted that, although territorial issues remain today, the current order in Northeast Asia is also a legacy, and this order will be the venue in which the parties concerned ultimately resolve those issues. Yokote's paper generated a considerable amount of detailed discussion about the treaty's precise implications for the oversight and management of railroad assets in Manchuria. In general, the participants felt that the treaty was deliberately vague on these matters; it thereby forced Japan and Russia to negotiate settlements on the ground. In short, Yokote's cooperation thesis seemed to have at least some validity.

Ouimet stated that the greatest legacy of the Portsmouth Treaty is the currently disputed Northern Territories question, because the treaty made null and void all previous territorial claims. He noted that Japan persistently turns to these pre-Portsmouth claims to support its case whereas it relied on the Portsmouth Treaty for nearly all of its twentieth-century dealings with Russia. By taking half of Sakhalin as a prize of war in 1905, Japan set the precedent that Russia would invoke after World War II when it claimed the Northern Territories. He suggested that Yokote's argument has implications for current Russian-Japanese disputes: if Portsmouth is understood as a treaty that created tacit cooperation in Manchuria against Chinese interests, then perhaps it could be the model, based on similar fears of China today, for a resolution of the Northern Territories dispute.

Session 4: The Portsmouth Treaty and Asia-Pacific Relations Today

The fourth session dealt with contemporary implications of the Portsmouth settlement. Framing the discussion were papers by David Wolff and Vladimir I. Ivanov, with Wolff arguing that American participation in the Portsmouth settlement was the genesis of contemporary anti-Americanism in Asia and Ivanov suggesting that growing economic cooperation between Russia and Japan may supersede any need to be overly concerned with historical legacies.

Wayne Merry, the discussant, opened his comments by stating that in many ways the Russo-Japanese War was the first concrete step leading to the demise of the Eurocentric world. In many respects, the war marked the beginning of the European imperialist retreat from Asia and, for East Asia, the start of the restoration of the global economic and political status it had held before the period of European imperialism. In that regard, the fall of Port Arthur and the Battles of Mukden and Tsushima were natural precursors to the fall of Singapore, the sinking of *The Prince of Wales* and *The Repulse,* and the Battle of Dien Bien Phu.

Merry stated that Japan's role in this process is well known. It was the first Asian country to embrace modernity in response to the challenge of European imperialism, the first one able to meet the imperialist powers on their own terms and to win, doing so most dramatically in this first conflict of the twentieth century. Japan's model has been so successful that almost every other country in East Asia has copied it. Japan now finds itself challenged in business and in other areas not by the European powers but by other Asian countries. Meanwhile, Russia's position has historically been less understood. The Russian case of imperialist expansion in Asia was unique among the Western powers in being an overland as well as overseas engagement, but land links were slow to develop, a situation that made the Russo-Japanese War as much a naval conflict as a land war. With 90 percent of its population living in Europe, Russia today is concerned about the tenability and permanence of its position in East Asia, in light of the expense of maintaining a presence almost halfway around the world. Moscow views Japanese economic engagement with the Russian Far East as essential to keeping Russia in Asia. The focus of Russian concerns, however, is not on Japan but rather on China, for much of the Russian Far East consists of territories that the Manchus ceded under two unequal treaties dating back to 1858 and 1860, territories that are on China's long-term agenda. In some respects, the United States also became an Asian power through a combination of overland and overseas expansion, but because Asia lacks an integrated alliance system like NATO, Washington engages in the region through a hub-and-spoke system in which it has separate alliances with various Asia-Pacific countries, the U.S. role being the only thing that unites them. To a large extent, the fact that America is the world's premier sea power defines much of its relationship with that part of the world, since the geography of East Asia inevitably places a premium on naval power and maritime trade. From early in the nineteenth century to this day, the United States has always focused its interest in Asia on China, which continues to loom large in the American mind in a way no other country in the world does or is likely to do in the future.

Merry then raised two current issues of concern in the region: the future of Korea and the territorial dispute between Russia and Japan. On Korea, he stated that in a significant way the role of the United States differs from those of other countries with conflicted histories involving Korea, namely,

China, Russia, and Japan. Though an Asian power, America is not an Asian country; if talks with North Korea go badly, it can walk away. By contrast, neighboring countries have much larger stakes, which require them to think about the future of Korea more seriously than Washington is likely to do. According to Merry, North Korea may well be approaching a systemic crisis of the kind that required outside interventions in places like Afghanistan and Liberia. Such an intervention in North Korea is not one that the United States could effectively perform. For historical reasons, Japan would have to play a largely economic role. One could imagine joint action by China and Russia to protect their regional interests in the event of a collapse of social order in North Korea, a scenario that others need to understand may become a necessity. Through their recent military exercises, China and Russia partly intended to send Pyongyang a message that such a move is within their capabilities.

On the territorial question, Merry stated: "there is no such thing as an easy territorial dispute." The Russo-Japanese one is unusual in the extent to which the two sides politically talk past each other; one is struck by how much the political elites in each country imagine that for the other country the issue is artificial. Merry further asserted that, in his experience, economics never solves territorial disputes. The expectation that the benefits of trade and investment will somehow overcome historical or political difficulties has simply never come to fruition. Economics will always be a key element of a solution, but alone it will never create the basis for a solution. In his view, the starting point in this case is for members of the two legislatures and political elites to communicate and meet with each other and at least come to understand that for the other side the issue is a serious one.

Edward Berger (American College of Physicians) asked about the motivations that led to the recent sudden settlement of the Sino-Russian dispute over islands in the Amur River and the lessons we might draw from that example. David Wolff responded to Merry and Berger by stating that resolution of a territorial dispute does not have to be a long-term project. In the Amur River case, Putin decided to reach a settlement without consulting regional officials; he acted similarly in resolving a border dispute with Kazakhstan. Wolff thought Putin could behave in the exact same way with regard to the Northern Territories, though taking such action on the Japanese side is much harder. Merry countered that Russia's recent border agreements differ from a settlement in which it would give up inhabited land that its constitution specifies as being part of the national territory. Moscow often sees the Kuril Islands dispute as related to the questions of Kaliningrad and Chechnya: Russia believes it would be more difficult to hold on to such areas, were it to begin the process of unraveling the federation by handing over the disputed islands to Japan.

Several participants commented on the history and nature of regionalism in Northeast Asia. Akira Iriye (Harvard University) suggested that a continuous theme since 1905 has been the relative success or failure of Russia, Japan, China, and the United States to negotiate their regional interests. In 1905 the parties concerned were aware that something like a regional structure was emerging in Northeast Asia. Whether that "something" will develop successfully into a stable regional system in the twenty-first century depends to a great extent on the ability of these four nations to arrange their regional affairs amicably. According to Yokote, Russia and Japan somehow managed to do so in the decades after Portsmouth; so did the United States and China. Today Russia and Japan cannot solve any of their outstanding issues without some kind of system that comes to terms with China and the Chinese-U.S. relationship. Viewing such issues as the territorial dispute within a regional context rather than in bilateral or national terms may be a way to solve them. Iriye went on to say that, if the United States is part of the equation, then we are not talking about an East Asian order but rather a North Pacific regional community. Should a Northeast Asia plus Pacific community develop, we could well go back to the Russo-Japanese War and see it as the starting point of that development.

Thomas Simons (Harvard University) cautioned that the problem of coalitions today is different from what it was earlier in the last century when China was weak. The rise of China has changed most of the givens, making it difficult to extrapolate from Portsmouth out into the twenty-first century, from a situation where Japan, Russia, and the United States were dealing with a declining China to one where they are engaging a China that is becoming stronger.

Togo outlined several possibilities for an emerging regionalism in Asia: an exclusive East Asia club such as "ASEAN Plus Three"; an inclusive Asia-Pacific on the model, for example, of APEC; and an inclusive Northeast Asia along the lines of the six-party talks on the denuclearization of North Korea. Wolff observed that regions are constructed: no such thing as a natural region exists. He suggested that the right scale for dealing with the Korea issue is Northeast Asia plus the United States because that combination represents the footprint of the Korean diaspora. The fact that a million or more Koreans live in each of the principal diasporic countries—Japan, Russia, China, and the United States—could be a powerful galvanizing force for reaching an acceptable settlement. Ivanov stated that Japan and South Korea speak mostly about an East Asian community, but for the last few years Seoul has actively pursued the concept of South Korea as an economic hub. Although this approach is somewhat narrow, it shows a willingness to engage in regional institution building. Ivanov noted that, in comparison to Europe and ASEAN, Northeast Asia has the opportunity, as a first step, to pursue functional cooperation in such areas as energy, the environment, transportation, and visa regulations.

Kaoru Iokibe questioned Wolff's characterization of Japanese anti-Americanism as a direct reaction to the Portsmouth Treaty. He argued that one should place anti-American sentiment in a broader historical context, beginning with the "scramble for concessions" in China in the late 1890s, a division of spoils that deepened Japanese distrust toward the Western powers. The Japanese also directed that distrust toward the United States for exercising power politics while proclaiming the Open Door and published articles critical of perceived American hypocrisy even before the Russo-Japanese War. Shin'ichi Kitaoka (Deputy Permanent Representative of Japan to the United Nations) seconded Iokibe's point, claiming that anti-Americanism had more to do with national interest and geopolitical concerns over Manchuria than with the Treaty of Portsmouth.

On economic issues, Togo remarked that the question of energy and specifically of oil-pipeline development has been one of the most critical in Russo-Japanese relations in recent years and that the problem has become more difficult in the past year. He wondered why Ivanov suggested otherwise, painting a more promising picture of the bilateral economic relationship. Kenneth Yalowitz (Dartmouth College) asked whether, in spite of Merry's negative comments about economics, a significant development of energy trade could contribute to some kind of solution to the Northern Territories dispute.

Ivanov replied that first of all he based his optimism about the future of Northeast Asia on growing economic interdependence in the region. China has become the leading trading partner of Japan and South Korea and soon will become number one for Russia. International consortia, including Japanese companies, have invested close to $40 billion in the two Sakhalin oil and gas projects, and Japan has already contracted half the output of Sakhalin's first-phase liquid natural gas (LNG) plant. These trends represent "a very sturdy sign of interdependence; no one wants to risk commercial and energy-supply stability." On the other hand, Russia's regional pipeline project remains a stumbling block. The Japanese government has expressed a willingness to help with the project in any way but on the condition that Russia channel all the oil to the Pacific coast, not to China. Russia cannot accept this condition, since China is a major trading partner. In Ivanov's view, the dilemma is more of a symbolic political issue than a true economic one, because everyone knows that China will consume half the oil, wherever Russia ships it. In the final analysis, Ivanov maintained, "Energy trade is going to be a major pillar of economic integration in Northeast Asia."

Open Discussion

In a wrap-up session, the organizers invited comments and suggestions on future directions in the study of Portsmouth and its legacies. Kitaoka began the session by pointing out that the problem of domestic political systems and values was missing from the previous discussion. Foreign policies are by and large the outward expression of those systems. He said that today the private sector is playing a more important role in Russo-Japanese relations; this development is the result of change in domestic political systems, specifically democratization. One should include this dimension in any discussion of regionalism.

Charles Doleac (Portsmouth Treaty Anniversary Committee) noted that also absent from the discussion so far was the history of the Portsmouth peace process itself. As a matter of diplomatic history, what happened a hundred years ago was quite unique, irrespective of its ultimate effects on the region: The president of the United States offered his good offices to two combatants in the largest war that two nations had ever fought until that time. The process he used to enable the two parties to resolve their differences on their own terms, the way he employed the U.S. Navy as host and the government of New Hampshire and local people as facilitators—much as private business may serve to foster the diplomatic process in the future—was an example of "multitrack diplomacy," which Portsmouth suggested could be successful in cases where the formal, governmental track alone cannot achieve peace. Japan, for one, has used this Portsmouth legacy to help resolve disputes in Cambodia and Sri Lanka.

Alexei Bogaturov (Moscow State Institute of International Relations) stated that Asian regionalism exists but that it does not resemble regionalism in Europe or elsewhere. He emphasized that we need to distinguish between formal and criminal, informal regionalism. Otherwise, we will fail to understand what is happening among China, Russia, Japan, and Korea; what we find there is strongly transnationalized cooperation among criminal organizations in all four countries. Smuggling in gold, fishery products, and timber is producing extraordinary amounts of money, strongly affecting local authorities in all those countries. When discussing territorial issues, we should bear in mind the indirect impact on the decision-making process of active criminal structures and the local authorities they influence.

James Collins (Akin Gump Strauss Hauer & Feld) offered thoughts on what to do next. First, we have an almost unique case study in which certain states saw their relationship devolve into conflict and subsequently made peace. We also have a formal reconfiguration of international arrangements that lasted for quite some time, albeit in an evolving way. Collins suggested that we could create a model around this particular set of circumstances that might help students understand what it means to conduct diplomacy and to have a diplomatic solution to a conflict. One of his tasks during the Camp David peace process, he explained, was to research the Treaty of Portsmouth and in particular the American role. He found that Portsmouth was in fact a model in many respects. It showed that mutual images, real power relationships, and timing all matter in setting the context. Also, people clearly matter. Creativity and the willingness to take political risks—such personal characteristics are important. Finally, Collins noted, history matters, too. How people got to where they are today is part of how they define their options for tomorrow. It is worth pulling together what we have learned about Portsmouth and seeing what model we can distill from it. All in all, the Portsmouth centennial offers a good commemorative moment for us to think about how these matters can affect our conduct and perception of issues today.

David Wolff commented on the unfortunate circumstance that neither Korea nor China was present at Portsmouth; both were shut out of the process. He then pointed to the irony that we have paralleled that situation in the way we have set up this conference. We need to include those countries, especially if we are going to look at contemporary regional issues as well. Wolff also noted that Roosevelt took a strong leadership role in the Portsmouth process and wondered who can provide such leadership today in building some kind of regional community.

Ronald Edsforth stated that the conference has largely overlooked the history of peace, which scholars have been actively writing. Norway, for example, had already developed a peace political culture that came out of its effort to separate peacefully from Sweden at the end of the nineteenth century. One can construct a narrative sequence that draws a connection between Norway's role in that period and its role in recent years as a mediator in peace negotiations between warring parties. If we are looking for leaders who can make peace, we need to teach young people the possibility of peace and the way that countries have made peace in various parts of the world. An article that appeared in *The New Republic* in May 2005 titled "The End of War?" offers convincing evidence that we may be in the most peaceful period in recent centuries, that war and threats between states are on the decline, that peacekeeping efforts are in the main successful, and that much of what we hear in the United States is in fact framed within a history that sees the past as nothing but a sequence of wars and preparation for war rather than a movement toward a new world order that people who have embraced the possibility of peace have increasingly made a reality. Edsforth proposed that one could think about locating Portsmouth in a different constructed historical narrative that picks up on some of what seem to be characteristics of the current international order.

Notes

Introduction (pages 1–7)

1. The "World War Zero" project was one of several international projects that involved centennial conferences and the production of edited volumes. The organizers of "World War 0: Reappraising the War of 1904–5," held at Keiō University in Tokyo, Japan, on May 23–27, 2005, edited a two-volume set: John W. Steinberg, Bruce W. Menning, David Schimmelpenninck van der Oye, David Wolff, and Shinji Yokote, eds., *The Russo-Japanese War in Global Perspective: World War Zero*, vol. 1 (Leiden and Boston: Brill Academic Publishers, 2005); and David Wolff, Steven G. Marks, Bruce W. Menning, David Schimmelpenninck van der Oye, John W. Steinberg, and Shinji Yokote, eds., *The Russo-Japanese War in Global Perspective: World War Zero*, vol. 2 (Leiden and Boston: Brill Academic Publishers, 2007). Another two-volume set draws on the papers presented at an international conference, "The Russo-Japanese War and the 20th Century: An Assessment from a Centennial Perspective," held in Israel on February 8–12, 2004, and at the "Centenary International Symposium on the Russo-Japanese War and the Portsmouth Peace Treaty," held in Nichinan, Japan: Rotem Kowner and Ben-Ami Shillony, eds., *Rethinking the Russo-Japanese War, 1904–5*, vol. 1: *Centennial Perspectives* (Folkestone, Kent, UK: Global Oriental Publishers, 2007); and Chiharu Inaba, John Chapman, and Matsumura Masayoshi, eds., *Rethinking the Russo-Japanese War, 1904–5*, vol. 2: *The Nichinan Papers* (Folkestone, Kent, UK: Global Oriental Publishers, 2007). Two other recent books of note are Rotem Kowner, *Historical Dictionary of the Russo-Japanese War* (Lanham, Md., Toronto, and Oxford: Scarecrow Press, 2006), which includes an extensive bibliography (pp. 471–535), and Rotem Kowner, ed., *The Impact of the Russo-Japanese War* (London and New York: Routledge, 2007), which examines the wide-ranging short- and near-term effects of the war and in which the editor argues that the Russo-Japanese conflict, though not really a world war, was nevertheless global in its repercussions (p. 4).

2. Schimmelpenninck and Teramoto had co-authored a paper for the conference but developed separate essays for this volume.

Chapter 1. Russia's Relations with Japan Before and After the War:
An Episode in the Diplomacy of Imperialism (pages 11–23)

1. Portions of this paper are condensed from the second part of David Schimmelpenninck van der Oye, *Toward the Rising Sun: Russian Ideologies of Empire on the*

Path to War with Japan (Dekalb: Northern Illinois University Press, 2001) and appear here with the kind permission of the publisher. Dates are according to the Georgian calendar.

2. Joseph W. Esherick, *The Origins of the Boxer Uprising* (Berkeley: University of California Press, 1987), 123–27.

3. Arthur Julius Irmer, "Die Erwerbung von Kiautschou, 1894–1898" (Inaugural dissertation, Rheinischen Friedrich-Wilhelm Universität zu Bonn, 1930), 9–12; Ralph A. Norem, *Kiaochow Leased Territory* (Berkeley: University of California Press, 1936), 11; O. Franke, *Die Großmächte in Ostasien von 1894 bis 1914: Ein Beitrag zur Vorgeschichte des Krieges* (Brunswick: George Westermann, 1923), 124–25.

4. Alfred von Tirpitz, *Erinnerungen* (Berlin: K. F. Koehler, 1927), 61–62. The German debate about a suitable location for a naval station is described in Irmer, "Erwerbung," 15–41; and Norem, *Kiaochow*, 13–27.

5. Georg Franzius, *Kiautschou: Deutschlands Erwerbung in Ostasien* (Berlin: Alfred Schall, 1902), 129–42; John Schrecker, *Imperialism and Chinese Nationalism: Germany in Shantung* (Cambridge, Mass.: Harvard University Press, 1971), 34; Henri Cordier, *Histoire des relations de la Chine avec les puissances occidentales, 1860–1902* (Paris: Félix Alcan, 1902), 3:352–53.

6. M. N. Murav'ev to Nicholas II, memorandum, October 26, 1897, Krasnyi Arkhiv (hereafter KA), 87:37–38; M. N. Murav'ev to P. P. Tyrtov, letter, October 26, 1897, Arkhiv vneshnei politiki Rossiiskoi Imperii (hereafter AVPRI), f. 138, op. 467, d. 166, l. 18, also in KA, 87:38; M. N. Murav'ev to Pahlen, telegram, October 27, 1897, AVPRI, f. 133, op. 470, d. 54, l. 290; M. N. Murav'ev to Pahlen, telegram, October 28, 1897, AVPRI, f. 133, op. 470, d. 54, l. 291. These last two telegrams are also in KA, 87:38–40 (translated from French), and excerpts are published in Johannes Lepsius et al., eds., *Die grosse Politik der europäischen Kabinette, 1871–1914: Sammlung der diplomatischen Akten des Auswärtigen Amtes* (Berlin: Deutsche Veragsgesellschaft für Politik und Geschichte, 1922–27), 14:73–74 (hereafter GP). Malozemoff explains that European powers often invoked "the right of first anchorage" when claiming areas on unsettled or "uncivilized" coasts; however, he adds, it was probably not applicable to established nations such as China: Andrew Malozemoff, *Russia's Far Eastern Policy* (Berkeley: University of California Press, 1958), 281, n40.

7. N. D. Osten-Sacken to N. M. Murav'ev, telegram, October 31, 1897, Gosudarstvennyi arkhiv Rossiiskoi Federatsii (hereafter GARF), f. 568, op. 1, d. 127, l. 6; also in KA, 87:40.

8. P. P. Tyrtov to F. V. Dubasov, telegram, GARF, f. 568, op. 1, d. 127, ll. 33–34.

9. Wilhelm II to Nicholas II, telegram, December 19, 1897, GP, 14:129–30.

10. Westel W. Willoughby, *Foreign Rights and Interests in China* (Baltimore: Johns Hopkins University Press, 1920), 228–44.

11. F. M. Knobel to W. H. de Beaufort, memorandum, January 7, 1898, *Rijksgeschiedkundige Publicatiën, Grote Serie* (The Hague: Martinus Nijhoff, 1905–), 138:578 (hereafter RGP); W. H. de Beaufort to F. M. Knobel, letter, February 21, 1898, RGP, 138:609; Michael H. Hunt, *Frontier Defense and the Open Door: Manchuria in Chinese-American Relations, 1895–1911* (New Haven: Yale University Press, 1973), 29–30.

12. The phrase is lifted from the title of William Langer's classic study of European diplomacy at the turn of the twentieth century, *The Diplomacy of Imperialism* (New York: Knopf, 1956).

13. The Choristers' Bridge refers to the tsarist foreign ministry, after a bridge near the quarters of the palace chapel choir that spanned the canal behind the ministry.

14. Prince Lobanov's proposal was merely one of several options he had dutifully submitted for his master's consideration, but there are indications that Tokyo might well have welcomed such a move. On the day after Japan's conditions for peace were announced, a Japanese diplomat in Berlin hinted that his government would not oppose a Russian move to secure a portion of northern Manchuria and a Korean port, as long as Japan's demand for the Liaodong Peninsula was assured: Otto von Mühlberg, memorandum, April 2, 1895, *GP,* 14:260; Langer, *Diplomacy,* 180–81.

15. S. Iu. Witte to Nicholas II, memorandum, August 11, 1900, Rossiiskii gosudarstvennyi istoricheskii arkhiv (hereafter RGIA), f. 560, op. 28, d. 218, l. 69.

16. Witte to Nicholas II, August 11, 1900, l. 71.

17. For the text, see General-Maior P. N. Simanskii, *Sobytiia na Dalnem Vostoke* (St. Petersburg: Voennaia tipografiia, 1910), 2:109–10; B. B. Glinskii, ed., *Prolog Russko-Iaponskoi voiny: materialy iz arkhiva Grafa S. Iu. Vitte* (Petrograd: Brokgauz-Efron, 1916), 137.

18. V. N. Lamsdorf to A. N. Kuropatkin, letter, March 31, 1900, Rossiiskii Gosudarstvennyi voenno-istoricheskii arkhiv (hereafter RGVIA), f. 165, op. 1, d. 759, ll. 1–2. See also V. N. Kuropatkin to V. V. Sakharov, letter, July 1, 1901, RGVIA, f. 165, op. 1, d. 702, l. 2.

19. A. Suvorin, "Malenkiia pisma," *Novoe Vremia,* 2/22/1903 (old style), 3; "Kitaiskaia zheleznaia doroga," *Novoe Vremia,* 5/3/1902 (old style), 2; N. Kravchenko, "S Dal'niago Vostoka, pis'mo XVXIV," *Novoe Vremia,* 10/22/1902 (old style), 2; B. H. Sumner, *Tsardom and Imperialism* (Hamden, Conn.: Archon Books, 1968), 17.

20. E. Kh. Nilus, ed., *Istoricheskii obzor Kitaiskoi vostochnoi zheleznoi dorogi, 1896–1923 gg* (Harbin: Tipografiia K. V. Zh. D., 1923), 1:122; Chancellery of the Finance Ministry, "Istoricheskaia Spravka o vazhneishchikh dlia Rossii sobytiiakh na Dal'nem Vostoke v trekhletie 1898–1900," RGIA, f. 1622, op. 1, d. 935, l. 92.

21. David Wolff, *To the Harbin Station: The Liberal Alternative in Russian Manchuria, 1898–1914* (Stanford: Stanford University Press, 1999), 25–29, 35–41; Nilus, *Istoricheskii obzor,* 126–33.

22. Nilus, *Istoricheskii obzor,* 131–34, 156–73. There was much sparring between Witte and War Minister Kuropatkin over who would have jurisdiction over the port. In 1899 it was resolved to put the entire leasehold under the authority of a navy officer, although the Finance Ministry would retain much responsibility over Dal'nii, with Port Arthur becoming a Russian military base: Minutes, Council of January 12, 1899, and March 19, 1899, RGIA, f. 560, op. 38, d. 179, ll. 23–39; Minutes, Council of April 17, 1899, RGIA, f. 1622, op. 1, d. 167, l. 1.

23. Nilus, *Istoricheskii obzor,* 200, 503–11; Glinskii, *Prolog,* 111; Rosemary Quested, *"Matey" Imperialists? The Tsarist Russians in Manchuria, 1895–1917* (Hong Kong:

University of Hong Kong, 1982), 99–100; David MacLaren McDonald, *United Government and Foreign Policy in Russia, 1900–1914* (Cambridge, Mass.: Harvard University Press, 1992), 12. The guards' most famous veteran was Aleksandr Guchkov, the future leader of the moderately conservative Octobrist Party in the Duma, Russia's prerevolutionary legislature: Nilus, *Istoricheskii obzor,* 507.

24. A good example of such reasoning is in I. P. Balashev to Nicholas II, memorandum, March 25, 1902, GARF, f. 543, op. 1, d. 180, ll. 1–26.

25. V. N. Lamsdorf to L. P. Urusov, letter, October 18, 1899, box 1, Urusov Papers, Bakhmeteff Archive of Russian and East European Culture, Columbia University, New York.

26. E. I. Alekseev to A. N. Kuropatkin, letter, March 19, 1901, Rossiiski gosudarstvennyi arkhiv Voenno-Morskogo Flota (hereafter RGAVMF), f. 32, op. 1, d. 123, ll. 1–7; E. I. Alekseev to A. N. Kuropatkin, telegram, August 9, 1901, RGVIA, f. 165, op. 1, d. 704, l. 1.

27. Alekseev to Kuropatkin, March 19, 1901, l. 6.

28. A. N. Kuropatkin, diary, September 12, 1901, RGVIA, f. 165, op. 1, d. 1871, ll. 51–52; A. N. Kuropatkin, diary, February 17, 1902, RGVIA, f. 165, op. 1, d. 1871, l. 68; A. N. Kuropatkin, diary, November 2, 1902, RGVIA, f. 165, op. 1, d. 1871, l. 92; V. N. Lamsdorf, note, April 1, 1902, AVPRI, f. 138, op. 467, d. 205/206, l. 1; V. N. Kuropatkin, diary, December 31, 1902, KA 2:17; Ministerial conference, minutes, January 25, 1903, KA, 52:119.

29. A. N. Kuropatkin to Nicholas II, memorandum, August 9, 1903, d. 27, n. 2, Witte Papers, Bakhmeteff Archive. Although written before Russia's occupation of Manchuria, the extensive *tour d'horizon* of Russia's strategic position that the war minister presented to the tsar is an excellent example of his thinking: see A. N. Kuropatkin to Nicholas II, memorandum, March 27, 1900, RGIA, f. 1622, op. 1, d. 269. A brief summary of this remarkable document is in William C. Fuller, *Strategy and Power in Russia, 1600–1914* (New York: Free Press, 1992), 377–79.

30. Bezobrazov's role in Russian Far Eastern diplomacy remains highly controversial, but it has probably been exaggerated. For more details about his scheme, see Igor Lukoianov, "The Bezobrazovtsy," in *The Russo-Japanese War in Global Perspective: World War Zero,* ed. John W. Steinberg et al. (Leiden and Boston: Brill, 2005), 65–86.

31. For the text, see Glinskii, *Prolog,* 180–83.

32. V. N. Lamsdorf, notes for report, December 3, 1901, GARF, f. 568, op. 1, d. 62, ll. 43–45; V. N. Lamsdorf to Nicholas II, memorandum, December 5, 1901, KA, 63:44–45; V. N. Lamsdorf to A. P. Izvol'skii, telegram, December 5, 1901, KA, 63:47–48; Ian Nish, *The Anglo-Japanese Alliance: The Diplomacy of Two Island Empires, 1894–1907* (London: Athlone Press, 1966), 186, 196–200; Simanskii, *Sobytiia,* 2:159–72; Langer, *Diplomacy,* 764–70; G. Trubetzkoi, *Russland als Grossmacht* (Stuttgart: Deutsche Verlags-Anhalt, 1917), 68–69.

33. B. Bülow, memorandum, November 4, 1901, *GP,* 18–1: 39. The navy minister was equally opposed to a Japanese presence in Korea, since it would deprive him of the possibility of a naval station on the peninsula: P. P. Tyrtov to V. N. Lamsdorf, letter, December 13, 1901, GARF, f. 568, op. 1, d. 177, ll. 1–3.

34. Although Nicholas coined the term, B. A. Romanov popularized it among historians to describe the growing ascendance of Bezobrazov. See B. A. Romanov, *Russia in Manchuria, 1892–1906*, trans. Susan Wilbur Jones (Ann Arbor, Mich.: J. W. Edwards, 1952).

35. Romanov, *Russia in Manchuria*, 284.

36. Romanov, *Russia in Manchuria*, 284. Citation paraphrased from translation for clarity.

37. Malozemoff, *Russia's Far Eastern Policy*, 218.

38. George Alexander Lensen, ed., *Korea and Manchuria between Russia and Japan, 1895–1904: The Observations of Sir Ernest Satow* (Tallahassee: Diplomatic Press, 1966), 210.

39. Nicholas II to E. I. Alekseev, telegram, September 10, 1903, RGAVMF, f. 417, op. 1, d. 2865, l. 31.

40. Nicholas II to S. Iu. Witte, letter, August 16, 1903, RGIA, f. 1622, op. 1, d. 34, l. 1.

41. Baron Roman Romanovich Rosen, *Forty Years of Diplomacy* (London: Allen & Unwyn, 1922), 1:219.

42. V. I. Gurko, *Facts and Features of the Past* (Stanford: Stanford University Press, 1939), 281.

43. William L. Langer, "The Origins of the Russo-Japanese War," in *Explorations in Crisis: Papers on International History*, ed. C. E. and E. Schorske (Cambridge, Mass.: Harvard University Press, 1969), 26–28.

44. A. P. Cassini to V. N. Lamsdorf, telegram, June 12, 1903, AVPRI, f. 143, op. 491, d. 45, l. 138; A. P. Cassini to V. N. Lamsdorf, telegram, June 13, 1903, AVPRI, f. 143, op. 491, d. 45, l. 146.

45. Langer, "Origins," 26–28.

46. David MacKenzie, *Imperial Dreams/Harsh Realities: Tsarist Russian Foreign Policy, 1815–1917* (Fort Worth: Harcourt Brace, 1994), 145.

47. Ian Nish, *The Origins of the Russo-Japanese War* (London and New York: Longman, 1985), 213.

48. Rosen, *Forty Years*, 1: 231.

49. A. V. Ignat'ev, *Vneshniaia politika Rossii v 1905–1907 gg* (Moscow: Nauka, 1986), 154.

50. Bruce W. Menning, *Bayonets before Bullets: The Imperial Russian Army, 1861–1914* (Bloomington: Indiana University Press, 1992), 217.

51. Fuller, *Strategy*, 415.

52. Based on Gorchakov's celebrated phrase "*La Russie ne boude pas, mais se receuille*" (Russia is not sulking. It is merely gathering its strength): Barbara Jelavich, *A Century of Russian Foreign Policy* (Philadelphia: J. B. Lippincott, 1964), 134.

53. V. A. Emets, "A. P. Izvol'skii i perestroika vneshnei politiki Rossii (soglashenie 1907 g.)," in *Rossiiskaia diplomatiia v portretakh*, ed. A. V. Ignat'ev et al. (Moscow: Mezhdunarodnye otnosheniia, 1992), 342–44.

54. Emets, "A. P. Izvol'skii," 342–44; V. A. Marinov, *Rossiia i Iaponiia pered pervoi mirovoi voinoi (1905–14 gody)* (Moscow: Nauka, 1974), 23–50; D.C.B. Lieven, *Russia and the Origins of the First World War* (New York: St. Martin's Press, 1983), 32.

55. A. A. Polivanov, *Iz dnevnikov i vospominanii po dolzhnosti voennogo ministra i ego pomoshnika 1907–1916 g* (Moscow: Vysshii voennyi redaktsionnyi sovet, 1924), 16.

56. For a thorough study based on Russian archives of the negotiations with Japan after Portsmouth, see Marinov, *Rossiia.* A good summary is Ignat'ev, *Vneshniaia politika,* 147–57, 172–81.

57. Ia. A. Shulatov, "Rossiisko-iaponskie otnosheniia v dalnevostochnoi politike Rossii (1905–1911 gg.)" (Prospectus for candidate's thesis, Khabarovsk State Pedagogical University, 2005), 21.

58. For the text, see E. D. Grimm, *Sbornik dogovorov i drugikh dokumentov po istorii mezhdunarodnykh otnoshenii na Dal'nem Vostoke (1842–1925)* (Moscow: Institut Vostokovedeniia, 1927), 169–70; Victor Yakhontoff, *Russia and the Soviet Union in the Far East* (New York: Coward-McCann, 1931), 374–76.

59. The best account of Russian activity in Manchuria during these years is Wolff, *Harbin Station.* For details about Mongolia, see Iwan Korostovetz, *Von Cinggis Khan zur Sowjetrepublic* (Berlin: Walter de Gruyter, 1926); and E. A. Belov, *Rossiia i Mongoliia (1911–1919 gg.)* (Moscow: IV RAN, 1999).

60. Similarly, the Anglo-Russian Accord of 1907 did not halt tsarist activity in Central Asia. See Jennifer Siegel, *Endgame: Britain, Russia and the Final Struggle for Central Asia* (London: I. B. Tauris, 2002).

Chapter 2. Japanese Diplomacy Before and After the War: The Turning Point on the Road to the Pacific War (pages 24–40)

1. In 1895 Russia, Germany, and France forced Japan to retrocede to China the leasehold it had negotiated on the Liaodong Peninsula as part of the terms of the peace treaty concluding the Sino-Japanese War of 1894–95.

2. When news of the Boxer Rebellion reached Beijing, Minister of War A. N. Kuropatkin said, "I am very glad. This will give us an excuse for seizing Manchuria. We will turn Manchuria into a second Bokhara": *The Memoirs of Count Witte,* trans. and ed. Abraham Yarmolinsky (New York: Doubleday, Page, 1921), 107–8; *Uitsutehaku kaisōki: Nichi-Ro sensō to Roshia kakumei* [The Memoirs of Count Witte: The Russo-Japanese War and the Russian Revolution], ed. Otake Hirokichi (Tokyo: Hara Shobō, 1972 reprint), 1:196–97.

3. *Katsura Tarō jiden* [The Autobiography of Katsura Tarō], annotated by Uno Shun'ichi (Tokyo: Heibonsha, 1993), 255.

4. *Kōshaku Katsura Tarō den* [Biography of Prince Katsura Tarō], annotated by Tokutomi Iichirō (Tokyo: Ko Katsura-kōshaku Kinen Jigyōkai, 1917), 1:1055–57.

5. *Yamagata Aritomo ikensho* [The Written Opinions of Yamagata Aritomo], ed. Ōyama Azusa (Tokyo: Hara Shobō, 1966), 196–97.

6. *Yamagata Aritomo ikensho,* 266; *Katsura Tarō jiden,* 300.

7. Ishii Kikujirō, *Gaikō yoroku* [Diplomatic Records] (Tokyo: Iwanami Shoten, 1930), 363–65; Honda Kumatarō, *Tamashii no gaikō* [The Diplomacy of Komura Jutarō] (Tokyo: Chikura Shobō, 1941), 5–6.

8. *Komura gaikō shi* [The History of Komura Diplomacy], ed. Gaimushō [Ministry of Foreign Affairs] (Tokyo: Beniya Shoten, 1953), 1:206–15.

9. *Nihon gaikō bunsho* [Japanese Diplomatic Documents], ed. Gaimushō [Ministry of Foreign Affairs] (Tokyo: Nihon Kokusai Rengō Kyōkai, 1957), 35:498–503.

10. *Nihon gaikō bunsho*, 33:699.

11. *Nihon gaikō bunsho*, 34:524.

12. *Nihon gaikō bunsho*, 34:66–67.

13. *Nihon gaikō bunsho*, 34:67.

14. *Nihon gaikō bunsho*, 34:67–69.

15. Honda, *Tamashii no gaikō*, 246–63; *Katsura Tarō jiden*, 259, 326.

16. Honda, *Tamashii no gaikō*, 322–23; *Katsura Tarō jiden*, 323–26.

17. Honda, *Tamashii no gaikō*, 243–46, 254–56.

18. *Hara Takashi nikki* [The Diary of Hara Takashi], ed. Hara Keiichirō (Tokyo: Fukumura Shuppan, 1981), 2:4; *Kōshaku Katsura Tarō den*, 1: 1066–67; *Katsura Tarō jiden*, 261–62, 299–300.

19. *Katsura Tarō jiden*, 256, 284, 300; *Kōshaku Katsura Tarō den*, 1:1057–58; *Hara Takashi nikki*, 2:6–7.

20. *Hara Takashi nikki*, 2:6; *Kōshaku Katsura Tarō den*, 1:1121.

21. *Katsura Tarō jiden*, 258–62. In a letter to Inoue Kaoru dated August 28, 1901, however, Katsura admitted that Japan had to negotiate with Russia to achive a favorable solution to the Korean problem: *Itō Hirobumi kankei monjo* [Documents Relating to Itō Hirobumi], ed. Itō Hirobumi Kankei Monjo Kenkyūkai (Tokyo: Hanawa Shobō, 1975), 3:359–60. It is not known when Katsura decided to call for an alliance with Britain as opposed to Itō's advocacy of a Russo-Japanese understanding: *Katsura Tarō jiden*, 359–60 (comment by the annotator).

Shumpei Okamoto regarded the attitude toward Russo-Japanese negotiations of oligarchs such as Itō as optimistic, but that of younger statesmen such as Katsura and Komura as pessimistic: Shumpei Okamoto, "Katō gaikō seisaku kettei no chōtan: Nichi-Ro sensō ni okeru Nippon no keiken" [The Oligarchic Control of Foreign-Policy-Making: Japan's Experience during the Russo-Japanese War], *Kokusai seiji* [International Politics] 41, no. 1 (1969): 9.

22. *Katsura Tarō jiden*, 259–60, 262, 300; *Kōshaku Katsura Tarō den*, 1:1106, 1113–14, 1121.

23. *Hara Takashi nikki*, 2:90–91; Tani Hisao, *Kimitsu Nichi-Ro senshi* [The Secret History of the Russo-Japanese War] (Tokyo: Hara Shobō, 1966), 49.

24. Tani, *Kimitsu Nichi-Ro senshi*, 49; *Sansen nijū shōsei Nichi-Ro taisen o kataru* [Twenty Campaign Generals' Memoirs of Russo-Japanese Land Battles] (Tokyo: Tokyo Nichinichi Shinbunsha and Osaka Mainichi Shinbunsha, 1935), 24–25 (memoir of Gen. Ōshima Ken'ichi); Navy Minister Yamamoto Gonnohyōe also explained the difficulty of funding the war, which was estimated to cost two billion yen: *Sansen nijū teitoku Nichi-Ro daikaisen o kataru* [Twenty Campaign Admirals' Memoirs of Russo-Japanese Naval Battles] (Tokyo: Tokyo Nichinichi Shinbunsha and Osaka Mainichi Shinbunsha, 1935), 38–39, 50; Komatsu Midori, *Shunpo-kō to Gansetsu-kō* [Prince Itō and Prince Yamagata] (Tokyo: Gakuji Shoin, 1934), 152.

25. Masumoto Uhei, *Shizen no hito Komura Jutarō* [Biography of Komura Jutarō] (Tokyo: Rakuyōdō, 1914), 657, 703.

26. *Itō Hirobumi den* [Biography of Itō Hirobumi] (Tokyo: Shunpo-kō Tsuishōkai, 1940), 3:579–80.

27. *Nihon gaikō bunsho*, 36–1: 452–644, 37–1: 641–49.

28. Komura to Kurino Shin'ichirō, August 20, 1903, and Komura to Uchida Yasuya, August 25, 1903, "Gaimushō kiroku" [Records of the Ministry of Foreign Affairs], Gaimushō Gaikō Shiryōkan [Diplomatic Archives, Ministry of Foreign Affairs], Tokyo.

29. *Meiji tennō ki* [Annals of the Meiji Emperor], ed. Kunaishō [Imperial Household Agency] (Tokyo: Yoshikawa Kōbunkan, 1974), 10:410; *Itō Hirobumi den*, 2:581. According to Witte, Bezobrazov urged that Russia establish influence in Korea by securing various concessions, ostensibly private but in reality backed and directed by St. Petersburg. And he conceived the idea of forming a semiofficial Eastern-Asiatic industrial corporation for the purpose of exploiting Korean forests; this enterprise had the earmarks of a politico-industrial adventure, although Witte argued that it would court disaster by provoking an armed clash with Japan: *Memoirs of Count Witte*, 116–17; *Uitsute-haku kaisōki*, 209–10.

30. A. N. Kuropatkin, *The Russian Army and the Japanese War*, trans. A. B. Lindsay (New York: E. P. Dutton, 1909), 1:169–79.

31. Kuropatkin, *The Russian Army and the Japanese War*, 2:312–13.

32. *Katsura Tarō jiden*, 272–74, 324–26; *Kōshaku Katsura Tarō den*, 2:119–22.

33. *Katsura Tarō jiden*, 272–74, 324–26.

34. *Katsura Tarō jiden*, 274.

35. Rikugun Sanbō Honbu [Army General Staff Office], ed., *Meiji sanjū-shichi-hachi nen himitsu Nichi-Ro senshi* [Secret Military History of the Russo-Japanese War of 1904–5] (unpublished, Bōeishō Bōei Kenkyūsho [National Institute for Defense Studies, Ministry of Defense], Tokyo), 1:26.

36. Rikugun Sanbō Honbu, *Meiji sanjū-shichi-hachi nen himitsu Nichi-Ro senshi*, 1:26–27, 45–46; *Nichi-Ro sensō to Iguchi Seigo* [The Russo-Japanese War and Iguchi Seigo] (Tokyo: Hara Shobō, 1994), 232; *Sansen nijū shōsei Nichi-Ro taisen o kataru*, 21–22. See the opinion expressed at this conference by Iguchi Seigo, general manager of the army General Staff Office and a central member of the midlevel officers' group: Rikugun Sanbō Honbu, *Meiji sanjū-shichi-hachi nen himitsu Nichi-Ro senshi*, 1:27–45.

37. Rikugun Sanbō Honbu, *Meiji sanjū-shichi-hachi nen himitsu Nichi-Ro senshi*, 1:47–50; *Nichi-Ro sensō to Iguchi Seigo*, 234–35. Ōyama did not get navy approval before submitting this memorandum.

38. Tani, *Kimitsu Nichi-Ro senshi*, 37.

39. Hosoya Chihiro has indicated that, in the pressure middle-echelon military officers exerted on the oligarchs, we can already discern at the time of the Russo-Japanese War the decentralized pattern of decision making that would characterize the process leading up to the Pacific War: Hosoya Chihiro, "Twenty Years after Pearl Harbor: A New Look at Japan's Decision for War," in *Imperial Japan and Asia: A Re-*

assessment, ed. Grant K. Goodman (New York: East Asian Institute, Columbia University, 1967), 61. Moreover, there was a slip of the tongue by Yamaza Enjirō, head of the Political Bureau in the Foreign Office, about plotting an assassination of Itō because of his weak stance toward Russia: Ichimata Masao, *Yamaza Enjirō den* [Biography of Yamaza Enjirō] (Tokyo: Hara Shobō, 1974), 33–37; Tani, *Kimitsu Nichi-Ro senshi,* 49; Komatsu, *Shunpo-kō to Gansetsu-kō,* 147–52.

40. *Nihon gaikō bunsho,* 36–1: 1–2.

41. *Nihon gaikō bunsho,* 36–1: 3.

42. *Katsura Tarō jiden,* 324, 326; *Kōshaku Katsura Tarō den,* 2:157–63, 184.

43. *Katsura Tarō jiden,* 259, 326, 328; *Kōshaku Yamagata Aritomo den* [Biography of Prince Yamagata Aritomo], ed. Tokutomi Iichirō (Tokyo: Yamagata Aritomo-kō Kinen Jigyōkai, 1933), 3:561–62; Honda, *Tamashii no gaikō,* 255–56, 258–59. On June 17, Komura sent a message to Uchida Yasuya, Japan's minister to China, indicating that he had already decided his policy toward Russia and thought the only option was war: *Uchida Yasuya,* ed. Uchida Yasuya Denki Hensan Iinkai (Tokyo: Kajima Kenkyūsho Shuppankai, 1969), 96–97.

44. *Yamamoto Gonnohyōe to Kaigun* [Yamamoto Gonnohyōe and the Navy], ed. Kaigun Daijin Kanbō [Navy Minister's Secretariat] (Tokyo: Hara Shobō, 1966), 134–36; *Hakushaku Yamamoto Gonnohyōe den* [Biography of Count Yamamoto Gonnohyōe] (Tokyo: Hara Shobō, 1968), 1:559–60.

45. *Yamamoto Gonnohyōe to Kaigun,* 144–48.

46. *Nihon gaikō bunsho,* 36–1: 12.

47. *Nichi-Ro sensō to Iguchi Seigo,* 257–58; Tani, *Kimitsu Nichi-Ro senshi,* 38–39.

48. *Meiji tennō ki,* 10:545–46; *Kōshaku Yamagata Aritomo den,* 3:573–74; *Itō Hirobumi den,* 3:620.

49. Honda, *Tamashii no gaikō,* 92, 288; Honda Kumatarō, *Senjin o kataru* [Memoirs of My Predecessors] (Tokyo: Chikura Shobō, 1939), 45–46; Tani, *Kimitsu Nichi-Ro senshi,* 41–42.

50. Tani, *Kimitsu Nichi-Ro senshi,* 42; *Kōshaku Katsura Tarō den,* 2:184–87; *Kōshaku Yamagata Aritomo den,* 3:574–76; *Itō Hirobumi den,* 3:620.

51. *Itō Hirobumi den,* 3:620–21; *Kōshaku Yamagata Aritomo den,* 3:573–74; Honda, *Tamashii no gaikō,* 288; *Shunpo-kō to Gansetsu-kō,* 178–81.

52. *Nihon gaikō bunsho,* 37–1: 13.

53. *Nihon gaikō bunsho,* 37–1: 86; Rikugun Sanbō Honbu, *Meiji sanjū-shichi-hachi nen himitsu Nichi-Ro senshi,* 1:103; Kaigun Sanbō Honbu [Navy General Staff Office], ed., *Gokuhi Meiji sanjū-shichi-hachi nen kaisenshi* [Top Secret History of Naval Battles during the Russo-Japanese War of 1904–5] (unpublished, Bōeishō Bōei Kenkyūsho [National Institute for Defense Studies, Ministry of Defense], Tokyo), 1–1: 72.

54. *Itō Hirobumi den,* 3:625–27; *Meiji tennō ki,* 10:590.

55. Rikugun Sanbō Honbu, *Meiji sanjū-shichi-hachi nen himitsu Nichi-Ro senshi,* 1:103–8.

56. *Nihon gaikō bunsho,* 37–1: 92–94.

57. *Nihon gaikō bunsho,* 37–1: 97–100. At the Hague Universal Peace Conference

in 1907, Dr. Louis Renault, a French judge on the Permanent Arbitration Court and a chief member of the committee considering the procedure for declaring war, admitted that there were no provisions prescribing such a procedure at the time of the Russo-Japanese War. This Hague Conference established the first convention concerning "the opening of hostilities": *Nihon gaikō bunsho, Heiwa kaigi kankei* [Documents Related to the Peace Conference], 2:489–90. See the bibliography by Hirama Yōichi in *Sen-kyūhyaku-shi-go nen Ro-Nichi kaisenshi* [History of Naval Battles between Russia and Japan in 1904–5], ed. Russian navy, trans. Japanese navy (Tokyo: Fuyō Shobō, 2004), 6; Ōe Shinobu, *Sekaishi toshite no Nichi-Ro sensō* [The Russo-Japanese War as World History] (Tokyo: Rippū Shobō, 2001), 398–400.

58. "Hayashi Tadasu kankei monjo" [Documents Relating to Hayashi Tadasu], archive 14, telegram 63, Gaimushō Gaikō Shiryōkan [Diplomatic Archives, Ministry of Foreign Affairs], Tokyo.

59. *Memoirs of Count Witte*, 123, 126.

60. *Memoirs of Count Witte*, 118; *Uitsute-haku kaisōki*, 1:270–71.

61. Mutsu Munemitsu, *Kenkenroku: A Diplomatic Record of the Sino-Japanese War, 1894–95*, ed. and trans. Gordon Mark Berger (Princeton and Tokyo: Princeton University Press and University of Tokyo Press, 1982), 17.

62. Iriye Akira, *Nihon no gaikō: Meiji ishin kara gendai made* [Japanese Diplomacy: From the Meiji Restoration to Today] (Tokyo: Chūō Kōronsha, 1966), 55, 62.

63. For more details, see Teramoto Yasutoshi, *Nichi-Ro sensō igo no Nihon gaikō: pawâ poritikusu no naka no Man-Kan mondai* [Japanese Diplomacy after the Russo-Japanese War: The Manchuria-Korea Problem in the Context of Power Politics] (Tokyo: Shinzansha, 1999), 10–12. For this section on postwar diplomacy and international politics, I have summarized the contents of the above book.

64. *Nihon gaikō bunsho, Nichi-Ro sensō* [The Russo-Japanese War], 3:505, 507; Rikugunshō [Army Ministry], ed., *Meiji sanjū-shichi-hachi nen sen'eki rikugun seishi* [Army Administration during the War of 1904–5] (Tokyo: Gannandō Shoten, 1982), 8:809–21. Regarding the decision-making process of the Japanese army after the Russo-Japanese War, see Kitaoka Shin'ichi, *Nihon Rikugun to tairiku seisaku* [The Japanese Army and Its Continental Policy] (Tokyo: University of Tokyo Press, 1978).

65. See, for example, the message Komura sent to Theodore Roosevelt on January 22, 1905: *Nihon gaikō bunsho, Nichi-Ro sensō*, 5:215–17.

66. *Nihon gaikō bunsho, 39–1*: 210–12; U.S. Department of State, ed., *Papers Relating to the Foreign Relations of the United States* (Washington, D.C.: Government Printing Office, 1909), 1906–1: 174–75.

67. *Nihon gaikō bunsho, 39–1*: 238; FO 410/47, inclosure in no. 92, March 31, 1906, Public Record Office, London.

68. *Nihon gaikō bunsho, Nichi-Ro sensō*, 3:588.

69. *Nihon gaikō bunsho, Nichi-Ro sensō*, 3:594.

70. *Nihon gaikō bunsho, 39–1*: 863.

71. "Gaimushō kiroku," 5.2.6.13.

72. Wakatsuki Reijirō, *Kofuan kaikoroku* [Memoir of Wakatsuki Reijirō] (Tokyo: Yomiuri Shinbunsha, 1950), 68–76.

73. *Itō Hirobumi hiroku* [Secret Documents of Itō Hirobumi], ed. Itō Hirokuni and Hiratsuka Atsushi (Tokyo: Shunjūsha, 1929), 1:392–408.

74. *Yamagata Aritomo ikensho*, 287; E. J. Dillon, "Japan and Russia: The Story of How Peace was Brought About," *Contemporary Review* 91 (February 1907): 288.

75. *Nihon teikoku no kokubō hōshin* [Japanese Imperial Defense Policy], 1907, "Miyazaki bunko" [Miyazaki papers], no. 39, Military Archives, Bōeishō Bōei Kenkyūsho [National Institute for Defense Studies, Ministry of Defense], Tokyo.

76. Akira Iriye has described Komura as "the conventional exponent of expansionism": Akira Iriye, "The Ideology of Japanese Imperialism: Imperial Japan and China," in *Imperial Japan and Asia*, 36. See also Shumpei Okamoto, "Meiji Nippon no tai-Chūgoku taido no ichi danmen: Komura Jutarō no baai" [One Aspect Regarding Meiji Japan's Attitude toward China: The Case of Komura Jutarō], in *Kindai Nihon no taigai taido* [The Foreign Attitude of Modern Japan], ed. Satō Seizaburō and Roger Dingman (Tokyo: University of Tokyo Press, 1974).

77. *Nihon gaikō bunsho*, 41–1: 687.

78. *Nihon gaikō bunsho*, 38–1: 106–7. On Komura's careful diplomacy in raising funds for the South Manchuria Railway through the special envoy Kaneko Kentarō after the revocation of the Harriman-Katsura memorandum on joint U.S.-Japanese financing of the railroad, see Matsumura Masayoshi, *Nichi-Ro sensō to Kaneko Kentarō: kōhō gaikō no kenkyū* [The Russo-Japanese War and Kaneko Kentarō: A Study in the Diplomacy of Public Relations], rev. ed. (Tokyo: Shin'yūdō, 1987), 480–84.

79. *Nihon gaikō bunsho*, 38–1: 203–4, 206.

80. For details, see Teramoto Yasutoshi, "Hayashi Tadasu no gaikō seisaku ni kansuru kenkyū: gōrisei to sono genkai" [A Study on the Foreign Policy of Hayashi Tadasu: Rationality and Its Limits], in *Nichi-Ro sensō kenkyū no shin shiten* [New Perspectives in the Study of the Russo-Japanese War], ed. Nichi-Ro Sensō Kenkyūkai (Yokohama: Seibunsha, 2005).

81. *Nochi wa mukashi no ki, hoka: Hayashi Tadasu kaikoroku* [Memoirs of Hayashi Tadasu], annotated by Yui Masaomi (Tokyo: Heibonsha, 1970), 306, 398 (comment by the annotator); Ukita Gōji, *Hakushaku Hayashi Tadasu den* [Biography of Count Hayashi Tadasu] (unpublished), 127.

82. Hayashi Tadasu, "Gaikō no dai hōshin o sadamu beshi" [A Major Diplomatic Policy Should Be Established], *Jiji shinpō*, May 28, 1895. On the role of Hermann Freiherr von Eckardstein, first secretary at the German embassy in London, see Ian H. Nish, *The Anglo-Japanese Alliance: The Diplomacy of Two Island Empires, 1894–1907* (London: Athlone Press, 1966), 124–27.

83. *Nihon gaikō bunsho*, 40–3: 803; A. M. Pooley, ed., *The Secret Memoirs of Count Tadasu Hayashi* (London: Eveleigh Nash, 1915), 225. *Secret Memoirs* is very important for understanding Hayashi's diplomatic thinking, because it includes his basic ideas on relations with China, America, and the European powers.

84. *Kanpō gōgai: Shūgiin giji sokkiroku* [Official Bulletin, Special Issue: Stenographic Record of Lower House Minutes], January 29, 1908.

85. "Nichi-Ei dōmei no genzai oyobi shōrai" [The Present Status and Future of the Anglo-Japanese Alliance], *Taiyō*, June 15, 1911.

86. "Hayashi Tadasu Kankei Monjo" [Papers Relating to Hayashi Tadasu], ar-

chive 40, Gaimushō Gaikō Shiryōkan [Diplomatic Archives, Ministry of Foreign Affairs], Tokyo; Pooley, *Secret Memoirs*, 260, 262.

87. *Nihon gaikō bunsho*, 40–3: 789–91; *Yamagata Aritomo ikensho*, 304–7; *Kōshaku Katsura Tarō den*, 2:335; Tsurumi Yūsuke, *Gotō Shinpei* [Biography of Gotō Shinpei] (Tokyo: Keisō Shobō, 1965), 2:977, 980–86; Gotō Shinpei, *Nihon shokumin seisaku ippan* [An Aspect of Japanese Colonial Policy] (Tokyo: Nihon Hyōronsha, 1944), 63.

88. "Hayashi Tadasu kankei monjo," archive 40; Pooley, *Secret Memoirs*, 253–54.

89. *Nihon gaikō bunsho*, 40–2: 396, 39–1: 612; "Itō Hirobumi kankei monjo" [Documents Relating to Itō Hirobumi], 57.9, Kensei Shiryō Shitsu [Modern Japanese Political History Materials Room], Kokuritsu Kokkai Toshokan [National Diet Library], Tokyo.

90. *Nihon gaikō bunsho*, 40–3: 580–84, 798–99.

91. "Gaimushō kiroku," 5.2.6.13.

92. Iguchi Kazuki, "Nippon teikokushugi no keisei to kokusai kankei" [The Formation of Japanese Imperialism and International Relations], in *Nihon no teikokushugi* [Japanese Imperialism], ed. Fujii Shūichi et al. (Tokyo: Gakuseisha, 1975), 131–36; Hosoya Chihiro and Honma Nagayo, eds., *Nichi-Bei kankeishi: masatsu to kyōchō no 140 nen* [A History of Japanese-American Relations: 140 years of Friction and Cooperation], 2nd ed. (Tokyo: Yūhikaku, 1982), 8.

93. Nakayama Jiichi, *Nichi-Ro sensō igo: Higashi Ajia o meguru teikokushugi no kokusai kankei* [After the Russo-Japanese War: The International Relations of Imperialism in East Asia] (Osaka: Sōgensha, 1957), 8–9; Oka Yoshitake, *Kokusai seiji shi* [A History of International Politics] (Tokyo: Iwanami Shoten, 1955), 161–62; Teramoto, *Nichi-Ro sensō igo no Nihon gaikō*, 10–11.

Chapter 3. The Portsmouth Peace (pages 41–61)

1. Shumpei Okamoto, *The Japanese Oligarchy and the Russo-Japanese War* (New York: Columbia University Press, 1970), 112–13.

2. B. A. Romanov, *Ocherki diplomaticheskoi istorii russko-iaponskoi voiny, 1895–1907* (Moscow: Izd-vo Akademii nauk SSSR, 1955), 323.

3. Romanov, *Ocherki diplomaticheskoi*, 325, 393.

4. Translation of the secret report of the Japanese ambassador to the United States, Takahira Kogorō to Komura Jutarō, June 27, 1904, Rossiiki gosudarstvenny arkiv Voenno-Morskogo Flota, St. Petersburg (hereafter RGAVMF), f. 467, op. 1, d. 430, ll. 2–3. This report was seized on the steamer *Kalakhas* in summer 1904.

5. Raymond A. Esthus, *Double Eagle and Rising Sun: The Russians and Japanese at Portsmouth in 1905* (Durham and London: Duke University Press, 1988), 16.

6. *Iz archiva S. Iu. Vitte: Vospominaniia*, vol. 2, *Rukopisnye zametki*, ed. B. V. Anan'ich et al. (St. Petersburg: D. Bulanin, 2003), 105–6.

7. Hayashi Tadasu to Komura Jutarō, July 26, 1904, Diplomatic Archives, Ministry of Foreign Affairs, Tokyo, no. 2.2.1.3–3, 49–50.

8. A. M. Abaza to E. I. Alekseev, June 21, 1904, RGAVMF, f. 32, op. 1, d. 212, ll. 34–39.

9. Notation by the Special Committee of the Far East about the coming Russo-Japanese War and the conditions of peace, RGAVMF, f. 32, op. 1, d. 301.

10. In an effort to weaken the central government, the Japanese sponsored the revolutionaries' liberation movement in Russia. In particular, there is evidence of the activity of one Colonel Akashi Motojirō, who financed the overseas purchase of weaponry for delivery to Russian revolutionaries on the steamship *John Grafton*. See Akashi Motojirō, *Rakka ryūsui: Colonel Akashi's Report on His Secret Cooperation with the Russian Revolutionary Parties during the Russo-Japanese War,* trans. Inaba Chiharu, ed. Olavi K. Fält and Antti Kujala (Helsinki: Suomen Historiallinen Seura, 1988). See also D. B. Pavlov and S. A. Petrov, *Iaponskie den'gi i russkaia revolutsiia: Russkaia razvedka i kontrrazvedka v voine 1904–1905 gg, dokumenty i materially* (Moscow: Progress, 1993). But the efforts of Akashi, though they promoted the development of revolution, failed to attain their goal of weakening the Russian war position. Contacts between Japanese intelligence and the Russian revolutionaries ended immediately after the conclusion of the Portsmouth Treaty.

11. Esthus, *Double Eagle and Rising Sun,* 8. The English ambassador in Russia, Charles Harding, noted the strengthening of antiwar sentiment in Moscow, especially in intellectual circles. See Ch. Harding to Lord Lansdowne, February 14, 1905, FO, no. 65/1698, 335–36, Public Record Office, London.

12. Hayashi Tadasu to Komura Jutarō, November 8, 1904, *Nihon gaikō bunsho* [Japanese Diplomatic Documents], *Nichi-Ro sensō* [The Russo-Japanese War], ed. Gaimushō [Ministry of Foreign Affairs] (Tokyo: Nihon Kokusai Rengō Kyōkai, 1960), 5:122–23.

13. Romanov, *Ocherki diplomaticheskoi,* 361–64, 370–72.

14. Romanov, *Ocherki diplomaticheskoi,* 360.

15. M. V. Rutkovskii to V. N. Kokovtsov, February 12 (25), 1905, Krasnyi Arkhiv, 1924, no. 6, 7–8.

16. V. N. Kokovtsov to M. V. Rutkovskii (undated telegram) and communication of V. N. Lamsdorf to V. N. Kokovtsov, February 12, 1905, Krasnyi Arkhiv, 1924, no. 6, 7–8.

17. Hayashi Tadasu to Komura Jutarō, March 2, 1905, Diplomatic Archives, Ministry of Foreign Affairs, Tokyo, no. 2.2.1.3–3, 156–57.

18. Witte, *Vospominaniia,* 2:573–74.

19. N. A. Raspopov to Ministerstvo Finansov, March 18 (31), 1905, Krasnyi Arkhiv, 1924, no. 6, 9.

20. Romanov, *Ocherki diplomaticheskoi,* 381.

21. Esthus, *Double Eagle and Rising Sun,* 28–29.

22. *Istoriia diplomatii,* ed. V. A. Zorin, 2nd ed. (Moscow: Gos. izd-vo polit. lit-ry, 1963), 2:581.

23. Motono Ichirō to Komura Jutarō, March 16, 1905, *Nihon gaikō bunsho, Nichi-Ro sensō,* 5:97–98.

24. T. Roosevelt to the Secretary of State, March 30, 1905, in *Theodore Roosevelt,*

Letters, ed. Elting E. Morison (Cambridge, Mass.: Harvard University Press, 1951), 4:1150.

25. V. N. Kokovtsov to Nicholas II (undated), Rossiiskii gosudarstvennyi is-toricheskii arkhiv (hereafter RGIA), f. 560, op. 28, d. 55, ll. 1, 10.

26. Konets russko-iaponskoi voiny (Voennoe sovechshanie 24 maia 1905 g. v Tsarskom Sele), Krasnyi Arkhiv, 1928, no. 3 (28), 182–204.

27. Wilhelm II to Nicholas II, June 3, 1905, *Perepiska Vil'gel'ma II s Nikolaem II 1894–1914 gg* (Moscow: Gos. izd-vo, 1923), 102–5.

28. Romanov, *Ocherki diplomaticheskoi,* 416.

29. Esthus, *Double Eagle and Rising Sun,* 40–41.

30. Ch. Harding to Lord Lansdowne, June 20, 1905, FO, no. 65/1701, 146, Public Record Office, London.

31. A. P. Cassini to V. N. Lamsdorf, June 3, 1905, *Sbornik diplomaticheskyh doku-mentov, kasaiuchshihsia peregovorov mezhdu Rossiei i Iaponiei o zakluchenii mirnogo dogovora, 24 maia–3 oktiabria 1905 goda* (hereafter *Sbornik*) (St. Petersburg: Russian Ministry of Foreign Affairs, 1906), 17.

32. N. V. Murav'ev's nomination displeased the Japanese, who believed that he had offended their delegation during the Hague Conference of 1899. See Small, *Zigzagi: Palomnichestvo S. Iu. Witte v Portsmut* (St. Petersburg, 1906), 19. However, his nomination cannot be considered a gesture pointed at Tokyo. The choice of Mu-rav'ev had been made in order to spite Witte, who was vigorously supported by V. N. Lamsdorf. See Ch. Harding to Lord Lansdowne, July 15, 1905, FO, no. 65/1701, 308, Public Record Office, London.

33. A. P. Cassini to V. N. Lamsdorf, May 31 (June 12), 1905, *Sbornik,* 15. It is clear that this information was deliberately leaked with the assumption that St. Peters-burg would appoint a figure of equivalent rank.

34. V. V. Sakharov to V. N. Lamsdorf, June 18 (July 1), 1905, *Sbornik,* 42–43.

35. F. K. Avelan to V. N. Lamsdorf, June 21 (July 4), 1905, *Sbornik,* 53–54.

36. V. N. Kokovtsov to V. N. Lamsdorf, June 20 (July 3), 1905, *Sbornik,* 47–53.

37. Instruktsiia stats-sekretariu N. V. Murav'evu, June 28 (July 11), 1905, *Sbornik,* 78–89.

38. As a worst-case scenario, the possibility of ransoming the railroad in ad-vance of negotiations was entertained. See Instruktsiia stats-sekretariu N. V. Mu-rav'evu, June 28 (July 11), 1905, *Sbornik,* 87.

39. On June 24 (July 7), 1905, the Japanese landed on the island and quickly over-came the resistance of weak and uncoordinated military command units. By July 16 (29), well prior to the beginning of negotiations in Portsmouth, the Japanese had seized most of Sakhalin. The question of its fate was a matter of serious concern in St. Petersburg, following a series of failures by the Russian army in early 1905. By then it was obvious that there was a very real danger that the Japanese would land on the island and capture it. Russia, moreover, did not have the forces to defend the island. Therefore, in March 1905, plans were made for the long-term leasing of all of Sakhalin to Russian and American businessmen. See E. I. Alekseev to V. N. Lams-dorf, March 20, 1905, Arkhiv vneshnei politiki Rossiiskoi Imperii (hereafter

AVPRI), f. 150, op. 493, d. 2016, l. 2. It was presumed that concessionaires would privately bind themselves to restoring their rights to Russia, if Russia demanded it. In the event of the handover of Sakhalin to the Japanese, the Russian treasury would receive half of the concessionaires' income. See Vsepoddanneishii doklad A. M. Abazy 19 aprelia, 1905, RGIA, f. 1337, op. 1, d. 176, l. 78. There was another plan as well: to sell Sakhalin to the Americans for 80–90 million rubles. But this was rejected after the envoy A. P. Cassini reported from Washington that the American government did not favor and would not support this deal. See A. P. Cassini to V. N. Lamsdorf, April 6 (19), 1905, AVPRI, f. 150, op. 493, d. 2016, ll. 15–16. A similar negative response was given by deputy E. I. Alekseev, who declared that, if the handover of Sakhalin to the Japanese were inevitable, it had to be on a temporary basis, with "certain conditions." See E. I. Alekseev to V. N. Lamsdorf, May 20, 1905, AVPRI, f. 150, op. 493, d. 2016, ll. 25–26. As a result Nicholas II rejected the next plan of the Bezobrazovites.

40. Instruktsiia N. V. Murav'evu, June 28 (July 11), 1905, *Sbornik*, 78–89.

41. Okamoto, *The Japanese Oligarchy and the Russo-Japanese War*, 124–25.

42. According to the story as told by General M. S. Komissarov, Russia installed a system for the mass decoding of diplomatic correspondence in 1904, after the outbreak of the Russo-Japanese War. "Twelve decoding systems were obtained" by him. "All foreign relations were monitored. . . . telegrams from abroad were received by our telegraph, copies were deciphered by the translator, and, if they were of no interest, were immediately sent on to the foreign embassy." In especially important instances—for example, during the negotiations in Portsmouth—the transmission of telegrams was held up for eight to twelve hours. What Komissarov confirmed is hardly surprising. "We knew all the American conditions before the American ambassador in St. Petersburg." The tsar was kept informed of all the most important news: "Not a day passed without one or two highly detailed reports being sent to him, based on intercepted correspondence." See Dopros M. S. Komissarova, May 4, 1917, Padenie tsarskogo regima, 1925, 3:141–42.

43. S. Iu. Witte to V. N. Lamsdorf, July 10–12 (23–25), 1905, Gosudarstvennyi arkhiv Rossiiskoi Federatsii (hereafter GARF), f. 568, op. 1, d. 381, l. 363.

44. *Sbornik*, 92–94.

45. Romanov, *Ocherki diplomaticheskoi*, 478–79. Witte precisely laid out the hand he had to play in Berlin: Germany was truly frightened by the revolutionary developments in Russia and was especially apprehensive of nationalist movements in adjacent areas. For this reason Germany was prepared to intervene to suppress revolutionary actions. See M. L. Ostretsova, "B'orkskii dogovor 1905 g. K voprosy o vliianii russko-iaponskoi voiny i revolutsii 1905 g. na razvitie russko-germanskikh otnoshenii," *Uchenye zapiski Moskovskogo gorodskogo pedagogicheskogo instituta im. V. P. Potemkina (Kafedra istorii Novogo vremeni, 4)* 83 (1958): 114–21.

46. A.V. Ignat'ev, *S. Iu. Vitte—diplomat* (Moscow: Mezhdunar otnoshenii, 1989), 215.

47. Motono Ichirō to Komura Jutarō, July 27, 1905, Diplomatic Archives, Ministry of Foreign Affairs, Tokyo, no. 2.2.1.3–3, 351–55.

48. B. V. Anan'ich and R. Sh. Ganelin, *Sergei Iul'evich Vitte i ego vremia* (St. Petersburg: D. Bulanin, 1999), 192–94. The idea of a war to win American public opinion was suggested to Witte by the American ambassador in Paris, R. McCormick. See S. Iu. Witte to V. N. Lamsdorf, July 12 (25), 1905, GARF, f. 568, op. 1, d. 381, ll. 372–74.

49. Hayashi Tadasu to Komura Jutarō, July 21, 1905, Diplomatic Archives, Ministry of Foreign Affairs, Tokyo, no 2.2.1.3–3, 334–36.

50. A Rafalovich to V. N. Kokovtsov, July 12 (25), 1905, Krasnyi Arkhiv, 1924, no. 6, 23. Hayashi Tadasu expressed his opinion to Gedemann, the London correspondent of the newspaper *Matin,* who was traveling to Portsmouth on the same steamship with Witte. It goes without saying that A. Rafalovich spoke with the reporter so that Hayashi's position could be communicated to St. Petersburg. This was most likely Hayashi's response to Witte's overture.

51. Romanov, *Ocherki diplomaticheskoi,* 472.

52. Ostretsova, "B'orkskii dogovor 1905," 101–3.

53. Romanov, *Ocherki diplomaticheskoi,* 467.

54. S. Iu. Witte to V. N. Lamsdorf, July 10–12 (23–25), 1905, GARF, f. 568, op. 1, d. 381, ll. 354–70.

55. I. Ia. Korostovets, "Mirnye peregovory v Portsmute v 1905 godu," *Byloe,* no. 29 (1918), 188. It is likely this was simply an excuse. A. I. Rusin did not appear in Portsmouth until July 27 (August 9). He reported that the army was in good spirits and was not expecting a peace settlement. Witte spoke for a long time with him "and came away with an unfavorable impression of the strategic situation and Russia's chances for victory" (219). Another member of the Russian delegation, Colonel M. K. Samoilov, a former military attaché in Japan, supported ending the war at any cost. Witte listened to his opinion more attentively. See A. I. Rusin, "K istorii mirnyh peregovorov v Portsmute v 1905 godu," *Morskiia zapiski* 2, no. 4 (1944): 253–54.

56. Witte, *Vospominaniia,* 2:156.

57. Anan'ich and Ganelin, *Sergei Iul'evich Vitte i ego vremia,* 193–94.

58. V. N. Lamsdorf to S. Iu. Witte, July 18 (August 1), 1905, *Sbornik,* 100–101.

59. Draft of a telegram from Witte to St. Petersburg, July 20 (August 2), 1905, GARF, f. 568, op. 1, d. 381, l. 374a.

60. R. R. Rosen to V. N. Lamsdorf, July 20 (August 2), 1905, *Sbornik,* 102.

61. S. Iu. Witte to V. N. Lamsdorf, July 22 (August 4), 1905, *Sbornik,* 103–4.

62. Korostovets, "Mirnye peregovory v Portsmute," 212–13.

63. I. P. Shipov to V. N. Kokovtsov, July 28, 1905, Krasnyi Arkhiv, 1924, no. 6, 28.

64. Roosevelt had been informed of the conditions prior to the beginning of negotiations and had advised the Japanese to moderate their demands, especially to refrain from attempts to force Russia to disarm Vladivostok and to hand over to Tokyo Russian vessels interned during the war in neutral ports. Further, he advised them to reduce as much as possible the amount of monetary compensation they were demanding and to avoid the word "indemnity." See Esthus, *Double Eagle and Rising Sun,* 71–72.

65. The demands were: (1) Russia, recognizing that Japan has major political, military, and economic interests in Korea, engages not to intervene or interfere with

any measures for government, protection, or oversight that Japan may find necessary to undertake in Korea. (2) Russia is required to withdraw completely from Manchuria within a determined time and to renounce all advantages deriving from preferential and exclusive concessions in the territory, as well as rights in this region, that violate Chinese sovereignty and are incompatible with the "principle of equivalent benefit." (3) Japan undertakes to return to China all those parts of Manchuria that are under its occupation, with the condition that reforms be introduced and improvements made in government, excepting those areas covered by the lease of the Liaodong Peninsula. (4) Japan and Russia mutually pledge not to interfere with measures that China recognizes it must take to further the development of trade and industry in Manchuria. (5) Sakhalin and all adjacent islands, with public buildings and property, are ceded to Japan. (6) The lease of Port Arthur and Dalian [the "Far" part—I. L.] as well as adjacent areas and territorial waters; all the rights, privileges, concessions, and the advantages gained by Russia from China in connection with or as part of this lease; and all public buildings and property are to be transferred to Japan. (7) Russia transfers to Japan, free from any claims and obligations, the railway between Harbin and Port Arthur and all its branches, together with its rights, privileges, and advantages, as well as all coal mines belonging to or being operated for the railway. (8) Russia retains and operates the Trans-Manchurian Railway in the eventuality of and dependent on its having the concession for its construction and also under condition that the railroad will be operated only for commercial and industrial purposes. (9) Russia compensates Japan for the actual costs of the war. The size and method of compensation will be determined subsequently. (10) All Russian warships that were given safe harbor in neutral ports because of damage sustained during the war and have been interned will be handed over to Japan as legitimate war prizes. (11) Russia pledges to limit its naval forces in Far Eastern waters. (12) Russia will offer Japanese subjects full fishing rights along the coast and in gulfs, harbors, bays, and rivers in its possession that are located in the Seas of Japan and Okhotsk and in the Bering Sea. See Korostovets, "Mirnye peregovory v Portsmute," 112–13.

66. G. A. Planson, Portsmutskaia mirnaia konferentsiia, Otchet sekretaria konferentsii, RGIA, f. 1622, op. 1, d. 982, l. 33. Why was Witte in such a hurry? If his explanation is true, it would mean that the Russian envoy was seriously counting on success at the negotiating table and his pessimism was feigned. But there is a more likely explanation. Witte's prompt reply provided insurance against changes of position in St. Petersburg. He had every reason to fear that "the war party" would gain the upper hand in the capital. Then the future hero of Portsmouth could refer to the fact that in its answer the Russian delegation had not exceeded its instructions. And, finally, Witte's step would induce St. Petersburg to accept his reply, without introducing serious corrections. Thus there were abundant reasons for haste. The desire to show the Japanese a readiness for dialogue would hardly be the primary one.

67. Planson, Portsmutskaia mirnaia konferentsiia, l. 34; Korostovets, "Mirnye peregovory v Portsmute," 115–16.

68. V. N. Lamsdorf to S. Iu. Witte, July 30 (August 12), 1905, *Sbornik*, 115–16.

69. Korostovets, "Mirnye peregovory v Portsmute," 134.

70. Telegram of Witte, August 1 (14), 1905, *Sbornik,* 120–21.

71. S. Iu. Witte to V. N. Lamsdorf , July 31 (August 13), 1905, *Sbornik,* 117–18.

72. Korostovets, "Mirnye peregovory v Portsmute," 126.

73. S. Iu. Witte to V. N. Lamsdorf, August 1 (14), 1905, *Sbornik,* 122–23.

74. S. Iu. Witte to V. N. Lamsdorf , August 4 (17), 1905, *Sbornik,* 137–39.

75. Telegram from Witte to St. Petersburg, August 5 (18), 1905, no. 15, RGIA, f. 560, op. 28, d. 321, ll. 51–52.

76. Telegram from Witte to St. Petersburg, August 5 (18), 1905, no. 22, RGIA, f. 560, op. 28, d. 321, ll. 54–55.

77. Esthus, *Double Eagle and Rising Sun,* 116–17.

78. S. Iu. Witte to V. N. Lamsdorf, August 7 (20), 1905, *Sbornik,* 162–63.

79. The basis for calculating the sum Japan wanted to receive from Russia was the size of the public debt, which had grown during the war from about 600 million to 2.4 billion yen. "Public opinion" held that 1.5–2 billion yen should be demanded. See Esthus, *Double Eagle and Rising Sun,* 109.

80. Witte to V. N. Kokovtsov, August 6 (19), 1905, Krasnyi Arkhiv, 1924, no. 6, 36–37.

81. V. N. Kokovtsov to V. N. Lamsdorf, August 7 (20), 1905, *Sbornik,* 149–53.

82. Resolution of Nicholas II in the telegram of S. Iu. Witte to V. N. Lamsdorf, August 4 (17), 1905, *Sbornik,* 137.

83. V. N. Kokovtsov, *Iz moego proshlogo: Vospominaniia, 1903–1919 gg* (Moscow: Nauka, 1992), 83–84. Instead, V. N. Lamsdorf, V. N. Kokovtsov, and D. M. Solsky presented to Nicholas II their view on the inadmissibility of this modus operandi. The tsar agreed with them.

84. S. Iu. Witte to V. N. Kokovtsov, August 11 (24), 1905, Krasnyi Arkhiv, 1924, no. 6, 38.

85. V. N. Kokovtsov to S. Iu. Witte, August 12 (25), 1905, Krasnyi Arkhiv, 1924, no. 6, 39–40.

86. S. Iu. Witte to V. N. Lamsdorf, August 8 (21), 1905, *Sbornik,* 163–64.

87. One can also interpret Nicholas' attempt to operate through the American ambassador as reflecting his wish to rein in the overly independent Witte, who continued to speak about concessions when the tsar had already decided everything for himself. Essentially Nicholas had left to his plenipotentiary only the matter of preparing optimal conditions for breaking off the talks. In this way all the blame for failure would fall "exclusively on Japan." See V. N. Lamsdorf to S. Iu. Witte, August 10 (23), 1905, *Sbornik,* 172–73.

88. T. Roosevelt to G. Meyer, August 9 (22), 1905 (perlustrated letter), RGIA, f. 1328, op. 2, d. 5, l. 73.

89. There is a discrepancy here. The German emperor wrote to Nicholas II that it would be well to raise the question of peace before the Duma and to decide the issue according to the people's will. See telegram of Wilhelm II, August 7 (20), 1905, in *Perepiska Vil'gel'ma II s Nikolaem II 1894–1914 gg,* 110–11. The answer, which Nicholas II read out loud to Meyer, probably went like this: "I daily receive telegrams, letters, petitions, and so forth asking me not to sign a peace on harsh terms. As long

as Japan insists on two things, every decent Russian is in agreement about continuing the war to the end. Our position is: not an inch of our territory, not a ruble of compensation for military expenses. But this is precisely what Japan will not concede. Nothing will force me to agree to these two demands. . . . I am ready to bear full responsibility. My conscience is clean, and I know that most of the people will support me." See telegram of Nicholas II (undated), in *Perepiska Vil'gel'ma II s Nikolaem II 1894–1914 gg,* 111. Such statements by the tsar were unquestionably meant more for the consumption of the American president than the German emperor. The game Berlin and Washington were playing was no mystery to St. Petersburg.

90. G. Meyer to the Secretary of State, August 11 (24), 1905 (opened letter), RGIA, f. 1328, op. 2, d. 5, l. 78.

91. Ch. Harding to Lord Lansdowne, August 13 (26), 1905 (opened letter), RGIA, f. 1328, op. 2, d. 5, l. 92. Harding reported what the American envoy had told him.

92. T. Roosevelt to G. Meyer, August 13 (26), 1905 (opened letter), RGIA, f. 1328, op. 2, d. 5, ll. 81–82.

93. Vsepoddanneishaia zapiska V. N. Lamsdorfa, August 12 (25), 1905, *Sbornik,* 182–83.

94. G. Meyer to T. Roosevelt, August 15 (28), 1905 (opened letter), RGIA, f. 1328, op. 2, d. 5, l. 83.

95. Kaneko Kentarō received letters from Roosevelt on August 22–23 informing him that Japan had to conclude the peace. Roosevelt presented copies of these letters to the tsar. See Roosevelt to Nicholas II, September 6, 1905, AVPRI, f. 150, op. 493, d. 200, ll. 272–73.

96. Nicholas II's resolution about Witte's telegram to V. N. Lamsdorf, August 14 (27), 1905, *Sbornik,* 191. Witte was informed about it the next day (193).

97. *Dnevniki imperatora Nikolaia II* (Moscow: Orbita, 1991), 275.

98. Planson, Portsmutskaia mirnaia konferentsiia, l. 114.

99. Makino Nobuaki to the Ministry of Foreign Affairs, August 6 and 7, 1905, Diplomatic Archives, Ministry of Foreign Affairs, Tokyo, no. 2.2.1.3–3, 379–80, 384.

100. Inoue Kaoru to the Ministry of Foreign Affairs, August 14 and 25, 1905, Diplomatic Archives, Ministry of Foreign Affairs, Tokyo, no. 2.2.1.3–3, 406–7, 436–37.

101. The Japanese government was informed about the details of the conversation in St. Petersburg by the English ambassador, K. McDonald. The information was immediately passed on to Komura Jutarō. See Katsura Tarō to Komura Jutarō, August 27, 1905, Diplomatic Archives, Ministry of Foreign Affairs, Tokyo, no. 2.2.1.3–3, 443.

102. Okamoto, *The Japanese Oligarchy and the Russo-Japanese War,* 150–55.

103. Korostovets, "Mirnye peregovory v Portsmute," 74.

104. I. P. Shipov to V. N. Kokovtsov, August 16 (29), 1905, RGIA, f. 560, op. 28, d. 321, l. 74. In the published copy the final phrase reads thus: "We do not share in the general joy, but with sorrow sigh in relief." See Krasnyi Arkhiv, 1924, no. 6, 41. One member of the Japanese delegation, a naval captain, after reading through the peace conditions, could not hide his feelings. "His face was distorted with rage and indignation." See Rusin, "K istorii mirnyh peregovorov v Portsmute v 1905 godu," 255.

105. Some among these were important. The delegations did not sign an armistice protocol until August 19 (September 1).

106. Okamoto, *The Japanese Oligarchy and the Russo-Japanese War,* 167.

107. Esthus, *Double Eagle and Rising Sun,* 167.

108. Donesenie belgiiskogo poslannika iz Tokyo, September 10, 1905 (opened letter), RGIA, f. 1328, op. 2, d. 6, ll. 32–33; Esthus, *Double Eagle and Rising Sun,* 184–86.

Chapter 4. Roosevelt and the U.S. Role: Perception Makes Policy (pages 62–74)

1. As quoted in Eugene P. Trani, *The Treaty of Portsmouth: An Adventure in American Diplomacy* (Lexington: University of Kentucky Press, 1969), 91, n. 26; for his Meyer article, see "Russia in 1905: The View from the American Embassy," *The Review of Politics* 31, no. 1 (January 1969): 48–65.

2. As quoted in Norman E. Saul, *Concord and Conflict: The United States and Russia, 1867–1914* (Lawrence: University Press of Kansas, 1996), 493, nn. 285, 286.

3. See, for instance, Paul A. Varg, *Open Door Diplomat: The Life of W. W. Rockhill* (Urbana: University of Illinois Press, 1952), 52, where he quotes Secretary of State John Hay to the effect that "dealing with a government with whom mendacity is a science is an extremely difficult and delicate matter."

4. Winston B. Thorson, "American Public Opinion and the Portsmouth Peace Conference," *American Historical Review* 53 (April 1948): 441, n. 4.

5. Thorson, "American Public Opinion," 443, 444.

6. Thorson, "American Public Opinion," 449, especially n. 44.

7. Thorson, "American Public Opinion," 450, 451, and quote on 453.

8. Thorson, "American Public Opinion," as quoted by Thorson, 457, nn. 83, 85.

9. Thorson, "American Public Opinion," 462.

10. *Foreign Relations of the United States, Diplomatic Papers, The Soviet Union, 1933–1939* (Washington, D.C.: Government Printing Office, 1952), 289–91, as quoted by William C. Bullitt to Secretary of State, March 4, 1936, with quote on 291; also see Norman E. Saul, *Distant Friends: The United States and Russia, 1763–1867* (Lawrence: University Press of Kansas, 1991), 170, 179. Saul notes: "Many later Russian and Soviet 'experts' would echo Brown's critical assessment of Russia," 170.

11. Frederick F. Travis, *George Kennan and the American-Russian Relationship, 1865–1924* (Athens: Ohio University Press, 1990), 250.

12. George Kennan [hereafter GK] to R. W. Gilder, November 3, 1888, box 53, The Century Company, New York Public Library.

13. Travis, *Kennan,* 251; especially see his n. 5 on p. 301.

14. Travis, *Kennan,* as quoted by Travis, 252, and see nn. 9 and 11 on p. 302.

15. "Japan must hold Port Arthur and she must hold Korea." TR as quoted by Trani, *Treaty of Portsmouth,* 91. As for the quote in the text, see Raymond A. Esthus, *Double Eagle and Rising Sun: The Russians and Japanese at Portsmouth in 1905* (Durham and London: Duke University Press, 1988), 21–22.

16. Travis, *Kennan,* 257, 258ff., 260, 262–63, and for the list of articles see 392–94.

17. Travis, *Kennan,* 263 and quote on 264; see also nn. 54–56 on p. 306 for important literature cited there.

18. For Kennan's impact in the 1890s, see Taylor Stults, "George Kennan: Russian Specialist of the 1890s," *Russian Review* 29 (July 1970): 275–85.

19. Preface to GK, "First Impressions of Japan," *Outlook* 77 (June 11, 1904): 355.

20. Preface to GK, "First Impressions," 358.

21. GK, "Japan at War," *Outlook* 77 (June 18, 1904): 401, 406.

22. GK, "War by Prearrangement," *Outlook* 77 (August 13, 1904): 891, 896.

23. GK, "A Japanese Naval School," *Outlook* 77 (August 27, 1904): 977.

24. GK, "The Japanese Red Cross," *Outlook* 78 (September 3, 1904): 35.

25. GK, "Japanese Tea-Houses and Russian Prisoners," *Outlook* 78 (September 10, 1904): 126.

26. GK, "A Visit to 'A Certain Place,'" *Outlook* 78 (September 17, 1904): 171, 174, 177, 178.

27. GK, "A Japanese Naval Base," *Outlook* 78 (September 24, 1904): 218, 224.

28. GK, "The Story of Port Arthur: I. A Journey to Dalny," *Outlook* 79 (March 4, 1905): 524, 526.

29. GK, "The Story of Port Arthur: II. In Dalny and at the Front," *Outlook* 79 (March 11, 1905): 633, 634.

30. GK, "The Story of Port Arthur: III. With the Besieging Army," *Outlook* 79 (April 1, 1905): 781.

31. GK, "The Story of Port Arthur: IV. The Assault That Failed," *Outlook* 79 (April 8, 1905): 888–92.

32. GK, "Port Arthur: IV," 893, 894–95.

33. GK, "The Story of Port Arthur: V. A General Bombardment," *Outlook* 79 (April 15, 1905): 940–41, 944.

34. For Kennan's sketch of the general position, see his number IV (n. 31 above), 889, as well as fort diagrams on p. 893.

35. GK, "The Story of Port Arthur: VI. The Second Attempt to Storm the Forts," *Outlook* 79 (April 22, 1905): 999–1001.

36. GK, "The Story of Port Arthur: VII. A Night Attack," *Outlook* 79 (April 29, 1905): 1042.

37. GK, "Port Arthur: VII," 1046.

38. GK, "The Story of Port Arthur: VIII. In the Advanced Trenches," *Outlook* 80 (May 20, 1905): 182. Also see his diagrams of the lines of the bombardment on p. 175 and a cross section of the defenses on p. 177 as well as the zigzag trench works on p. 180.

39. GK, "The Story of Port Arthur: IX. The Progress of the Siege," *Outlook* 80 (May 27, 1905): 233.

40. GK, "The Story of Port Arthur: X. Life in the Japanese Trenches," *Outlook* 80 (June 17, 1905): 419–20.

41. GK, "The Story of Port Arthur: XI. Saps, Mines, and Assaults," *Outlook* 80 (July 8, 1905): 622, quote on 624, 628.

42. GK, "The Story of Port Arthur: XII. The Surrender of Port Arthur," *Outlook* 81 (September 30, 1905): 257–59.

43. GK, "Port Arthur: XII," 260–65. This ends the 12-part series just on Port Arthur.

44. GK, "Russian Views of Kuropatkin and His Army," *Outlook* 79 (February 18, 1905): 428 and quote on 431.

45. Esthus, *Double Eagle and Rising Sun,* 24–25.

46. GK, "Admiral Tōgō," *Outlook* 80 (August 12, 1905): 920. See also GK, "The Struggle for Command of the Sea," *Outlook* 80 (June 10, 1905): 367–69.

47. GK, "The Destruction of the Baltic Fleet," *Outlook* 80 (July 29, 1905): 811, 817, 818–19.

48. GK, "Which Is the Civilized Power?" *Outlook* 78 (October 29, 1904): 515.

49. GK, "Civilized Power," 515–18, 519, quotes on 520–21.

50. H. W. Brands, *T. R.: The Last Romantic* (New York: Basic Books, 1997), 681 and especially 693, where TR is directly quoted when writing Cecil Spring Rice on August 22, 1911: "My fellow editors have the same high purpose and sanity that, for instance, the members of the Tennis Cabinet had. . . . I can work with them in complete sympathy."

51. GK, "The Sword of Peace in Japan," *Outlook* 81 (October 14, 1905): 357.

52. GK, "Sword of Peace," 358.

53. GK, "Sword of Peace," 359.

54. GK, "Sword of Peace," 360.

55. GK, "Sword of Peace," 360–61.

56. GK, "Sword of Peace," 362.

57. GK, "Sword of Peace," 364.

58. Travis, *Kennan,* 265.

59. Travis, *Kennan,* as quoted by Travis, 266 and n. 65 on p. 307, where Travis indicates that the letter was sent via Lyman Abbott, *Outlook*'s editor, to avoid its ending in the wrong hands; further criticism of Kennan was made to Abbott. See TR to GK, October 15, 1905, and TR to Lyman Abbott, October 16, 1905, both in the Roosevelt Papers in the Library of Congress.

60. Travis, *Kennan,* 266 and nn. 66–68 on p. 307.

61. For a detailed review of this nineteenth-century relationship, see Saul, *Distant Friends* and *Concord and Conflict.*

62. For this line of analysis, check Donald E. Davis and Eugene P. Trani, *The First Cold War: The Legacy of Woodrow Wilson in U.S.-Soviet Relations* (Columbia and London: University of Missouri Press, 2002), especially 200–206.

63. Perhaps Harry Hopkins best expressed FDR's hope immediately after Yalta: "The Russians had proved that they could be reasonable and farseeing and there wasn't any doubt in the minds of the President or any of us that we could live with them and get along with them peacefully for as far into the future as any of us could imagine." This was quoted by Robert E. Sherwood in *Roosevelt and Hopkins: An Intimate History* (New York: Enigma Books reprint, 2001, from the 1948 Harper Bros. first printing), 832.

64. For George F. Kennan's "Long Telegram," see his *Memoirs: 1925–1950* (Boston: Little, Brown and Company, 1967), 547–59; and for his "X" article check "The Sources of Soviet Conduct," *Foreign Affairs* 25 (July 1947): 566–82; for Paul H. Nitze's NSC-68, refer to Kenneth W. Thompson and Steven L. Rearden, eds., *Paul H. Nitze on National Security and Arms Control* (Lanham, Md.: University Press of America, 1990), 5–31. For Reagan, see Jack F. Matlock, Jr., *Reagan and Gorbachev: How the Cold War Ended* (New York: Random House, 2004), especially 59–60.

Chapter 5. Lessons Lessened: The Near-Term Military Legacy of 1904–5 in Imperial Russia (pages 77–97)

1. With respect to conventions, all dates herein are rendered according to the Julian calendar, which lagged behind the Gregorian by 13 days at the beginning of the twentieth century. All transliterations from Russian are rendered according to the modified U.S. Library of Congress system, except for proper and place names that have come into common English usage through other systems, e.g., Nicholas, Alexander, St. Petersburg, Moscow.

2. For why the army lacked offensive capability, see F. Immanuel, "Poucheniia izvlechennye iz opyta russko-iaponskoi voiny maiorom germanskoi sluzhby Immanuelem," in *Russko-iaponskaia voina v nabliudeniiakh i suzhdeniiakh inostrantsev,* ed. K. M. Adaridi, 32 vols. (St. Petersburg: Komissioner Voenno-Uchebnykh Zavedenii, 1906–14), 1:36.

3. Boris Ananich, "Financing the War," in *The Russo-Japanese War in Global Perspective: World War Zero,* ed. John W. Steinberg et al., 2 vols. (Leiden and Boston: Brill, 2005, 2007), 1:463.

4. See, for example, Bruce W. Menning, *Bayonets before Bullets: The Imperial Russian Army, 1861–1914* (Bloomington: Indiana University Press, 1992), 161–71, and Oleg R. Airapetov, "The Russian Army's Fatal Flaws," in *The Russo-Japanese War in Global Perspective,* 1:164, 168.

5. This intent was very clear in A. K. Baiov, ed., *Russko-iaponskaia voina v soobshcheniiakh v Nikolaevskoi Akademii General'nago Shtaba,* 2 vols. (St. Petersburg: Tip. S. G. Knorus, 1906–7), 1:iii–iv.

6. V. A. Zolotarev and Iu. F. Sokolov, *Tragediia na Dal'nem Vostoke: Russko-iaponskia voina, 1904–1905 gg.,* 2 vols. (Moscow: Animi Fortitudo, 2004), 2:390–97.

7. See, for example, Donald Wright, "'That Vital Spark': Japanese Patriotism, The Russian Officer Corps and the Lessons of the Russo-Japanese War," in *The Russo-Japanese War in Global Perspective,* 1:605–8; and Bruce W. Menning, "Mukden to Tannenberg: Defeat to Defeat, 1905–1914," in *The Military History of Tsarist Russia,* ed. Frederick W. Kagan and Robin Higham (New York: Palgrave, 2002), 208–17.

8. A. F. Geiden, *Itogi russko-iaponskoi voiny* (Petrograd: Tip. Morskogo Ministerstva, 1914).

9. Geiden, *Itogi russko-iaponskoi voiny,* 50.

10. Voenno-istoricheskaia komissiia, *Russko-iaponskaia voina, 1904–1905 g.g.*, 9 vols. (St. Petersburg: Tip. A. S. Suvorina, 1910–13), 1:751.

11. For the budgetary limits, see Peter Gatrell, *Government, Industry, and Rearmament in Russia, 1900–1914: The Last Argument of Tsarism* (Cambridge: Cambridge University Press, 1994), 91–95.

12. Menning, "Mukden to Tannenberg," 212–15.

13. Geiden, *Itogi russko-iaponskoi voiny,* 54–55.

14. Bruce W. Menning, "Neither Mahan nor Moltke: Strategy in the Russo-Japanese War," in *The Russo-Japanese War in Global Perspective,* 1:133–46.

15. Iu. F. Subbotin, "A. N. Kuropatkin i Dal'nevostochnyi konflikt," in *Rossiia: Mezhdunarodnoe polozhenie i voennyi potentsial v seredine XIX-nachale XX veka,* ed. I. S. Rybachenok, L. G. Zakharova, and A. V. Ignat'ev (Moscow: Institut rossiiskoi istorii RAN, 2003), 161–62.

16. For brief overviews of the war on land and sea, see John W. Steinberg, "The Operational Overview," in *The Russo-Japanese War in Global Perspective,* 1:105–28; Pertti Luntinen and Bruce W. Menning, "The Russian Navy at War, 1904–05," in *The Russo-Japanese War in Global Perspective,* 1:229–59; and David Schimmelpenninck van der Oye, "The Russo-Japanese War," in *Military History of Tsarist Russia,* 183–201.

17. L. G. Beskrovnyi, *Armiia i flot Rossii v nachale XX v.* (Moscow: Nauka, 1986), 49–50, 64–66.

18. Aleksandr Rediger, *Istoriia moei zhizni,* 2 vols. (Moscow: Kuchkovo pole, 1999), 1:411.

19. Beskrovnyi, *Armiia i flot Rossii v nachale XX v.,* 64–65.

20. Rediger, *Istoriia moei zhizni,* 1:429, 436–37, 452; and Walter Thomas Wilfong, "Rebuilding the Russian Army, 1904–1914: The Question of a Comprehensive Plan for National Defense" (Ph.D. diss., Indiana University, 1977), 42–43, 65–66.

21. David MacLaren McDonald, *United Government and Foreign Policy in Russia, 1900–1914* (Cambridge, Mass.: Harvard University Press, 1992), 83–87.

22. William C. Fuller, Jr., *Strategy and Power in Russia, 1600–1914* (New York: Free Press, 1992), 407–12.

23. N. A. Epanchin, *Na sluzhbe trekh imperatorov* (Moscow: Izd. zhurnala Nashe Nasledie, 1996), 328.

24. V. A. Sukhomlinov, *Vospominaniia* (Berlin: Russkoe universal'noe izd-vo, 1924), 156.

25. Quoted in P. A. Zaionchkovskii, "Vysshee voennoe upravlenie. Imperator i tsarstvuiushchii dom," in *P. A. Zaionchkovskii 1904–1983 gg.: Stat'i, publikatsii i vospominaniia o nem,* ed. L. G. Zakharova, Iu. S. Kukushkin, and T. Emmons (Moscow: ROSSPEN, 1998), 94–95.

26. McDonald, *United Government and Foreign Policy in Russia,* 89–92.

27. Rediger, *Istoriia moei zhizni,* 2:216.

28. A. G. Kavtaradze, "Iz istorii russkogo general'nogo shtaba," *Voenno-istoricheskii zhurnal,* no. 7 (July 1972): 87–88.

29. Kavtaradze, "Iz istorii russkogo general'nogo shtaba," 90.

30. Rediger, *Istoriia moei zhizni*, 2:226.

31. Evgenii F. Podsoblyaev, "The Russian Naval General Staff and the Evolution of Naval Policy, 1905–1914," *Journal of Military History* 66 (January 2002): 42.

32. M. A. Petrov, *Podgotovka Rossii k mirovoi voine na more* (Leningrad: Gosvoenizdat, 1926), 98–100.

33. Petrov, *Podgotovka Rossii k mirovoi voine na more*, 95.

34. Iu. N. Danilov, *Rossiia v mirovoi voine 1914–1915 gg.* (Berlin: Slovo, 1924), 32.

35. McDonald, *United Government and Foreign Policy in Russia*, 92–95, 103–11; and A. V. Ignat'ev, *Vneshniaia politika Rossii 1907–1914* (Moscow: Nauka, 2000), 33–43.

36. Rossiiskii gosudarstvennyi voenno-istoricheskii arkhiv, f. 2000, op. 1, d. 97, ll. 9–9 ob., 10–11, 23–24.

37. Petrov, *Podgotovka Rossii k mirovoi voine na more*, 100–107; see also Podsoblyaev, "The Russian Naval General Staff," 43–44, 49–50.

38. I. D. Spasskii, ed., *Istoriia otechestvennogo sudostroeniia*, 5 vols. (St. Petersburg: Sudostroenie, 1994–96), 3:17–19.

39. K. F. Shatsillo, *Ot Portsmutskogo mira k pervoi mirovoi voine* (Moscow: ROSSPEN, 2000), 91–92.

40. Shatsillo, *Ot Portsmutskogo*, 93.

41. Shatsillo, *Ot Portsmutskogo*, 94.

42. Spasskii, *Istoriia otechestvennogo sudostroeniia*, 3:20.

43. Petrov, *Podgotovka Rossii k pervoi mirovoi voine na more*, 112–13.

44. Shatsillo, *Ot Portsmutskogo*, 96–97.

45. Shatsillo, *Ot Portsmutskogo*, 97–99.

46. Shatsillo, *Ot Portsmutskogo*, 99.

47. Shatsillo, *Ot Portsmutskogo*, 100.

48. Petrov, *Podgotovka Rossii k pervoi mirovoi voine na more*, 122.

49. McDonald, *United Government and Foreign Policy in Russia*, 112–19; and Shatsillo, *Ot Portsmutskogo*, 37–51.

50. A. A. Polivanov, *Iz dnevnikov i vospominanii po dolzhnosti voennogo ministra i ego pomoshchnika 1907–1916 g.*, ed. A. M. Zaionchkovskii (Moscow: Vysshii voen. redaktsionnyi sovet, 1924), 43.

51. Beskrovnyi, *Armiia i flot Rossii v nachale XX v.*, 51, 66.

52. Geiden, *Itogi russko-iaponskoi voiny*, 81–83.

53. P. A. Zaionchkovskii, "Russkii ofitserskii korpus nakanune Pervoi mirovoi voiny," in *P. A. Zaionchkovskii 1904–1983 gg.*, 37–40.

54. A. G. Kavtaradze, "Military Reforms of 1905–12," *Great Soviet Encyclopedia*, 3rd ed., 31 vols. and suppl. (New York: Macmillan, 1973–83), 5:278–79.

55. See, for example, the commentary in Shatsillo, *Ot Portsmutskogo*, 334–38.

56. David M. McDonald, "The Military and Imperial Russian History," in *Reforming the Tsar's Army: Military Innovation in Imperial Russia from Peter the Great to the Revolution*, ed. David Schimmelpenninck van der Oye and Bruce W. Menning (Cambridge and Washington, D.C.: Cambridge University Press and Woodrow Wilson Center Press, 2004), 310.

Chapter 6. The Absence of Portsmouth in an Early Twentieth-Century Japanese Imagination of Peace (pages 98–105)

1. See, for example, "The Ground of Anti-Militarism," *Heimin shimbun* (September 4, 1904): 1.

2. Kōtoku Shūsui, "Nijusseiki no kaibutsu, teikokushugi" [The Monster of the Twentieth Century, Imperialism], in *Kōtoku Shūsui zenshū* [Complete Works] (Tokyo: Meiji Bunken, 1968), 3:105–96. Originally published in 1901 by Keiseisha Shoten, Tokyo.

3. *Taoka Reiun zenshū* [Complete Works] (Tokyo: Hōsei Daigaku Shuppankyoku, 1969), 5:68.

4. "Nihon shinshi batsu no kaibō" [Anatomy of Japan's Gentlemen's Cliques], *Chokugen* 2, no. 8 (March 26, 1905): 1. The historicity behind this "anatomy" was that the Meiji Revolution did not fulfill its potential as these cliques began to wield their power.

5. See John D. Pierson, *Tokutomi Sohō, 1863–1957: A Journalist for Modern Japan* (Princeton: Princeton University Press, 1980), 275–85.

6. Hattori Shisō and Konishi Shirō, eds., *Shūkan Heimin shimbun* [Weekly People's Newspaper], 4 vols. (Osaka: Sōgensha, 1953), 1:207.

7. *Volia,* no. 6 (May 7, 1906).

8. Sho Konishi, "Translation and Conversion beyond Western Modernity: Tolstoian Religion in Meiji Japan," in *Converting Cultures: Religion, Ideology, and Transformations of Modernity,* ed. Dennis Washburn and A. Kevin Reinhart (Leiden and Boston: Brill, 2007), 235–65.

9. *Shakaishugisha no shokan* [Letters of Socialists], ed. Waseda Daigaku Shakai Kagaku Kenkyūjo (Tokyo: Waseda University Press, 1974), 8.

10. See, for example, "Kuropotokin," in *Demokurashi* 1, no. 5 (July 1, 1919): 14.

Chapter 7. Political Legacies of the Portsmouth Treaty (pages 106–22)

1. S. Iu. Vitte, *Vospominaniia,* 1, book 2 (St. Petersburg: D. Bulanin, 2003), 852.

2. *Nis-So kōshō shi* [The History of Japanese-Soviet Diplomatic Negotiations], ed. Gaimushō [Ministry of Foreign Affairs] (Tokyo: Gannandō Shoten, 1969), 450–51. A part-time employee of Japan's Foreign Ministry wrote this book on the basis of diplomatic records. According to this source, in November 1938, the Soviet government asserted that Japan had violated the Portsmouth Treaty, pointing to the presence of the Japanese army in Manchuria and the restriction of free passage through the Sōya (La Pérouse) Strait.

3. In the case of China, see, for example, Min Tu-ki, *National Polity and Local Power: Transformation of Late Imperial China* (Cambridge, Mass.: Council on East Asian Studies, Harvard University, 1989), 140–41.

4. Tsunoda Jun, *Manshū mondai to kokubō hōshin* [The Manchurian Problem and National Defense Policy] (Tokyo: Hara Shobō, 1967), 330–31, 442–46.

5. S. S. Grigortsevich, *Dal'ne vostochnaia politika imperialisticheskikh derzhav v 1906–1917 gg.* (Tomsk: Izd-vo Tomskogo universiteta, 1965), 62–64.

6. *Komura gaikō shi* [The History of Komura Diplomacy], ed. Gaimushō [Ministry of Foreign Affairs] (Tokyo: Shinbun Gekkansha, 1953), 2:70–71.

7. Tsunoda, *Manshū mondai to kokubō hōshin*, 267–69. See also Tak Matsusaka's argument on Russian railway imperialism. According to Matsusaka, the Chinese Eastern Railway Company was in essence a Russian instrument for colonizing Manchuria, and Japan inherited the Russian scheme with the acquisition of the southern portion of that railway: Yoshihisa Tak Matsusaka, *The Making of Japanese Manchuria, 1904–1932* (Cambridge, Mass.: Harvard University Asia Center, 2001).

8. Yoshimura Michio, *Nippon to Roshia* [Japan and Russia], revised and enlarged ed. (Tokyo: Hara Shobō, 1991), 9–10.

9. Leonid Kutakov, *Rossiia i Iaponiia* (Moscow: Nauka, 1988), 349.

10. Sakai Tetsuya, *Taishō demokurashī-taisei no hōkai* [The Collapse of the Taishō Democracy System] (Tokyo: Tokyo Daigaku Shuppankai, 1992). Sakai argues that, in the Japanese politics of 1932–33, the anti-Soviet faction led by Araki Sadao was defeated and disappeared from the political scene.

11. V. P. Safronov, *SSSR, SShA, i Iaponskaia agressiia na Dal'nem Vostokei Tikhom Okeana, 1931–1945 gg.* (Moscow: Rossiiskaia akademiia nauk, In-t rossiiskoi istorii, 2001).

12. Safronov, *SSSR, SShA*, 17.

13. *Nihon gaikō bunsho* [Japanese Diplomatic Documents], ed. Gaimushō [Ministry of Foreign Affairs], 73 vols. (Tokyo: Nihon Kokusai Rengō Kyōkai, 1936–63), 41–1: 730–34.

14. Michael H. Hunt, *Frontier Defense and the Open Door* (New Haven: Yale University Press, 1973), 141–42.

15. The argument here is mainly based on the documents in Iu. V. Basenko, V. I. Zhuravleva, and E. Iu. Sergeev, *Rossiia i SShA: diplomaticheskie otnosheniia, 1900–1917* (Moscow: Mezhdunarodnyi fond Demokratiia, 1999), 122–26; and Okumura Shinji, *Man-Mō no kokusai kankei oyobi jōyaku* [International Relations and Treaties of Manchuria and Mongolia] (n.p., 1921), 53–56.

16. Okumura, *Man-Mō no kokusai kankei oyobi jōyaku*, 56–57.

17. Basenko, Zhuravleva, and Sergeev, *Rossiia i SShA*, 141–43.

18. Grigortsevich, *Dal'ne vostochnaia politika*, 209. There is a corresponding document in *Nihon gaikō bunsho* 42–1: 360. But in the Japanese document Motono's words are not as straightforward as in the Russian one. The discrepancy is probably due to the difference in impressions that the foreign minister and ambassador received. I followed the Japanese document for the time of the talks.

19. On the discussions over policy orientation among Russia's high-ranking bureaucrats and statesmen to this time, see Basenko, Zhuravleva, and Sergeev, *Rossiia i SShA*, 128–32, 133–38, 144–49.

20. On the analysis of these treaties, see E. B. Price, *The Russo-Japanese Treaties of 1907–1916 Concerning Manchuria and Mongolia*, reprinted ed. (New York, 1971), 42–46.

21. George Alexander Lensen, *Japanese Recognition of the USSR: Soviet-Japanese Relations, 1921–1930* (Tokyo: Sophia University Press, 1970), 12–13.

22. Lensen, *Japanese Recognition of the USSR*, 85–86.

23. This is in the documents relating to Shimada Shigeru (a Japanese diplomat who served in the 1920s and 1930s) held at Hitotsubashi University Library in Tokyo.

24. Lensen, *Japanese Recognition of the USSR*, 112, 128, 149, for the Gotō-Ioffe talks, Kawakami-Ioffe negotiations, and Karakhan-Yoshizawa negotiations. See also *Nis-So kōshō shi*, 73, 75, 89.

25. S. T. Leong, *Sino-Soviet Diplomatic Relations, 1917–1926* (Honolulu: University of Hawaii Press, 1976); Bruce Elleman, *Diplomacy and Deception: The Secret History of Sino-Soviet Diplomatic Relations, 1917–1927* (New York: M. E. Sharpe, 1997).

26. *Nihon gaikō bunsho*, 1924 (Tokyo: Gaimushō, 1981), 2:588–94.

27. *Nihon gaikō bunsho*, 1924, 2:687.

28. *Nihon gaikō bunsho*, 1924, 2:731.

29. This is from Lensen, *Japanese Recognition of the USSR*, 187.

30. *Nis-So kōshō shi*, 93. A more detailed description is given in a document dated 1926 in the above-mentioned Shimada papers, Hitotsubashi University Library. This document is titled "Nichi-Ro kōshō keika gaiyō" [Outline of the Progress of Russo-Japanese Negotiations].

31. *Pravda*, September 3, 1945.

Chapter 8. Riding Rough: Portsmouth, Regionalism, and the Birth
of Anti-Americanism in Northeast Asia (pages 125–41)

1. Dr. Kajima worked in the Japanese Foreign Ministry from 1920 until 1930. After the war, in addition to running his own giant construction firm, he served several terms in the Diet Upper House, including a long stint in the early 1960s as head of the Foreign Relations Research Committee of the Liberal Democratic Party.

2. Tyler Dennett, *Roosevelt and the Russo-Japanese War: A Critical Study of American Policy in Eastern Asia in 1902–5, Based Primarily upon the Private Papers of Theodore Roosevelt* (Garden City, N.Y.: Doubleday, Page, 1925), 243.

3. For example, see Peter G. Peterson, "Riding for a Fall," *Foreign Affairs* 83 (September/October 2004): 111–25. Peterson, a former secretary of commerce, was serving in 2004 as the chairman of both the Council of Foreign Relations and the related Institute of International Economics.

4. The Pew survey interviewed more than sixteen thousand people in the United States and fifteen other countries, including Britain, Canada, France, Germany, Spain, the Netherlands, Russia, Poland, Turkey, Pakistan, India, Lebanon, Jordan, Indonesia, and China during April and May. In ten of the countries surveyed, the majority of the public held unfavorable views of the United States. Several of those countries were in Western Europe, where opposition to the Iraq war was very high. More than 40 percent of French, Germans, and Spaniards said they did not have a favorable view of the United States.

5. Many citations below refer to the two-volume set in which I participated as an editor: John W. Steinberg et al., eds., *The Russo-Japanese War in Global Perspective: World War Zero*, vol. 1 (Leiden and Boston: Brill, 2005); and David Wolff et al., eds., *The Russo-Japanese War in Global Perspective: World War Zero*, vol. 2 (Leiden and Boston: Brill, 2007).

6. Ku Daeyeol, "A Damocles Sword? Korean Hopes Betrayed," in *The Russo-Japanese War in Global Perspective*, 2:435–65. The Americans did not appreciate King Kojong's geopolitical efforts, with the American minister, Horace N. Allen, labeling the monarch "morbidly superstitious." This characterization suggests that, at least in the eyes of a former medical missionary, the king was neither moral nor rational.

7. Bōei Chō Bōei Kenkyūsho Senshi-shitsu [National Defense Agency, National Defense Institute, War History Office], *Hawai sakusen* [The Hawaii Operation], Senshi Sōsho [War History Series] (Tokyo: Asagumo Shinbunsha, 1967), 84, quoted in Aizawa Kiyoshi, "Differences Regarding Togo's Surprise Attack on Port Arthur," in *The Russo-Japanese War in Global Perspective*, 2:81.

8. After the war, Japan tried to build both its army and navy simultaneously, despite budgetary issues. In the end, unwillingness to reconcile two "realisms" led to an unsustainable course of action. See Tadokoro Masayuki, "Why Did Japan Fail to Become the 'Britain' of Asia?" in *The Russo-Japanese War in Global Perspective*, 2:295–323.

9. Akira Iriye, *After Imperialism* (Cambridge, Mass.: Harvard University Press, 1965), 302.

10. On the naval buildup instituted under the construction plan of 1898, see Nicholas Papastratigakis with Dominic Lieven, "The Russian Far Eastern Squadron's Operational Plans," in *The Russo-Japanese War in Global Perspective*, 1:203–27. On Japanese tracking of the Trans-Siberian's rate of completion, see David Wolff, *To the Harbin Station: The Liberal Alternative in Russian Manchuria, 1898–1914* (Stanford: Stanford University Press, 1999), chapter 2. On dwindling oil reserves as a trigger of war in 1941, see W. G. Beasley, *Japanese Imperialism, 1894–1945* (Oxford: Clarendon Press, 1987), 232.

11. See Tohmatsu Haruo, "Approaching Total War: Ivan Bloch's Disturbing Vision," in *The Russo-Japanese War in Global Perspective*, 2:179–202.

12. *Pravda*, September 3, 1945.

13. Egawa's *manga* are probably the most read version of the Russo-Japanese War, with *Spirits'* print run in the hundreds of thousands. In addition, sixteen volumes of the collected "Russo-Japanese War Story" (*Nichi-Ro sensō monogatari*) have already appeared. Ishiwara in *Spirits*, August 22–29, 2005, 376–94.

14. Dennett, *Roosevelt*, 265.

15. For example, in spring 1905 Roosevelt expressed his views on the war for transmission to the Japanese in the following terms: "I have, from the beginning, favored Japan and have done all I could, consistent with international law, to advance her interests. I thoroughly admire and believe in the Japanese. They have always told the truth and the Russians have not": Norman E. Saul, "The Kittery Peace," in *The*

Russo-Japanese War in Global Perpective, 1:489. On Schiff's role and motivations, see Cyrus Adler, ed., *Jacob H. Schiff: His Life and Letters* (New York: Doubleday, 1929).

16. Winston Thorson, "American Public Opinion and the Portsmouth Peace Conference," *American Historical Review* 53 (April 1948) suggests that American public opinion was firmly behind Japan during the peace conference. This contradicts Roosevelt's representation.

17. See Edward S. Miller, "Japan's Other Victory: Overseas Financing of the Russo-Japanese War," in *The Russo-Japanese War in Global Perspective,* 1:465–83. The veteran Russian historian B. A. Romanov wrote in his *Ocherki diplomaticheskoi istorii russko-iaponskoi voiny, 1895–1907,* 2nd ed. (Moscow: Izd-vo Akademii nauk SSSR, 1955), 567, that the precise timing of Roosevelt's pressure and Schiff's advice was more coincidence than he could bear.

18. Dennett, *Roosevelt,* 285. Another accusation involved Roosevelt's not informing the Japanese delegation to Portsmouth of the tsar's willingness to cede half of Sakhalin, although the information arrived just in time via London. Tosh Minohara, "The 'Rat Minister': Komura Jutaro and U.S.-Japan Relations," in *The Russo-Japanese War in Global Perspective,* 2:561–66, suggests that the British leak may well have been intentional to provide the Japanese with key intelligence without compromising Roosevelt's neutral status, thus absolving Roosevelt of any anti-Japanese intentions.

19. A. Whitney Griswold, *The Far Eastern Policy of the United States* (New York: Harcourt, Brace, 1938), 121, 138n, citing Tatsuji Takeuchi, *War and Diplomacy in the Japanese Empire* (Garden City, N.Y.: Doubleday, Doran, 1935). The largest political parties, the Seiyūkai and the Shimpotō, had both passed resolutions calling for an indemnity: Dennett, *Roosevelt,* 204. Of course, one could just as easily argue that the Katsura-Harriman agreement was signed in the course of the peace negotiations to encourage American preference for Japan, but without intent to follow through on the agreement.

20. *Hitomede wakaru Nichi-Ro sensō* [Understanding the Russo-Japanese War at a Glance] (Tokyo: Gakken, 2004), 86. This work is a popular publication filled with excellent pictures, selling for the reasonable price of ¥950. In the photo of Roosevelt, he looks mean with a cold-blooded stare.

21. Kazuhiko Togo, *Japan's Foreign Policy, 1945–2003: The Quest for a Proactive Policy* (Leiden: Brill, 2005), 8.

22. Yokote Shinji, *Nichi-Ro sensō shi: 20-seiki saisho no taikokukan sensō* [History of the Russo-Japanese War: The First War between Great Powers in the Twentieth Century] (Tokyo: Chūō Kōron Shinsha, 2005), 200. Edward S. Miller, *War Plan Orange: The U.S. Strategy to Defeat Japan, 1897–1945* (Annapolis, Md.: Naval Institute Press, 1991).

23. Dennett, *Roosevelt,* 265–66; Romanov, *Ocherki diplomaticheskoi istorii,* 557.

24. Saul, "Kittery Peace," 506, citing Meyer and Roosevelt private papers in the Library of Congress. For imperial complaints, see Romanov, *Ocherki diplomaticheskoi istorii,* 571. The empress was even more upset than the emperor, with both of them speaking "sharply about all who put their hand to the peace, which in their ex-

pression is a [source of] shame for Russia": Romanov, *Ocherki diplomaticheskoi istorii*, 571. Meyer had earlier spoken of her as watching him "like a cat—She is for continuing the war": Saul, "Kittery Peace," 491.

25. Witte was nonetheless granted the title of "Count" for his diplomatic services, but wits dubbed him "Count Half-Sakhalin" (*Graf Polsakhalinskii*).

26. Saul, "Kittery Peace," 506.

27. Morinosuke Kajima, *The Diplomatic Theses and Documents* (Tokyo: Japan Times, 1969), 169. Kazuhiko Togo notes that "both countries shared a common concern *vis-à-vis* the United States": Togo, *Japan's Foreign Policy*, 12.

28. L. N. Kutakov, *Portsmutskii mirnyi dogovor: iz istorii otnoshenii Iaponii s Rossiei i SSSR, 1905–1945 gg.* (Moscow: Izd-vo sotsialno-ekon. lit-ry, 1961), 12, speaks of Roosevelt's "blackmail." V. A. Marinov, *Rossia i Iaponiia pered pervoi mirovoi voinoi* (Moscow: Nauka, 1974), 15, accuses the United States of practicing "divide and conquer."

29. For more on the impact of the war on Northeast China, see David Wolff, "Intelligence Intermediaries: The Competition for Chinese Spies," in *The Russo-Japanese War in Global Perspective*, 1:305–30.

30. Rosemary Quested, *"Matey" Imperialists? The Tsarist Russians in Manchuria, 1895–1917* (Hong Kong: University of Hong Kong, 1982), 140, 142.

31. Lu Hsun, *Selected Stories of Lu Hsun*, trans. Yang Hsien-yi and Gladys Yang, 3rd ed. (Beijing: Foreign Languages Press, 1972), 2–3.

32. Other important figures who were inspired to revolutionary nationalism by China's impotence during the Russo-Japanese War were the country's most famous female martyr, Qiu Jin, who was executed for planning an uprising in 1907, and Zhou Enlai, whose direct influence lasted much longer.

33. The discussion below is based on Hirakawa Sachiko, "Portsmouth Denied: The Chinese Attempt to Attend," in *The Russo-Japanese War in Global Perspective*, 2:531–49.

34. Hirakawa, "Portsmouth Denied," 538.

35. Hirakawa, "Portsmouth Denied," 542.

36. Hirakawa, "Portsmouth Denied," 545.

37. Hirakawa, "Portsmouth Denied," 542–43.

38. See Kim Ki-Jung, "The War and U.S.-Korean Relations," in *The Russo-Japanese War in Global Perspective*, 2:467–89.

39. Fred Harvey Harrington, *God, Mammon, and the Japanese: Dr. Horace N. Allen and Korean-American Relations, 1884–1905* (Madison: University of Wisconsin Press, 1944), 320–21, 326.

40. Che Mun-hyon, *Nichi-Ro sensō no sekaishi* [A Global History of The Russo-Japanese War] (Fujiwara Shoten, 2004), 237–57. Although this work is the latest interpretation of American actions as detrimental to Korean history, it is hardly the first. See, for example, Jong-suk Chay, "The United States and the Closing Door in Korea, American-Korean Relations, 1894–1905" (Ph.D. diss., University of Michigan, 1965).

41. On August 12, the day the Anglo-Japanese Treaty was renewed, the Russian plenipotentiary Witte surprised all present with an impassioned plea for the preser-

vation of Korean sovereignty, but then he swiftly agreed in Article II of the peace treaty to accept Japanese measures of "guidance, protection and control" in Korea. His key strategic goal was the avoidance of indemnity payment.

42. In fact, the day before the Russian and Japanese delegations were formally presented to each other at Roosevelt's Long Island estate, the president was visited by a two-man Korean delegation asking for "the good office of the United States" to preserve "the integrity of our country." The junior member, a student at George Washington University, was Syngman Rhee, future president of the Republic of Korea, ever suspicious of the fickleness of American support. Howard K. Beale, *Theodore Roosevelt and the Rise of America to World Power* (Baltimore: Johns Hopkins Press, 1956), 323.

43. Beale, *Theodore Roosevelt*, 318–19, 322; Harrington, *God, Mammon, and the Japanese*, 335.

44. For more on those "Isms," see Akira Iyire, "Introduction," in *The Russo-Japanese War in Global Perspective*, 2:1–9.

45. In February 1945, the Japanese consul at Harbin visited Soviet ambassador Ia. A. Malik at his post in Tokyo, part of the Japanese effort to obtain Soviet mediation to end the war. The consul began his disposition by wondering out loud "if the Soviet Union was always going to follow [the lead] of America and England." He then suggested that the moment had arrived for "one of the top international actors, with enough prestige, authority and force to be convincing, to take on the role of peacemaker [*mirotvorets*]. . . . Only Marshal Stalin could be such an authoritative figure": Arkhiv vneshnei politiki Rossiiskoi Federatsii, February 18, 1945.

46. Edward J. Lincoln, *East Asian Economic Regionalism* (New York: Council on Foreign Relations, 2004); Gilbert Rozman, *Northeast Asia's Stunted Regionalism: Bilateral Distrust in the Shadow of Globalization* (Cambridge: Cambridge University Press, 2004).

47. Russo-Chinese joint military maneuvers—"Mission Peace 2005"—on both sides of the Korean Peninsula in August 2005 produced a wide range of images that would satisfy those nostalgic for the earliest stages of the Cold War.

Chapter 9. Economic Engagement: Coping with the Realities of the Globalized World (pages 142–56)

1. The decision on the Pacific pipeline was officially announced on December 31, 2004. The pipeline will be built in two phases, first to Skovorodino (2006–8), then to Perevoznaya Bay (from 2008), and the chief contractor for the project is Transneft. It is not clear yet how the project will be financed, but one option is to use the extra revenue accumulated in the Stabilization Fund. An alternative is to employ the transportation tariff levied by Transneft as well as taxation preferences and customs benefits extended to companies involved in the project.

2. Currently, the annual level of funding for geological exploration and development in eastern Russia is a little more than $100 million, only about 10 percent of the required investment level.

3. Nippon Keidanren [Japan Business Federation], "Looking to Japan's Future: Keidanren's Perspective on Constitutional Policy Issues," January 18, 2005, available online at www.keidanren.or.jp/english/policy/2005/002.html.

4. The Russian government decided to ratify the Kyoto Protocol to the United Nations Framework Convention on Climate Change on September 30, 2004. The ratification bill was approved in the State Duma on October 22 and in the Council of Federation on October 27, 2004. After the president's signing, the instrument of ratification was deposited with the U.N. secretary-general, and the protocol went into effect ninety days later.

5. See Sawa Takamatsu, "Let Taxes Spur Carbon Cuts," *Japan Times*, March 8, 2005, 16. Professor Sawa of Kyoto University concludes his article by arguing that "Japan should do everything possible to avoid having to buy these credits [originating from Russia]."

6. GIS is not bound by criteria of additional emission reductions in 2008–12. Reductions before 2008 could be credited and transferred to investors as a forward trade of emission units. GIS is based on the income from sale of surplus units, meaning that from the start a GIS project will have a source of finance. See Kristian Tangen et al., *A Russian Green Investment Scheme: Securing Environmental Benefits from International Emissions Trading* (Climate Strategies, 2002), 30, 65.

7. With eighty-nine such projects in operation, Russia is using only about 1 percent of its small-hydro potential. Small hydroelectric power stations can help provide power supply at the local level, in remote regions in particular. According to the International Energy Agency, the best near-term option could be to modernize and rehabilitate existing stations, including abandoned ones. Also, a small station can be constructed in the Far Eastern region in about one and a half years, with a payback period of up to five years.

8. The Pacific Intertie has displaced fossil-fueled power plants in California, reducing emissions. In 1986–2000, the net displacement of CO_2 amounted to 173 Mt. If these emissions were valued at $20 per ton of carbon dioxide, the total amount of saving would be about $3.5 billion: *Electric Power Grid Interconnections in the APEC Region* (Tokyo: Asia Pacific Energy Research Center, 2004), 49.

9. Annually, about 16–17 million Japanese go abroad, and 2 million foreigners come to Japan. In 2003 about 87,000 Japanese visited Russia while 44,000 Russians visited Japan. At the same time, the number of Japanese who visit South Korea and China annually reaches about 2.3 million and 2.4 million, respectively, and the reverse flows from those countries come to around 1.5 million and 0.5 million.

Chapter 10. The Contemporary Implications of the Russo-Japanese War: A Japanese Perspective (pages 157–82)

1. See Peter Katzenstein and Rudra Sil, "Rethinking Asian Security, a Case for Analytical Eclecticism," in *Rethinking Security in East Asia: Identity, Power, and Efficiency,* ed. J. J. Suh, Peter Katzenstein, and Allen Carlson (Stanford: Stanford University Press, 2004), 1–33. See also John Ikenberry and Michael Mastanduno, "In-

ternational Relations Theory and the Search for Regional Stability," in *International Relations Theory and the Asia-Pacific,* ed. John Ikenberry and Michael Mastanduno (New York: Columbia University Press, 2003), 1–21.

2. Akira Iriye, "Japan's Drive to Great-Power Status," in *The Cambridge History of Japan,* ed. Marius B. Jansen, vol. 5 (Cambridge: Cambridge University Press, 1989), 721–82.

3. See, for example, Matsumura Masayoshi, *Nichi-Ro sensō 100 nen* [100 Years from the Russo-Japanese War] (Yokohama: Seibunsha, 2003); Yokote Shinji, *Nichi-Ro sensō shi* [History of the Russo-Japanese War] (Tokyo: Chūō Kōron Shinsha, 2005); Yamamuro Shin'ichi, *Nichi-Ro sensō no seiki* [The Century of the Russo-Japanese War] (Tokyo: Iwanami, 2005); and Katō Yōko, *Sensō no ronri: Nichi-Ro sensō kara Taiheiyō sensō made* [Logic of War: From the Russo-Japanese War to the Pacific War] (Tokyo: Keisō Shobō, 2005).

4. See S. C. M. Paine, *The Sino-Japanese War of 1894–1895: Perceptions, Power, and Primacy* (Cambridge: Cambridge University Press, 2004), 3–20, for an excellent analysis on the changing status of China and Japan before and after the Sino-Japanese War of 1894–95.

5. The full extent of this confidential agreement came to Japan's knowledge only after the disruption caused by the Russo-Japanese War, but those portions regarding the Chinese Eastern Railway were known earlier through analysis of contracts on the establishment of the railway. See Kawashima Shin, "Nichi-Ro sensō to Chūgoku no chūritsu mondai" [The Russo-Japanese War and the Question of China's Neutrality], in *Nichi-Ro sensō (1): kokusaiteki bunmyaku* [The Russo-Japansese War (1): The International Context], ed. Gunji Shigakkai [Military History Society] (Tokyo: Kinseisha, 2004), 80. Construction of the Chinese Eastern Railway began in 1898. After the Triple Intervention and the return of the Liaodong Peninsula in 1898, Russia also received the rights to the South Manchuria Railway, which connects Harbin and Port Arthur. Both railways were constructed by 1901, and full operation began in 1903.

6. See Okazaki Hisahiko, *Komura Jutarō to sono jidai* [Komura Jutarō and His Era] (Tokyo: PHP, 1998), 123, 134, 167, and 172. See also Kanno Naoki, "Ōryo-kukō engan no shinrin riken mondai to Nihon rikugun" [Timber Rights along the Yalu River and the Japanese Army], in *Nichi-Ro sensō (1): kokusaiteki bunmyaku,* 260–68.

7. Li Yon-sun, Chon Je-jong, and So Ui-sik, *Wakamono ni tsutaetai Kankoku no rekishi* [Korean History to Be Told to the Young Generation] (Tokyo: Akashi Shoten, 2004), 78–79.

8. See Djun Kil Kim, *The History of Korea* (Westport, Conn.: Greenwood Press, 2005), 111–15.

9. Ikei Masaru, *Nihon gaikō shi gaisetsu* [An Outline of Japanese Diplomatic History] (Tokyo: Keiō University Press, 1992), 82–85.

10. Recent Japanese scholarly works emphasize that the image that Japan moved toward a head-on collision with Russia after the humiliation of the Triple Intervention is wrong, that a strong mood of *ensen kibun* (antiwar feeling) dominated public opinion, and that the Meiji leadership exhausted all threads of diplomacy to leave war as the last option. See Katō, *Sensō no ronri,* 55–56.

11. See Okazaki, *Komura Jutarō to sono jidai*, 173–79.

12. Shinji Yokote, "Political Legacies of the Portsmouth Treaty," chapter 7 of this volume.

13. See Matsumura, *Nichi-Ro sensō 100 nen*, 164–65.

14. See Yokote, *Nichi-Ro sensō shi*, 199.

15. Kim, *History of Korea*, 115; Li et al., *Wakamono ni tsutaetai Kankoku no rekishi*, 84–85.

16. See Okazaki, *Komura Jutarō to sono jidai*, 293.

17. See Geoffrey Jukes, *The Russo-Japanese War, 1904–1905* (Wellingborough, UK: Osprey Publishing, 2002), 30.

18. See Jukes, *Russo-Japanese War*, 30; and Okazaki, *Komura Jutarō to sono jidai*, 292, 297.

19. See Kim, *History of Korea*, 120.

20. Li et al., *Wakamono ni tsutaetai Kankoku no rekishi*, 86. Okazaki observes that the Korean court had no intention to cooperate with Japan but that resistance against this protocol came mostly from Koreans who supported Russia: Okazaki, *Komura Jutarō to sono jidai*, 293, 306.

21. See Kim, *History of Korea*, 120.

22. F. A. McKenzie, *The Tragedy of Korea* (Seoul: Yonsei University Press, 1969 reprint), 109–10. Alexis Dudden has also written about "Japan's repeated assurances to Korea that Korean independence would be fully restored after the war with Russia (promises publicized in the popular press to the Korean people)." Alexis Dudden, *Japan's Colonization of Korea: Discourse and Power* (Honolulu: University of Hawaii Press, 2005), 80.

23. McKenzie, *Tragedy of Korea*, foreword, 17.

24. There are many writings published on An Chung-gun in Japan, but my observations are based on Nakano Yasuo, *An Jūkon: Nik-Kan kankei no genzō* [An Chung-gun: The Original Image of Japanese-Korean Relations] (Tokyo: Aki Shobō, 1991); Nakano Yasuo, *An Jūkon to Itō Hirobumi* [An Chung-gun and Itō Hirobumi] (Tokyo: Kōbunsha, 1996); and Saitō Yasuhiko, *An Jūkon* [An Chung-gun] (Tokyo: Satsuki Shobō, 1997).

25. See Nakano, *An Jūkon*, 210.

26. In his analysis of An Chung-gun's "Thesis on Oriental Peace," Hong Sohoon-ho reiterates (1) An's view that the Korean people believed in Japan's promise to ensure Oriental peace and Korean independence and (2) An's view on the fight between the yellows and the whites. See Hong Sohoon-ho, "An Chung-gun eui Dongyang Pyounghwa Ron" [An Chung-gun's Thesis on Oriental Peace], in *Kyoheoi-sa Yaengoo* [Research on Church History] (Seoul: The Research Foundation of Korean Church History, 1994), 9:53–54. Choi Kiyoung confirms that "most Korean intellectuals [initially] considered the Russo-Japanese War as a war for the maintenance of Oriental peace and Korean independence." See Choi Kiyoung, "An Chung-gun eui Dongyang Pyounghwa Ron e daehan Nonpyung" [A Review on An Chung-gun's Thesis on Oriental Peace], in *Kyoheoi-sa Yaengoo* [Research on Church History] (Seoul: The Research Foundation of Korean Church History, 1994), 9:64. Hyun Kwang-ho argues: "most Korean scholarship stated that Koreans saw Japan-

ese as friends and did not have anti-Japanese feelings before the Russo-Japanese War." See Hyun Kwang-ho, "An Chung-gun eui Dongyang Pyounghwa Ron gwa Gu Sungkyuk" [The Nature of An Chung-gun's Thesis on Oriental Peace], in *Asea Yeongoo* [The Journal of Asiatic Studies] (Asiatic Research Center, Korea University, Seoul) 46, no. 3 (2003): 163.

27. The editorial was written on November 20 by Chang Chiyon; see Kim, *The History of Korea*, 122.

28. See Lee Ki-Baik, *A New History of Korea*, trans. Edward W. Wagner with Edward J. Shultz (Seoul: Ilchokak Publishers, 1984), 310.

29. See Okazaki, *Komura Jutarō to sono jidai*, 299.

30. See Okazaki, *Komura Jutarō to sono jidai*, 302.

31. See Kim, *History of Korea*, 122–24.

32. See Okazaki, *Komura Jutarō to sono jidai*, 302–3.

33. See Che Mun-hyon, *Nichi-Ro sensō no sekaishi* [A Global History of the Russo-Japanese War] (Tokyo: Fujiwara Shoten, 2004), 237–45; see also chapter 8 in this volume: David Wolff, "Riding Rough: Portsmouth, Regionalism, and the Birth of Anti-Americanism in Northeast Asia."

34. Nagata Akifumi, *Nihon no Chōsen tōchi to kokusai kankei* [Japan's Rule of Korea and International Relations] (Tokyo: Heibonsha, 2005), 32; Nagata Akifumi, *Seodoa Rūzuberuto to Kankoku* [Theodore Roosevelt and Korea] (Tokyo: Miraisha, 1992), 152–57, 184–90; Kim, *History of Korea*, 121.

35. See Okazaki, *Komura Jutarō to sono jidai*, 308.

36. See Kawashima, "Nichi-Ro sensō to Chūgoku no chūritsu mondai," 81–82.

37. See Kawashima, "Nichi-Ro sensō to Chūgoku no chūritsu mondai," 82.

38. See Kawashima, "Nichi-Ro sensō to Chūgoku no chūritsu mondai," 80.

39. Interview with a director of a think tank on June 22, 2005, in Shanghai.

40. See Yamamuro, *Nichi-Ro sensō no seiki*, 228.

41. See Jukes, *Russo-Japanese War*, 84–85.

42. Sun made this speech in 1924 and, while acknowledging the positive impact that the Russo-Japanese War had had on the Asian independence movement, sternly criticized Japan for failing to meet the expectations of oppressed people throughout the world. See Yamamuro, *Nichi-Ro sensō no seiki*, 94, 164–65.

43. Yokote, "Political Legacies of the Portsmouth Treaty," 108.

44. See Okazaki, *Komura Jutarō to sono jidai*, 63–64.

45. See Kawashima, "Nichi-Ro sensō to Chūgoku no chūritsu mondai," 84, and Che, *Nichi-Ro sensō no sekaishi*, 49–56.

46. "Germany seized Jiaozhou in Shandong; Russia got Liaodong; Britain leased Weihaiwei in Shandong and the New Territories next to Hong Kong; France leased Guangzhou bay near Hainan Island." See Patricia Buckley Erby, *China* (Cambridge: Cambridge University Press, 1996), 254.

47. See Okazaki, *Komura Jutarō to sono jidai*, 61.

48. See Kawashima, "Nichi-Ro sensō to Chūgoku no chūritsu mondai," 84–85.

49. See Katō, *Sensō no ronri*, 63.

50. See Ikei, *Nihon gaikō shi gaisetsu*, 98; Yokote, "Political Legacies of the Portsmouth Treaty."

51. Emperor Meiji died in 1912; his son's succession to the throne began the Taishō Era.

52. See J.A.G. Roberts, *The Complete History of China* (Stroud, UK: Sutton Publishing, 2003), 350–51.

53. See Yamamuro, *Nichi-Ro sensō no seiki*, 201.

54. See Ikei, *Nihon gaikō shi gaisetsu*, 116. Katsuoka states that Asian support of Japan's victory can be traced in India, Indonesia, and Vietnam; Egypt, Turkey, and countries under Russian occupation such as Poland and Finland also responded positively: Katsuoka Kanji, ed., *Kyōkasho kara mita Nichi-Ro sensō* [The Russo-Japanese War as Seen from Textbooks] (Tokyo: Tentensha, 2004), 40–49. Uzbekistan and other Central Asian countries had similar reactions.

55. See Okazaki, *Komura Jutarō to sono jidai*, 64.

56. See Che, *Nichi-Ro sensō no sekaishi*, 98.

57. See Okazaki, *Komura Jutarō to sono jidai*, 175.

58. See Roberts, *Complete History of China*, 358.

59. See Che, *Nichi-Ro sensō no sekaishi*, 36–44.

60. http://www.loc.gov/rr/hispanic/1898/intro.html [October 1, 2005].

61. Hawaii was a sovereign kingdom until 1893, when the monarchy was deposed and a provisional government was established with American support. The annexation took place five years later, and Hawaii became a territory of the United States in 1900. See http://www.hawaii-nation.org/moolelo.html [October 1, 2005].

62. Yui Daizaburō, "Amerika no seiki wa dō tsukuraretaka" [How Was the American Century Made?], in Ariga Natsuki and Yui Daizaburō, eds., *Amerika no rekishi* [American History] (Tokyo: Yūhikaku, 2003), 295–97; Che, *Nichi-Ro sensō no sekaishi*, 48.

63. See Che, *Nichi-Ro sensō no sekaishi*, 33–36.

64. On July 18, 1903; see Okazaki, *Komura Jutarō to sono jidai*, 176.

65. See Che, *Nichi-Ro sensō no sekaishi*, 163–64.

66. The second paragraph of Article V of the Portsmouth Treaty prescribed that the two governments would "engage to obtain the consent of the Chinese government" on the transfer of the South Manchuria Railway from Russia to Japan.

67. See Che, *Nichi-Ro sensō no sekaishi*, 290–94; and Okazaki, *Komura Jutarō to sono jidai*, 280–84.

68. See Che, *Nichi-Ro sensō no sekaishi*, 292.

69. See Yui, "Amerika no seiki wa dō tsukuraretaka," 292–94.

70. See Okazaki, *Komura Jutarō to sono jidai*, 285–86.

71. See Yamamuro, *Nichi-Ro sensō no seiki*, 212.

72. See Ikei, *Nihon gaikō shi gaisetsu*, 105; Okazaki, *Komura Jutarō to sono jidai*, 314–16; and Che, *Nichi-Ro sensō no sekaishi*, 320–25.

73. Tsuyoshi Hasegawa, *The Northern Territories Dispute and Russo-Japanese Relations*, 2 vols. (Berkeley: University of California, International and Area Studies, 1998), 1:31–32.

74. The Treaty of Nerchinsk was concluded in 1689 between Russia and China.

75. See Togawa Tsuneo, *Roshia to Sorenpō* [Russia and the Soviet Union] (Tokyo:

Kōdansha, 1991), 294–95; Ikei, *Nihon gaikō shi gaisetsu,* 86–87; and Okazaki, *Komura Jutarō to sono jidai,* 168–69.

76. David Schimmelpenninck van der Oye, "The Immediate Origin of the War," in John W. Steinberg et al. eds., *The Russo-Japanese War in Global Perspective, World War Zero,* vol. 1 (Leiden and Boston: Brill, 2005), 44. See also Yokote Shinji, "Nichi-Ro sensō ni kansuru saikin no Ōbei no kenkyū" [Recent Study on the Russo-Japanese War in the West], in *Nichi-Ro sensō (1): kokusaiteki bunmyaku,* 277–84; and Igor Lukoianov, "The Bezobrazovtsy," in Steinberg et al., *The Russo-Japanese War in Global Perspective,* 79–81.

77. See Togawa, *Roshia to Sorenpō,* 297–98.

78. See Yokote, *Nichi-Ro sensō shi,* 191–92.

79. See Yokote, *Nichi-Ro sensō shi,* 188.

80. See Matsumura, *Nichi-Ro sensō 100 nen,* 156–68.

81. See Matsumura *Nichi-Ro sensō 100 nen,* 163.

82. See Yokote, *Nichi-Ro sensō shi,* 202.

83. See Hasegawa, *The Northern Territories Dispute and Russo-Japanese Relations,* 29.

84. President Franklin D. Roosevelt's priority at Yalta was to ensure Soviet entry into the war against Japan in order to limit American military casualties. But it remains unclear why a briefing paper that correctly described the history of the Kuriles was omitted from Roosevelt's Yalta briefing. See Lim Robyn, *The Geopolitics of East Asia* (London: Routledge, 2003), 81.

85. The Chinese Eastern Railway had been sold to Manchukuo in 1935 as a result of negotiations between Japan and the Soviet Union.

86. Shimotomai Nobuo, *Ajia reisenshi* [History of the Cold War in Asia] (Tokyo: Chūō Kōron Shinsha, 2004), 97–98.

87. Habomai, Shikotan, Kunashiri, and Etorofu were demarcated as Japanese territory by the 1855 treaty.

88. For their valuable comments, the author profoundly thanks Professor Sheldon Garon, Mr. Thomas Pepper, Professor Gilbert Rozman, Mr. Jai-Hoon Yang, and participants in the seminar held in Amsterdam on October 8, 2005, "How the Balance Swung: A Hundred Years after the Russo-Japanese War," organized by the International Institute for Asian Studies (IIAS), including Professor Touraj Atabaki, Dr. Victor Van Bijlert, Dr. Koen De Ceuster, Professor Marcel van der Linden, Dr. Roald Maliangkay, and Dr. Ethan Mark. He is also indebted to Ms. Mayumi Komoda for her helpful research in Seoul.

Appendix: Summary of Conference Discussions (pages 183–200)

1. Steven Ericson, Allen Hockley, and Kenneth Yalowitz, *Portsmouth and Its Legacies: Commemorating the Centennial of the Russo-Japanese Peace Treaty of 1905,* Occasional Paper, John Sloan Dickey Center for International Understanding (Hanover, N.H.: Dartmouth College, 2006).

Contributors

DONALD E. DAVIS is Professor Emeritus of History at Illinois State University. He is a specialist in Russian history and editor of the memoir of Paul B. Anderson, *No East or West* (1985). He is the coauthor, with Eugene Trani, of *The First Cold War: The Legacy of Woodrow Wilson in U.S.-Soviet Relations* (2002), which was published in English, Russian, and Chinese. He is currently finishing, with Eugene Trani, *Distorted Mirrors: American Relations with Russia and China, 1891–1991*, due to be published in English, Russian, Chinese, and Spanish. He is a graduate of San Francisco State University and earned his master's and doctoral degrees from Indiana University.

STEVEN ERICSON is an Associate Professor of History and Chair of the Asian and Middle Eastern Studies Program at Dartmouth College. Professor Ericson specializes in the history of Japan with a focus on the country's modern transformation. His research centers on government financial and industrial policies and their economic and social effects in the late nineteenth and early twentieth centuries. He is author of *The Sound of the Whistle: Railroads and the State in Meiji Japan* (Harvard, 1996). Dr. Ericson graduated from Michigan State University and received his master's and doctoral degrees from Harvard University.

ALLEN HOCKLEY is an Associate Professor in the Department of Art History at Dartmouth College. He specializes in the histories of Japanese prints and early Japanese photography. In addition to numerous articles, essays, and reviews, he is the author of *The Prints of Isoda Koryūsai: Floating World Culture and Its Consumers in Eighteenth-Century Japan* (2003) and *Inside the Floating World: Japanese Prints from the Lenoir C. Wright Collection* (2002). Recently he has been authoring websites for MIT's Visualizing Cultures project. Dr. Hockley received degrees from the University of Victoria (B.A.), University of British Columbia (M.A.), and University of Toronto (Ph.D.).

VLADIMIR I. IVANOV is Deputy Chief Representative of Rosneft Oil Company in Beijing, China. He is also former Senior Economist and Director of the Research Division at the Economic Research Institute for Northeast Asia in Niigata, Japan, and former head of the Asia-Pacific Studies Department at the Institute of World Economy and International Relations of the Russian Academy of Sciences. He was a visiting scholar at Harvard University and the University of Tokyo and a research fellow at the U.S. Institute of Peace at the Center for International and Strategic Studies in Washington, D.C., and at the East-West Center in Honolulu. He has published extensively on economic, social, political, and security issues involving Northeast Asia and the larger Asia-Pacific region, including Russia's economic relations with her neighbors and prospects for regional cooperation. He received his Ph.D. in Political Economy from the Institute of Oriental Studies of the Russian Academy of Sciences.

SHO KONISHI is University Lecturer of Modern Japanese History in the Faculty of History at the University of Oxford. He is also a faculty fellow of St. Antony's College and of the Nissan Institute of Japanese Studies at Oxford. Before coming to Oxford, he was an Assistant Professor of History at the University of Illinois, Urbana-Champaign. He studies the cultural, intellectual, and transnational history of Japan from 1700. His publications include "Reopening the 'Opening of Japan': A Russian-Japanese Revolutionary Encounter and the Vision of Anarchist Progress" in *The American Historical Review*, February 2007.

I. V. LUKOIANOV is a Research Associate at the Institute of Russian History in St. Petersburg. In 2004–5 he was a Visiting Fellow at the Slavic Research Center of Hokkaido University. A specialist in the history of tsarist diplomacy in East Asia, he received his Ph.D. from the St. Petersburg Institute of History and was a research fellow at the Russian Academy of Sciences. His fields of interest include the political and diplomatic history of Russia in the nineteenth and twentieth centuries. He is the author of *U istokov rossiiskogo parlamentarizma* (At the Sources of Russian Parliamentarism) and *Rossiiskie conservatory: konets XVIII–nachalo XX* (Russian Conservatives: From the End of the 18th Century to the Beginning of the 20th Century). Recent publications include *Delo Mendelia Beilisa* (The Mandel Beilis Affair), *Zemskii Sobor* (Ignat'ev N. P. Zemsky Congress), and *Iz archiva S. Iu. Vitte: Vospominaniia* (From the Archive of Sergei Witte: Memoirs).

COL. (RET.) BRUCE W. MENNING is a Professor of Military Strategy with the Department of Joint and Multinational Operations at the U.S. Army Command and General Staff College in Fort Leavenworth. A specialist in Russian history and Russian, Soviet, and post-Soviet military history and strategy, he is the author of *Bayonets before Bullets: The Imperial Russian Army, 1861–1914* (1992) and coeditor of *The Russo-Japanese War in Global Perspective: World War Zero*, 2 vols. (2005–7). He has lectured at the National Defense University, the Royal Military Academy at Sandhurst, and the former Soviet Institute of Military History in Moscow.

DAVID SCHIMMELPENNINCK VAN DER OYE is Associate Professor of Russian History and Chair of the History Department at Brock University, St. Catharines, Ontario, Canada. A specialist in imperial Russian diplomatic, intellectual, and cultural history, he is the author of *Toward the Rising Sun: Ideologies of Empire and the Path to War with Japan, 1895–1904* (2001) and a coeditor of *The Russo-Japanese War in Global Perspective: World War Zero*, 2 vols. (2005–7). He is now completing a book under contract with Yale University Press titled *Russian Orientalism: Asia in the Russian Mind from Catherine the Great to the Emigration*.

JOHN W. STEINBERG, a graduate of Ohio State University, is Associate Professor of History at Georgia Southern University. He has also been the Fulbright Professor of Russian History at Helsinki University and was trained as an instructor of strategy, tactics, and doctrine by the U.S. Air Force. His research focuses on the history of the Imperial Russian Army. He is coeditor of *The Russo-Japanese War in Global Perspective: World War Zero,* 2 vols. (2005–7). He has published several articles on the Imperial Army and currently has under contract with the Woodrow Wilson Center Press a book manuscript titled *All the Tsar's Men: Russia's General Staff and the Fate of the Empire, 1898–1914.*

YASUTOSHI TERAMOTO is Professor in the Graduate School of Social Science at Hiroshima University. An expert in Japanese diplomatic history, particularly Japanese foreign policy during and after the Russo-Japanese War, he is the author of *Nichi-Ro sensō igo no Nihon gaikō: pawā poritikusu no naka no Man-Kan mondai* (Japanese Diplomacy after the Russo-Japanese War: The Manchuria-Korea Problem in the Context of Power Politics) (1999) and "Hayashi Tadasu no gaikō seisaku ni kansuru kenkyū: gōrisei to sono genkai" (A Study in the Foreign Policy of Hayashi Tadasu: His Rationality and Its Limits), in *Nichi-Ro sensō kenkyū no shin shiten* (New Perspectives on the Study of the Russo-Japanese War), ed. Nichi-Ro Sensō Kenkyūkai (2005).

KAZUHIKO TOGO joined the Foreign Ministry of Japan in 1968 and worked altogether 17 years on Soviet-Russian affairs. He also held posts related to Europe, the United States, and international law and economics and served as Ambassador of Japan to the Netherlands. He retired from the Foreign Ministry in 2002. From 1995 he began teaching at universities in Moscow and Tokyo and since retirement has taught at Leiden, Princeton, and Seoul National, among other universities. His recent publications include *Japan's Foreign Policy, 1945–2003: The Quest for a Proactive Policy* (2005) and *Hoppō ryōdo kōshō hiroku: ushinawareta gotabi no kikai* (The Inside Story of the Negotiations on the Northern Territories: Five Lost Windows of Opportunity) (2007).

EUGENE P. TRANI is President of Virginia Commonwealth University and a scholar of history and U.S. foreign affairs. He is the author or coauthor of various books: *The Treaty of Portsmouth: An Adventure in American Diplomacy* (1969), *The Presidency of Warren G. Harding* (1977), and *The First Cold War: The Legacy of Woodrow Wilson in U.S.-Soviet Relations* (2002). He is currently finishing his next book, with Donald Davis, titled *Distorted Mirrors: American Relations with Russia and China, 1891–1991.* He previously served as Vice President for Academic Affairs and Professor of History in the University of Wisconsin System; Fellow at St. John's College in Cambridge, England; Visiting Professor at University College Dublin in Ireland; and Senior Visiting Scholar at Lincoln College, Oxford. He is a graduate of the University of Notre Dame and earned his master's and doctoral degrees from Indiana University.

DAVID WOLFF is Professor of Eurasian History at the Slavic Research Center of Hokkaido University in Sapporo, Japan. He is also a former Director of the Cold War International History Project at the Woodrow Wilson Center for International Scholars in Washington, D.C. He is the author of *To the Harbin Station: The Liberal Alternative in Russian Manchuria, 1898–1914* (1999) and coeditor of *The Russo-Japanese War in Global Perspective: World War Zero*, 2 vols. (2005–7). He has also served as an International Affairs Fellow of the Council on Foreign Relations.

SHINJI YOKOTE is Professor of Russian History and Politics in the Faculty of Law and Politics at Keiō University in Tokyo, Japan. He specializes in the history of Russian foreign policy, and his research covers Russo-Japanese relations in the twentieth century. He was the chief editor of *Roshia shi kenkyū* (Studies in Russian History), the journal of the Japanese Society for the Study of Russian History, from 2002 to 2004. He is the editor of *Higashi Ajia no Roshia* (Russia in East Asia) (2004), author of *Nichi-Ro sensō shi: 20-seiki saisho no taikokukan sensō* (History of the Russo-Japanese War: The First War between Great Powers in the Twentieth Century) (2005), and coeditor of *History of the Russo-Japanese War in Global Perspective: World War Zero*, 2 vols. (2005–7).

Index